I0232836

Love versus Liquor

Books by Ray Green
Buyout – A Roy Groves Thriller (1)

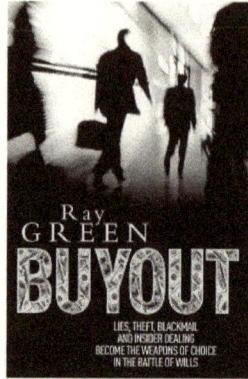

For five ordinary guys and one rather extraordinary woman, the only escape from the corporate rat-race is to buy the company they're working for: take it all to a new level, save hundreds of jobs and make some serious money.

But it quickly becomes clear that nothing is as easy as it seems. The bid is quickly undercut as twisted corporate politics and personal vendettas take over.

When the buyout becomes all or nothing for the management buyout team, it all spins out of control: marriages fall apart, lurid secrets are discovered; life savings are spent on the stock market; illegal insider dealing becomes a matter of fact; and blackmail, theft, betrayal, and manipulation are the new rules of the game.

A once-in-a-life-time opportunity turns into a lurid nightmare.

BUYOUT is a gripping and compulsive page-turner about the power of money to unveil the deepest in human nature. It's also a story about chasing one extraordinary dream. At an extraordinary price.

Books by Ray Green
Payback – A Roy Groves Thriller (2)

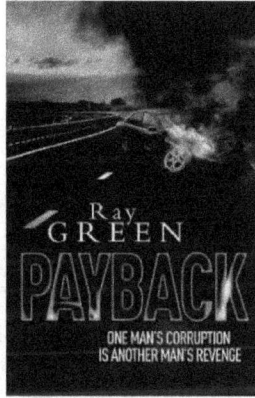

Roy Groves is Operations Director of a successful company manufacturing dashboard instruments for luxury cars.

A fatal motorway fire is traced back to a fault in the product supplied by Roy's company. Was it a tragic accident or something more sinister? As Roy and his colleagues battle to establish the cause of the fire, and save the company from bankruptcy, they discover that they have been the victims of sabotage.

Eventually, it emerges that an old enemy of Roy and the rest of the team has reappeared and is intent on destroying the company and every member of its management team. Once just a business adversary, their nemesis is now so consumed with hatred that he is on the edge of insanity; he resorts to blackmail and even murder in the pursuit of his goal.

PAYBACK is a chilling tale of how hatred can twist and corrupt the human soul.

Books by Ray Green
Chinese Whispers – A Roy Groves Thriller (3)

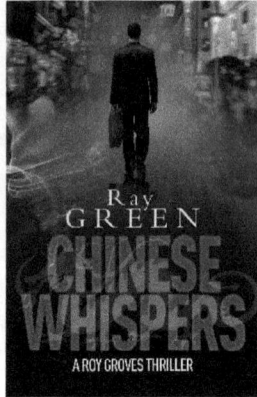

Chuck Kabel is on a business trip to China, visiting the factory to which his UK-based company subcontracts the manufacture of its products. He unexpectedly collapses and dies at the airport before he is able to report on his visit. When the Chinese authorities are evasive about the exact cause of death, the suspicions of his boss, Roy Groves, are raised.

Roy decides to investigate further; it soon becomes clear that there are serious financial irregularities within the Chinese company, and that dark forces are in play, intent on ensuring that these do not come to light. When Roy edges closer to uncovering the truth, he is warned off but refuses to back down, unaware that he is about to confront the Chinese Mafia, who will stop at nothing to achieve their objectives.

When his own family are targeted by his opponents, Roy embarks on a desperate battle to protect them, now well aware that if he should turn to the police, their lives will be in even greater danger.

CHINESE WHISPERS is a frightening tale of organised crime and the way in which it uses and abuses legitimate business for its own illegal purposes, relentlessly destroying the lives of anyone who stands in the way.

Books by Ray Green
Horizontal Living: A Tale of Expats Abroad - A Roy Groves Thriller (4)

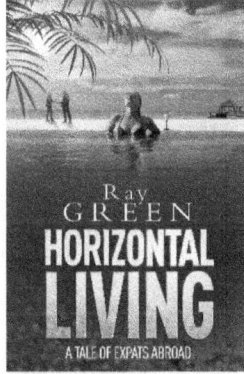

Roy Groves has led a colourful career in business, during which he battled with corporate politics, deception, and even vicious criminals. But now Roy has retired, and he is looking forward to a quieter life. He and his wife, Donna, have bought an apartment in an exclusive development on Spain's Costa del Sol.

He soon learns, however, that there are financial problems: the community is, in effect, bankrupt. Roy is persuaded to take on the role of President of the community, confident that, with his extensive business experience, he should easily be able to sort things out. It soon becomes clear, however, that nothing is as simple as it seems. As he tries to come up with a rescue plan, Roy discovers that a poorly constructed retaining wall has begun to collapse, threatening the development with a landslide. And this is just the start …

As the problems mount up, Roy becomes entangled with an astonishingly diverse cast of characters: the devious building developer; the vengeful former President; the Russian prostitute, and her mafia minders; the deranged Middle Eastern doctor; the devastatingly glamorous French girl next door; and many more …

HORIZONTAL LIVING is an illuminating insight into the shenanigans which pervade an ex-pat community abroad: sometimes hilarious, sometimes hard to believe, but sometimes darkly disturbing.

Books by Ray Green
Lost Identity - The Identity Thrillers Series – Book 1

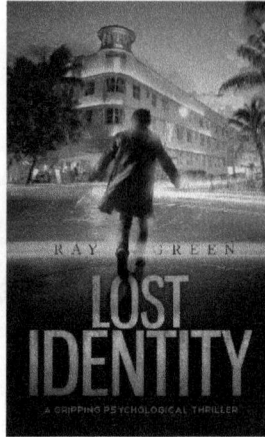

When research scientist, Stephen Lewis, wakes from a coma in a Miami hospital bed, he remembers nothing about his head injury, how he came to be in Florida, or even who he really is.

As fragments of his memory return, Stephen is shocked to find that even those closest to him seem not to know him. And when another man turns up, claiming to be the real Stephen Lewis, he begins to doubt his own sanity.

Desperate to learn the truth, Stephen is unwittingly drawn into a murky web of drug trafficking and murder. At its heart lies a terrifying conspiracy and a secret so appalling that, even if he survives, he knows his life can never be the same again.

Books by Ray Green
Identity Found - The Identity Thrillers Series – Book 2

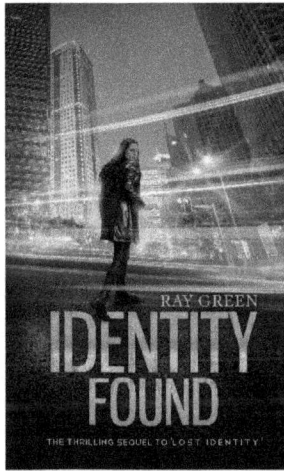

Stephen Lewis and Carla Fernandez fled from Miami, Florida a year ago, to escape a terrifying battle with drug trafficking cartels and professional assassins. Now they are living a quiet life in Canada, under false identities.

But when a young female journalist is murdered in New York City, Stephen recognises that the killing has all the hallmarks of one of the world's most highly paid and notorious assassins. Why should this man, who can command a fee of millions of dollars for a single hit, be hired for such a seemingly insignificant contract? He concludes that the journalist must have been investigating something big – very big – and had been murdered to shut her up.

The police seem not to have made this link, and Stephen cannot approach them directly, as he is wanted in connection with the events in Miami. Fearful that there may be some terrible plot underway, possibly with many lives at stake, he decides to investigate. Carla insists on helping him.

Before long, Stephen and Carla find themselves battling for their lives once again.

Books by Ray Green
New Identity - The Identity Thrillers Series – Book 3

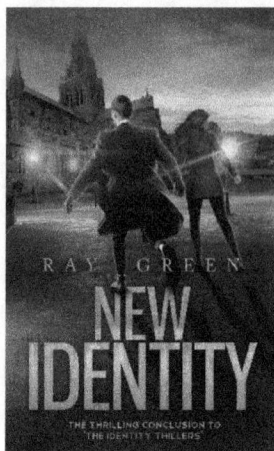

Jason Hardwick and Gabriela Suarez have been on the run for almost three years – pursued by a network of professional assassins. Now they are living under false identities in the market town of Chichester, in England.

Mark Bowman was the detective who helped the couple escape from a terrifying confrontation with their pursuers in New York City some fifteen months ago. Now he has been murdered. His killer is Jade Lacroix: a beautiful, highly intelligent, bisexual assassin. Jason and Gabriela are her next targets. When Jason and Gabriela learn of Mark's death, they realise that these people will never give up. What can they do to fight back?

Alexis Miller – also an NYPD detective – was Mark's girlfriend. She has vowed to bring his killer, and those she works for, to justice.

Will Alexis track down the assassin before she gets to Jason and Gabriela? Will she become a target herself? Who is the shadowy figure behind this murderous network?

'New Identity' is the thrilling, shocking conclusion to the 'Identity Thrillers' trilogy.

Books by Ray Green
The Ultima Variant – A Coronavirus Conspiracy Thriller

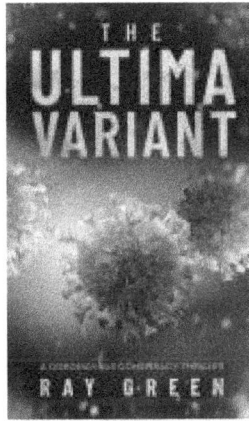

It is ten years since the Covid pandemic which had crippled countries throughout the entire world, and life is more or less back to normal. But then a deadly new coronavirus emerges, highly transmissible and capable of evading all existing vaccines. The scientists are, once again, racing against time to find a new vaccine, but just as one research team succeed in developing such a vaccine, the scientist leading the team, Professor Felicity Maddocks, is murdered. Why?

Meanwhile James and Tessa Blackmore, who lost their first baby to Cot Death, are trying for another child. Although Tessa fell pregnant with their first child almost immediately they started trying, she now finds herself unable to conceive. Before long, their plight is replicated by couples around the entire world. What is causing this worldwide decline in the birth rate?

The mysterious murder of Professor Maddocks is investigated by Detective Inspector David Prendergast. His investigation leads him to a shadowy group of scientists and academics who have no obvious connection but who meet in secret for some unknown purpose. Are they somehow connected with the rise of the new coronavirus or the unexplained decline in global birth rate?

The answer is shocking.

Love versus Liquor

Love versus Liquor
Can a mother's love save her son from alcohol addiction?

By Madeleine Fisher
and
Ray Green

Based on a true story

mainsail
books

Love versus Liquor

Published in Great Britain by Mainsail Books in 2026
First Edition

Copyright © Madeleine Fisher and Ray Green 2026

Madeleine Fisher and Ray Green have asserted their rights under the Copyright, Designs and Patents Act 1988 to be identified as the authors of this work.

This book is based on a true story. Most of the events contained within it actually happened, but the names of characters, entities, and places are fictitious, unless otherwise stated.

All rights reserved. No part of this publication may be reproduced, stored in, or introduced into a retrieval system, or transmitted, in any form, or by any means (electronic, mechanical, photocopying, recording or otherwise) without the prior written permission of the authors, nor to be otherwise circulated in any form of binding or cover, other than that in which it is published, without a similar condition being imposed on the subsequent purchaser. Any person who carries out any unauthorised act in relation to this publication may be liable to criminal prosecution and civil claims for damages.

ISBN 978-1-7397047-3-5

Published by Mainsail Books
www.mainsailbooks.co.uk

Cover design by Ana Grigoriu-Voicu
ana@books-design.com

Preface

by Ray Green

I am an author ... as will be evident from the shameless plug at the beginning of this book for my previous work! But this is not my story; it belongs to Madeleine Fisher, a hardworking nurse and single mother.

I met Madeleine (not her real name) some years ago while undergoing treatment for a skin condition on my forearms brought about by far too much sun exposure in my earlier years. My treatment had to be repeated several times over a period of months and years, so I got to spend quite a bit of time with Madeleine. We chatted about her life and mine and, over time, became good friends.

As we shared experiences, I learned that, in addition to the demands of bringing up four children, she had suffered an abusive relationship (now thankfully behind her) and faced the agonising scenario of one of her children sliding into alcohol addiction.

As she revealed more and more of the devastating effects of her son's addiction, and her struggles to help him, I realised there was a story there begging to be told, if for no other reason than to provide some support and solidarity for others out there struggling to help a loved one battling this horrible disease.

As we discussed the matter, it became clear that Madeleine was desperate to share her story but had little idea how to go about writing or publishing a book, so I offered to help her. This book is the result. It is a fictionalised account of true events based on Madeleine's experiences: most of the events described are real, but not the names of the characters depicted; they are the product of the authors' imaginations.

So here it is: a story about a young man's descent into addiction and mental health issues; about a mother's struggles to help him while trying to cope with all the stresses and strains of bringing up a large family on her own. But most of all, it is a story about a mother's unconditional love for her son.

If this book helps just one person out there who is dealing with similar issues, then it will have been well worth writing.

Ray Green

Dedications

by Madeleine Fisher

Writing this book has been a bittersweet journey; the story is one of chaos, heartbreak, and an uncertain future yet, somehow, love always shines through.

I dedicate this book to my son, Liam, and to his sisters Amelia, Grace, and Megan, who were a source of strength when mine ran out.

I would also like to mention my mum. Without knowing it, she prepared me for life's challenges which would lie in my path. Mum, I love you.

Finally, I dedicate this book to families and individuals who may be walking a similar path or even trying to understand it. I offer you strength and understanding but, mainly, I offer you love.

Madeleine Fisher

Prologue

'Judged'

My child became an addict in his teens, lured to drugs and alcohol by a culture that glorifies substance use – the same culture that now, so ignorantly and harshly, passes judgement on him. *And me.*

I am judged for helping, fixing, and pushing (or not helping, fixing, or pushing enough) this sick child of mine who won't be helped or fixed or pushed. I am judged for over-reacting and under-reacting, enabling and letting go. Most hurtful of all, I am judged to be a mother whose love must be somehow flawed.

When my child became an addict I became the mom of an addict – a role I wasn't prepared for and certainly didn't want. It's a role the whole world seems to have an opinion about, whether they know anything about addiction or not. Whatever I do (or don't do), I am judged to be wrong, but I no longer pay attention to that. I just keep doing what I'm doing, with love.

Sandy Swenson

***

Judge tenderly, if you must. There is usually a side you have not heard, a story you know nothing about, and a battle waged that you are not having to fight.

Traci Lea LaRussa

***

The words above are not mine, but those of others whom society has cruelly judged. However, they express perfectly some of the feelings which I, too, have experienced during the heartbreaking journey which I have travelled, and which provided the inspiration for this book.

Madeleine Fisher

Chapter 1

'Peas'

Let me tell you about peas. They seem inoffensive enough: small, round, unassuming little vegetables. But believe me, if you live with an alcoholic, they become the work of the Devil, turning into venomous balls of trouble.

Let me explain: it's all down to the ever-present tremors. They give the green light for peas carefully balanced on a fork to head off in all directions: across the table, onto the floor, occasionally even onto someone else's plate. I do believe that peas have minds of their own, conspiring to highlight, name, and shame the unfortunate individual who has released them.

No, peas are not the innocent little things they purport to be; they are evil.

***

Today, my family and I are sitting around the dining table trying to be a normal family enjoying a Sunday roast. And we *were* a normal family once … but not anymore. Liam's descent into alcoholism has seen to that. Liam is my son; he's twenty-three years old and the source of the escaping peas which the rest of us are pretending not to notice. When I say 'the rest of us' that's not strictly true; my youngest daughter, Amelia – she's ten years old – is delighting in giving a running commentary on the unpredictable trajectories of the dancing peas!

Amelia is a bright, funny, confident kid: in many ways mature beyond her years. Maybe living with an alcoholic has made her like

1

that … or maybe that's just the way she is. At least she doesn't seem to have suffered psychologically from Liam's antics, some of which, as you will later learn, have been extreme, to say the least. But right now, she seems unable to resist the temptation to draw attention to the errant peas despite everyone else's studious efforts to ignore them.

Beside Amelia sits Grace, her elder sister, aged twenty-two. She's a beautiful girl, both physically and in temperament. She's tired of the situation, but she would never do anything to make things any worse than they already are; she's far too kind a person to embarrass her brother like that.

There are a couple of empty chairs. My eldest daughter, Megan, aged twenty-five, lives locally but, for reasons which will become clear, is seldom around for one of these awkward family gatherings.

And then there's me. I'm Madeleine, the harassed mum trying to hold this dysfunctional family together. I'm in my late forties now, wondering if things will ever return to anything resembling 'normal'. People say I'm attractive, and false modesty aside, I think I do actually scrub up pretty well when I can be bothered to attend properly to my hair, makeup, and clothes. However, there is no husband or partner in my life these days; it's hard to find a good, single man who could accommodate my chaotic, unstable, and pea-infested life!

I suppose peas may seem an odd subject with which to begin my story, but in a strange sort of way, I fancy they are almost symbolic of some of the friends, family, and other people in my life. You can see some of them roll away a short distance but not beyond the reach of possible retrieval. Others scoot off into the distance never to be seen again. Yet others, who are thought to have been lost forever, turn up weeks or months later, stuck to the bottom of a table mat or nestled in the corner, up against the skirting board.

Then there are those very few *real* friends: the ones who stick with you through thick and thin; the ones who are not fazed by talking about Liam, his bizarre behaviours, or his regular thirty-five units per day alcohol habit. They're not like the peas at all; if anything, they are more like the heavy, solid oak table around which we are currently seated. Sadly, friends like this are few and far between; it's amazing how alcoholism drives people away once you really start to talk about it.

***

Lunch is almost finished now. Compared to some of our recent family gatherings, I'd say it went quite well. Sure, there were a few niggles. Amelia was particularly persistent in needling Liam about the peas making their bids for freedom, and none of my disapproving frowns shot in her direction had any effect whatsoever. Finally, when a whole forkful of peas went flying, she shrieked with laughter. This rather undermined my efforts to play down the incident.

Liam, for his part, insisted on telling us – several times – about his very busy morning. As far as I can determine, the most eventful and strenuous part of his morning was getting out of bed at 11a.m. consuming his customary morning tumblerful of vodka and bringing down the dirty dishes which had lingered in his bedroom for the previous couple of days. Still, at least he *did* bring them down, which was, I suppose, something.

Amelia is really fidgeting now, so I tell her she can leave the table; Liam takes his cue to do likewise. He slopes off towards the stairs, no doubt to retire to his room and begin the non-stop drinking which will probably characterise the rest of his day.

Grace helps me clear away the dishes and load the dishwasher, which, inevitably, will only accommodate about half of the mountain of pots, pans, and dishes which has accumulated on the worktop. Once the machine is running, Grace informs me she is meeting some girlfriends this afternoon and excuses herself. I soon find myself alone with a stack of dirty dishes and my own thoughts.

Yes, all things considered, this was a pretty good family lunch by our standards. Maybe the two-and-a-half hours I spent preparing it was worthwhile.

I decide to hand-wash some of the pots and pans which are still dirty, rather than wait for the dishwasher to complete its cycle and cool down. As I stand at the sink, gazing out of the window, watching the traffic pass by, I wonder where everyone is going and what they are going to do when they get there. Many will be heading back to their normal families, I guess.

We were once a normal family, too … how on earth did things come to this?

Chapter 2

23 years earlier

'A beautiful child'

> *A beautiful child I birth and hold*
> *The deep love I feel just can't be told*
> *Such perfect fingers, such perfect toes*
> *The biggest blue eyes, and a cute button nose*
> *Today life's journey starts, my son*
> *What will you do? What will you become?*

Liam wasn't my first baby; that was Megan. I was just twenty-two years old when she was born. She's a lively two-year-old now: an irrepressible bundle of energy. Thankfully, she's just settled down for her afternoon nap which will, hopefully, allow me one of those rare occasions when I can feed Liam without constant interruptions.

As I shift position and move him from one breast to the other, he gazes up at me with those beautiful, big blue eyes, and I feel that surge of love, that bond which only another mother can truly appreciate. As he settles to his feeding once again, he makes those contented little gurgling noises which make my heart sing.

After ten more minutes, his suckling becomes less urgent; his eyelids begin to close. After a few more minutes, he is fast asleep. I stand up carefully, anxious not to wake him, and ease him into his cot, laying a light blanket over him.

With both my children fast asleep, it's so tempting to grab a little 'me time': read a book, watch a bit of TV … even catch an hour or so of much-needed sleep myself. But no … there's always so much that needs to be done around the house. And it won't be so very long before James gets home. James is my partner, Megan and Liam's father. He's twenty-six years older than me, a gap that so many people have told me is far too much for a girl of my age to accept.

'Think about when you're sixty,' they'd say. 'He'll be eighty-six!'

I don't care. I'm just twenty-four; I can scarcely think a month ahead, let alone decades. I'm OK with his age; I just wish he'd do more to help out around the house.

James is a 'white goods' repair engineer: self-employed, so his hours vary considerably depending on his workload. Today, he only has three calls to make and is expecting to be home by about 4p.m. He doesn't much like me doing housework after he gets home from work, and he certainly doesn't like doing any himself. To keep the peace, I try to squeeze in as much housework as possible in those fleeting daytime intervals between caring for and playing with my kids, shopping, and trying to figure out how to pay the bills.

I glance up at the clock: 2.45p.m. Should be enough time to hang up the washing and clean the bathrooms; maybe even grab a cup of tea too. With a deep sigh, I head to the kitchen to check whether the washing machine has finished its cycle.

James is a bit later than expected getting home so, when I've completed the planned chores, I have a little time to sit down in front of the TV to watch the news. Not that the news is very uplifting: war in the Middle East, a devastating earthquake in Japan, and here at home, the economy tanking.

Before I can soak up any more doom and gloom from the TV, I hear the front door opening; James is home.

'What …' he says, his tone joking, but with an underlying familiar edge, 'got time to sit and watch TV during the day?' Those first few words set the tone for the evening.

I'm just about to let fly when Liam's first intermittent cries announce that he has woken up.

'Oh,' says James, dumping his tool-bag on the cream rug just inside the door – the precise place that I've asked him a million times not to – 'I guess you'd better go and see to him.'

I bite my lip and head off to attend to Liam.

***

By the time I have changed Liam's nappy and fed him, I have calmed down. When I come back into the living room, James is watching TV, while Megan is sitting on the floor happily brushing the hair of one of her dolls.

'How was your day?' I venture.

'Oh, OK ... pretty quiet really. Actually, business has been a bit *too* quiet lately. Since you've been off work, we're not really bringing in enough in to keep things on an even keel.'

Tell me something I don't know, I think. Trying to eke out the money available for food, clothes, and household essentials has become a daily struggle. And luxuries like occasionally eating out have become a distant dream.

For several years now, I've been working in a care home for special needs kids: not well-paid work, but oh so rewarding in other ways. I took a break when Megan was born, and now of course, with another small baby to care for, I'm off work again.

'I know,' I reply. 'Look, I'll be going back to work as soon as Liam's old enough to be left with a childminder, but in the meantime can't we do anything to perk up the business a bit?'

'Like what?'

'What about advertising?'

'Well, I've already got the signage on the van and an entry in Yellow Pages.'

'Hmm ... that slot in Yellow Pages is so tiny, and with a name like "Williams Washing Machine Repair", it's right near the end of the alphabetical listing.'

'Well ... that's my name,' he says, spreading his hands helplessly.

'And,' I add, 'how many people do you suppose happen to see your van at the exact time that their washing machine or dishwasher breaks down?'

'Hmm ... 'spose you're right,' he grunts.

'So, don't you think it's worth a try ... advertising, I mean?'

'I'm not sure if I can find the time to—'

I interrupt him. 'Then let *me* have a go ... it's something I could do, working from home until I go back to work.'

He looks up at me, finally showing some interest in what I'm saying. 'That's not a bad idea, babe. After all, you're here at home all day at the moment, with time on your hands.'

I don't take the bait.

'OK, well let's give it a try. We'll need to agree how much money we can afford to spend on it but then leave the rest to me.'

'O ... K,' he says, drawing out the letters.

'Now I need to go and start the dinner if we're to eat before Liam wakes up again.'

'Great ... I'm starving. What are we having?'

'Lasagne ... I'll just—'

I'm interrupted by a piercing scream.

'Megan, what is it? What's wrong?'

'Belinda's arm has come off,' she cries, rushing to me, her lower lip quivering as she holds up the dismembered doll.

'Don't worry, Daddy will fix it,' I assure her, guiding her towards her father, 'and then he'll play with you.'

'But I really wanted to watch the football,' he protests.

I shoot him my most withering glare. 'You want some dinner tonight, or not?'

He gets the message.

Chapter 3

4 months later

'The murder mystery party'

Things are looking up a bit.

The advertising seems to be working; business is up by around twenty percent, and the additional income is now more than covering the cost of the advertising. Money is still tight, but it won't be that long now before I can go back to work. My mum – bless her – has offered to provide free childcare while I'm at work.

Liam is now sleeping solidly through the night, meaning that I am no longer dead on my feet throughout the day.

James is still doing very little to help around the house or share any childcare duties but at least he's keeping busy at work now.

Are we in danger of entering a phase of our lives which could be considered 'normal'? We decide to test the theory by hosting one of those 'murder mystery' parties. You know the sort of thing: a boxed game, in which a small group of friends come round, and they are each assigned character roles according to the instructions in the box. Everyone then questions everyone else in an effort to try to identify which participant is the perpetrator of a fictitious murder. Past experience suggests it will expose absolutely appalling acting skills and everyone will fail miserably to identify the murderer – apart from the murderer him or herself of course: they are told on the individual card they are given.

It's a severe test: if we can get though the complete thing without it all turning to shit at some point, then we are indeed on the road to 'normal'.

***

Saturday evening; it's just after 9p.m. The kids were settled and asleep by 7p.m. in spite of vociferous protests from Megan, who could not see any just cause for being bundled off to bed so early. Promise of a trip to Rossi's ice cream parlour and a visit to the local duckpond to feed the ducks tomorrow morning settled the dispute.

We've been playing the game for almost two hours now and everyone is starting to get distinctly tipsy, which is doing nothing for the quality of the role play. I still don't have the first idea who the murderer is; the only thing I do know is that it's not me. I could cheerfully become one, though, if James doesn't stop his drunken flirting with our neighbour, Lisa. Mind you, she's doing nothing to discourage him. Disgraceful! He's old enough to be her father. But then again, I suppose he's old enough to be mine.

We reach one of those lulls in conversation which mysteriously occur from time to time for no obvious reason. Everyone seems to be intently studying their notes as though trying to make some kind of sense of their incoherent scribbles. Seems like a good time to take a break.

'Right,' I declare, 'while everyone's taking a few moments to try to work it out, I'll go and get some nibbles.'

My close friend, Debbie, pipes up. 'Oh, let me come and help … I don't think any amount of gazing at my notes is going to get me any closer to working it out.'

Now, Debbie has recently announced that she is pregnant, so I make the obligatory protest. 'No, in your condition, you should take it easy.'

'Oh nonsense, I'm only three months gone.'

'James,' I call out, 'perhaps you could help?'

He tears his gaze away from Lisa's cleavage, pretending to have been studying his notes before looking up. 'Uh, yes … in a moment … I … I think I'm onto something here … I just need to …'

By now, Debbie is on her feet. 'Come on, let's leave Sherlock to solve the crime, while you and I sort out the nibbles.'

I stare James a volley of daggers, none of which appear to find their target.

Debbie and I head for the kitchen.

'Right …' I say, waving a hand towards the numerous plates arrayed on the worktop, 'well, there's not much to do really. It's mostly all prepared. All we need to do is remove the cling film and take it all through to the living room. I'm so annoyed that James wouldn't even help with that.'

'Oh, never mind,' she says, her tone conspiratorial. 'Look, I wanted to get you alone for a moment anyway.'

I'm intrigued. 'Why … what is it?'

'You look … different.'

'Different … how, different?'

'Your face … it's sort of fuller, and you've got more colour in your cheeks.'

'What?' I reply, taking a few steps towards the mirrored door of one of the kitchen cabinets. I run my fingers down my cheeks. 'Well maybe I'm a bit flushed; it's pretty hot in the other room.'

Debbie gives a knowing shake of her head. 'I don't think it's that.'

I wasn't quite sure why she had picked up her handbag before we came into the kitchen, but now her reason becomes clear. She delves into the bag and hands me two small, blue, cardboard boxes. 'I still have a couple of these, left over from when I was testing myself.'

'Don't be ridiculous!' I laugh. 'I'm still breastfeeding, my periods haven't started up yet, and now I'm back on the pill. It's impossible.'

'Humour me,' she says. 'Go on, nip upstairs and do it now. I'll sort out the snacks while you're gone.'

***

I gaze in disbelief at the small, plastic device I am holding. It is only a few minutes since I have taken the test, but already there are two blue lines showing. Can this actually be true? Can I really be pregnant again? One of the lines is quite faint, so maybe it's a false positive.

I place the device on the windowsill, sitting back down for a couple of minutes before checking it again: both lines are now strong and distinct. I still don't believe it.

Can I squeeze out enough pee to use the second test? I think so; I've been drinking rather too much this evening.

Same procedure, same result: I'm pregnant ... just four months after giving birth to Liam.

In a daze, I pull up my knickers and jeans before heading down to re-join the party.

***

As soon as I enter the room, Debbie shoots me a significant glance.

'You OK?' says James. 'You've been gone for ages.'

'I ... er ... well, I do feel a bit ...'

My knees turn to jelly, and I feel as though I'm about to faint. Debbie rushes to my aid, propping me up and helping me out of the room.

'Well?' she says when we get out into the hallway.

I look her in the eyes and nod, helplessly.

She gives a little shriek of delight. 'I knew ... I just *knew* it. Can we tell everyone?'

Debbie is a great friend, but very impulsive, and to be honest, a bit pushy at times.

I'm too stunned to argue. 'I ... yes, well I suppose so.'

She drags me back into the living room where everyone is eating and chatting. There is no sign whatsoever that the murder mystery enquiry has been resumed.

Debbie grabs an empty glass from the coffee table and taps it with a spoon to attract everyone's attention. The conversation abruptly stops.

'We have an announcement,' she declares, before pausing a few seconds for dramatic effect. 'Madeleine is pregnant.'

As if this news wasn't momentous enough, Debbie reinforces it with a piercing scream of delight.

One by one, as the guests digest this unexpected news, they all begin to offer their congratulations. James just slumps back in his chair, his expression incredulous.

And that is the end of the murder mystery game. My unexpected pregnancy is now the only topic of conversation.

It turns out James was the murderer, which meant he never had to spend time working it out, and he could devote all his attention to studying Lisa's impressive bust.

Well, now he's got something else to think about.

Chapter 4

1 year later

'... and then we were five.'

Grace, our third child, was born one year, almost to the day, after Liam. So now we find ourselves with three children all under the age of four. I say 'we', but James is still contributing very little to bringing up the kids or helping around the house. Whenever I bring up the subject he argues, reasonably I suppose, that as my return to work is now on indefinite hold, he needs to concentrate on the business to bring in as much money as possible to fund our modest lifestyle. The trouble is ... it just isn't working.

The income from the business is starting to decline, and I just don't have time anymore to help with this. Grace is a delightful baby, but like all babies, demanding. With a three-year-old, a one-year-old, and a new baby to care for, plus a household to run, I just have no spare time whatsoever.

James is, as usual, reluctant to confront the issue, but I finally pin him down one evening to discuss what we're going to do.

***

'Look,' I say, 'when we started the extra advertising a year or so back, it really seemed to help bring in some extra business, but it just doesn't seem to be working as well now.'

He nods, gloomily. 'You're right. Not sure why, though.'

'Well, I'm no expert, but the advertising has probably become a bit too … familiar … stale, if you like. We probably need to pep it up and try some new ideas.'

'Good idea.' he agrees. 'What are you thinking of doing?'

I sigh. 'Look, I'm sorry, but I just can't help much right now. By the time I've fed and changed Grace, looked after Liam, taken Megan to and from nursery, done the shopping, done the housework, cooked our meals, and got the kids off to bed, I literally don't have *any* time left at all.'

'Oh,' he says, in a tone which suggests none of this has ever occurred to him.

We descend into silence for several long seconds, and then, uncharacteristically, he begins to show some initiative.

He leans forward and places his hand on mine. 'You're right … I'm going to have to pick up the advertising stuff myself. And truth be told, I'm getting behind on a lot of my paperwork, too. I think I need to allocate an hour or two at the end of each day, after I've finished all my house calls, to spend on admin.'

'That'd be great,' I say, reciprocating with a squeeze of his hand. 'And then, once I can get back to work myself as well, we should be more comfortable again.'

His brow furrows as he starts to process what might be required for this idea to work.

'I'll need somewhere quiet to work, with a desk, laptop, printer, and so on. Since the spare room has now been turned into a nursery for Grace, we just don't have any space at all.'

He does have a point. If he's serious about spending a couple of hours every day on admin he really needs some sort of dedicated work area. I don't want this plan to fall at the very first hurdle, so I make a suggestion.

'Why don't you see if you can rent some space in a small office somewhere nearby? Then maybe you could go there at the end of the day, after all your calls are finished, and do your admin before coming home. If you've properly finished all your work for the day, you might be able to relax a bit more in the evenings as well.'

He now looks positively animated – by his standards anyway. 'That's a great idea babe.' But then his face falls as quickly as it had brightened. 'But it'll cost … we can't afford to blow too much money on it.'

Back to the old James … always seeing problems rather than opportunities. He needs another nudge.

'Well, a small piece of office space shouldn't cost too much, and hopefully the extra work you'll be putting in will more than pay back.'

His brow furrows as he considers my words, before finally declaring. 'You're right … let's do it.'

This is about the most positive I've seen him for months. I hope it works out …

Chapter 5

3 years later

'Chocolate biscuits'

I'm back at work now. The daily routine is hectic. I drop Megan off at school and the two younger ones at nursery before starting work at 9.15a.m. in the care home. Mum picks them all up in the afternoon and looks after them until I can collect them from her around 5.00p.m. Don't know what I'd do without her.

James did find an office, but it hasn't exactly worked out as I'd hoped. He never gets in much before 8.30p.m. and then expects a cooked dinner. The kids can't wait until then, so we end up eating around 6p.m. and then I have to prepare something separately for James to eat on his own around 9p.m. by which time Liam and Grace are in bed. Even Megan doesn't always stay up to see him before going to bed.

By the time I've given James his dinner, I'm usually exhausted, so once the kids are all settled, I head off to bed myself, while James pours himself a glass of wine and settles down to watch TV. If I'm lucky, he'll have put the dirty dishes in the dishwasher before coming to bed, but if that involves emptying the clean items from the machine first, he usually doesn't bother.

I could perhaps tolerate all this if his late nights were actually resulting in more business, but they're not. We're still short of money and, were it not for my meagre salary, we'd really be in trouble.

All in all, not a happy situation.

***

This morning, like every morning, I'm up before everyone else, in order to get breakfast ready. On weekdays, breakfast time is the only time the five of us spend together as a family; something to be cherished in this frantic, chaotic life.

As I enter the kitchen, I'm pleased to see there are no dirty dishes on the worktop; it's a good start to the day. I set about preparing everyone's breakfasts, before making up the children's packed lunches. With sandwiches, fruit, and yoghurt stacked in their lunchboxes, I go to get the individually wrapped chocolate biscuits which complete the meal. I am dismayed to find just one, solitary Penguin biscuit where there should have been an assortment of at least eight Penguin, Club, and Caramel bars. The creeping tendrils of suspicion snake through my mind; this is not the first time this has happened.

As the anger begins to burgeon within me, I go through to the living room.

In an instant, my previously sunny mood evaporates. Not only is the sofa littered with empty chocolate biscuit wrappers, but on the coffee table is an empty wine bottle. The cork is still impaled on the corkscrew which is lying on the table alongside. Worse still, James's dirty dinner plate from the previous evening still festers on the table.

Now I am seething.

I stomp up the stairs and into our bedroom; James is fast asleep, snoring gently.

I grab a spare pillow and hit him with it, as hard as I can. 'Get up you lazy bastard!' I yell.

'Wh-what the hell …?' he splutters, blinking at me in utter bewilderment.

'I said, "get up!".' I grab his pyjama sleeve and pull on it until I hear the seam begin to rip. He stumbles unsteadily to his feet.

'What the hell are you doing?' he protests, rubbing his eyes as he tries to focus.

I slap his face, hard. 'I'll show you what the hell I'm doing. Get down those stairs!' I give him an encouraging shove from behind. Unfortunately, he maintains his balance and doesn't go head over heels down the stairs.

At the bottom of the stairs he pauses, evidently still disoriented. I shove him into the living room.

'Why the fuck,' I yell, pointing at the evidence on the sofa, 'did you eat all the kids' chocolate bars?'

He looks at me as though I'm totally demented – and to be honest, I *am* pretty close at this moment. 'I was hungry … only had a sandwich for lunch yesterday.'

I point at the empty plate on the coffee table. 'And steak pie and chips for dinner.'

'Well, I was still hungry … Christ! It's only a few chocolate bars.'

'And how, exactly, do I get the kids to eat the healthy stuff if I don't bribe them with a chocolate biscuit to finish?'

'Oh babe, come on … you're getting this all out of proportion.'

I ignore his last assertion. 'And what's with the wine?'

'Well, I always have a glass of wine in the evening.'

'A glass, yes … not a whole fucking bottle. I'm trying to watch every penny we spend, and you're just pissing it all away.'

'I-I'd had a hard day. I just—'

'Not as bloody hard as this one's going to be,' I seethe. 'And I suppose your plate was too heavy for you to carry through to the kitchen and put in the dishwasher?'

'Oh … yes … forgot about that. I can do it now.'

'Get out! Go and earn some money.'

'OK, as soon as I've had my breakfast, I'll—'

'Your breakfast?' I scream. 'I'll show you your breakfast.'

I drag him into the kitchen, show him the plate containing his breakfast, and scrape it all into the waste bin.'

His eyes widen in astonishment. 'Why the hell did you do that?'

'Work it out for yourself!' I yell. 'Now get dressed and get out of this house.'

He does.

***

Several weeks have passed since the flaming row over the chocolate biscuits although, in truth, it really wasn't all about the chocolate biscuits: they were just a trigger, a catalyst. It was about everything: our relationship, our circumstances, and to be frank, his infuriating lack of consideration. Still, things seem to have settled down a bit, and we have at least been civil to one another in recent weeks.

It's Saturday evening; my day hasn't been quite as frantic as a typical weekday. The kids are in bed, and after James drank himself silly with his golfing mates this afternoon, so is he.

Perfect! An evening all to myself in front of the TV.

I make myself a cup of tea and grab a couple of Hob Nobs from the biscuit barrel before curling up on the sofa. As I'm scrolling through the programme guide to see what's on, the front doorbell sounds. *Dammit! Who's this likely to be?*

I open the door to reveal a stranger: a man, probably aged around thirty, scruffy, hair dishevelled. I look at him enquiringly.

'Sorry to trouble you, love, but I wonder if you can help me?'

His words are slightly slurred; I'm immediately on edge.

'How can I help, exactly?'

'My car's broken down, and—'

I involuntarily close the door a few degrees. 'I'm sorry … I don't know anything about cars. Why don't you call a breakdown service?'

'Well that's the thing: I've lost my phone. Can I come in and use yours?'

Is this genuine? I'm not convinced.

'Wait a moment,' I say before turning my head and calling up to James.

'James! Can you come down here? There's someone at the door.'

No response.

The stranger waits, looking past me as though waiting for someone to appear.

I call out again, this time yelling at the top of my voice. 'James! Can you come down here?'

Finally, I hear a muffled reply, but the words are indistinguishable.

'He's coming,' I say, more in hope than expectation.

Then I hear the sound of footsteps on the creaky floorboards upstairs, followed by James's voice – louder now. 'What the hell is it? I was asleep.'

'Can you come down here … there's someone at the door who needs some help.'

'Oh Christ, Mads … can't you deal with it? I'm shattered.'

With that, I hear the floorboards creaking again, tracing his path back to the bedroom. *The bastard's actually going back to bed!*

'Look,' says the stranger, 'no need to get him up; I'll only need a couple of minutes.'

As he takes a step closer, I catch a waft of the alcohol on his breath. He gently pushes the door open a little further.

That's enough! There's something very wrong here.

'Sorry,' I say, 'but I'm afraid I can't help you.'

I go to close the door, but he pushes back.

'Come on, darlin' … I only want to—'

His plea is cut short as I stamp on his foot, as hard as I can. I'm only wearing bedroom slippers, so it can't have inflicted much pain, but the surprise is enough to make him relax his pressure against the door for a moment. I crouch slightly, tense, and then put my shoulder against the door, lunging forward as hard as I can,

It works: he staggers backwards as the door slams shut. I quickly slip the security bolt into place.

Now he's hammering furiously at the door. 'Let me in, bitch … I was only … LET ME IN!'

'You fuck off!' I scream. 'I'm calling the police … right now.'

The hammering ceases, and when I peep through the spyhole in the door, I can see him walking away, no doubt to try his luck elsewhere.

I slump down on the sofa, my heart pounding. As I go to take a sip of tea, my hand is shaking so much that it slops over the rim of the cup. I curse, steadying the cup with my other hand. The tea's half cold now anyway.

With all thoughts of watching TV now banished from my mind, I switch everything off and head up to bed.

James appears to be fast asleep, and I'm not ready to have another row with him right now, so I let him sleep while I slip into bed alongside him.

But he's not asleep. I feel his hand snake across and settle on my breast. He rolls towards me and starts nuzzling my neck. The stink of alcohol assaults my senses.

'Are you fucking kidding me?' I hiss, pulling away sharply.

'Aw, c'mon, babe, it's been quite a few days now.'

'And it'll be quite a few more,' I mutter.

I jump smartly out of bed.

'Oh … baaabe,' he protests.

'We'll talk about this tomorrow … GOOD NIGHT.'

I grab a blanket from the chest of drawers in the corner of the room and head downstairs to sleep on the sofa.

Chapter 6

'The last supper'

When, the following day, I relate the incident of the stranger trying to force his way into our house, James actually appears to be genuinely concerned. He swears he will never, ever, leave me in such a situation again.

But it's too little, too late. I've heard too many of his lame excuses, explanations, and apologies over the years. This incident is the last straw.

Now, three weeks later, I'm ready to make my move.

It's Sunday. James has been out playing golf for much of the day, but we agreed earlier to have a proper family meal, all together, at around 5.30p.m.

I really push the boat out: prawn cocktail starter, full Sunday roast to follow, and profiteroles for dessert. I haven't discussed my plans with either James or the children. Only I know it will be the last supper.

***

'That was fabulous, babe,' declares James. He turns to the children. 'Isn't your mummy a great cook, kids?'

They all nod in unison. Grace, the youngest, declares, 'The very best in the whole wide world.'

'Yes!' cry the other two.

I feel a surge of love towards all three of them. Soon, they will no longer have to endure their father's neglect. Soon, it will be just the four of us.

'Thank you,' I say. 'Everyone had enough?'

Assent all round.

'Then I'll get cleared up.'

'I'll help you, Mummy,' says Megan.

'Thank you.'

'And me,' adds Grace.

'Alright if I go and watch the football?' says James. 'Looks like you've already got two willing helpers.'

'That's fine,' I say, knowing it's the last time I will be taken for granted like this. 'Liam,' I add, 'you can watch the football with Daddy if you like … the girls are helping me with the clearing up.'

'OK,' he says skipping off alongside his father.

***

I don't sleep at all well that night, but nothing is going to deter me from my chosen course.

We all have breakfast together as usual, but I've taken care to make sure we're fifteen minutes or so ahead of schedule this morning. James doesn't seem to have noticed.

I send the kids upstairs to clean their teeth and gather all their things for school and nursery.

'We're a little bit early this morning, so you can play in your rooms for a while before we set off.'

'Yes!' exclaims Liam.

Once they're all upstairs I turn to James. 'Before you set off for work, I need to talk to you.'

'You do … what about?'

This is it … I take a deep breath. 'I'm leaving you.'

His eyebrows levitate and his jaw drops. For a second or two he appears to be dumbstruck.

Eventually he finds his voice. 'Is this a joke?'

'No joke. When you get back from work today, we'll be gone.'

'What? You can't just spring that on me, out of the blue.'

'Out of the blue? Now *you're* the one who's joking. You know full well that our relationship is shot to pieces. I just can't carry on bearing the whole burden of holding our family together without a scrap of support from you.'

He looks wounded. 'That's not fair … I mean, I know I'm not always around for you and the kids but …' his voice peters out.

'See,' I say, 'you can't even think of a credible "but".'

'We need to talk about this.'

'No, we don't … I'm done talking.'

His shoulders slump: it feels like his moment of realisation. 'What about the kids?'

'They're coming with me.'

'You can't take Liam.'

'Why just Liam … what about your daughters?'

'You know I already have four daughters from my previous marriage.'

'And how much attention do you ever pay to them? I'll tell you … NONE. I'm taking Liam, along with the girls. We don't need you, and we don't want you. Goodbye James.'

He looks me directly in the eyes. 'Let's talk about it when I get home.'

'We'll all be gone by then … now you'd better get going if you're going to make your first call at nine-thirty.'

He makes for the door, picking up his bag and turning to give me one last, imploring look. I maintain a stony countenance.

When the door closes behind him, I dissolve into tears. However determined I was – and that determination has not wavered – this is the end of an era: the closure of a chapter of my life. I have no idea what lies ahead, but I know this is what I have to do.

Chapter 7

'The house hunt'

My first priority is finding somewhere to live. Right now, we're all staying with Mum; as always, she's supportive of my choices and never judges me. I love her to bits. But this can only be a temporary solution; her house is way too small to accommodate all of us and it's just not fair to impose on her like this for any significant length of time.

Having scoured the local newspapers and the internet for several days, I quickly discover that finding and paying for somewhere to live is not going to be easy. There's quite a shortage of suitable rented properties in the local area, and the rents are, frankly, more than my meagre salary will support. What's more, most landlords want an initial deposit equivalent to six weeks' rent plus the first month's rent up-front. I just don't have that sort of money spare.

And it gets worse: it's only been days since we walked out on James, but already I know that I won't be able to carry on working at the care home as well as dealing with bringing up three kids on my own and running a household. If I *can* secure a suitable property for us, I'm going to have to quit my job and rely on whatever benefits I can claim; right now, I don't even know how much that might amount to.

That night, after the kids have gone to bed, I open the last bottle of wine which I had retrieved from the fridge at our previous home before leaving James. I retire to 'my' room – Mum's given me the larger of her two spare bedrooms, while Liam has the tiny third bedroom. The girls are sleeping on camp beds in what used to be my absent father's study. I pour myself a generous measure of wine and put the radio on low to provide some sort of aural backdrop while I contemplate my situation.

As I turn it all round and round in my head, the position seems to become more and more intractable. I know I didn't think all this through properly before leaving, but equally, I know it was something I had to do. I pour myself another glass of wine.

Mum has already offered to help financially, but I know she doesn't have much. She's already helped so much; I can't raid her little nest egg too.

Could I apply to the council to house us? Possibly, but who knows how long that might take? You hear all the time about long waiting lists for council accommodation. I pour myself another glass of wine.

Come on Mads ... there has to be a solution. But if there is, it just doesn't seem to be forthcoming. My head is starting to feel sort of fuzzy, and I'm *so* tired now. I pour the last of the wine into my glass, take a couple of sips, and lay my head back on the pillow.

***

I'm not sure what it was that woke me up: the crashing of the garbage bins being collected outside or the insistent pressure in my bladder. Either way, I feel like shit.

I blink to try to clear my blurred vision; the soft light of dawn is seeping through the thin curtains, suffusing the room with a gentle glow. I check the bedside clock: 5.15a.m. I'm still fully clothed.

Christ! I must have dropped off and slept right through.

Alongside the clock, on the bedside table, the wine bottle is empty, and only what was left in my glass remains. I give a wry smile as I think back to how I used to berate James for demolishing a whole bottle on his own in an evening. Still, I know it won't happen again as that was the only bottle I had, and I certainly can't afford to buy any more.

There's no point going to bed now; the kids will be up and about soon. I drag myself up to a sitting position; swing my legs over the edge of the bed; and sit there for a few moments, head in hands, as I try to pull myself together sufficiently to face the day ahead. I can't linger long, as I'm absolutely bursting for a pee. Wearily, I drag myself to my feet and head for the bathroom, taking my glass with me and tipping the last remnants of wine into the wash hand basin.

Having relieved myself and stripped off my crumpled clothes, I reach into the shower and turn on the water, waiting until the temperature has stabilised before stepping inside. As I let the soothing jets of water wash over me, my thoughts return to the dilemma I was wrestling with the previous evening.

Isn't it strange how a fresh mind and the cold light of day can begin to open a pathway through problems which seem completely insurmountable in the darkness of night?

As I turn the issue over and over in my mind, I start to feel a new resolve, a determination to succeed. It was my decision to leave James and strike out on my own with the kids, so *I* will be the one to make it work.

By the time I step out of the shower, ten minutes later, I have a plan.

***

Two hours later, having completed the school run, I settle down in front of my laptop, my phone alongside, and set to work. I've already booked a week off work to give myself a little time to try to sort out my situation, but that will fly by; there's no time to waste.

The first thing I need is some money … to pay the deposit and up-front rent on a house or apartment. I've never before checked my credit rating, but I've had two credit cards for years and I've never defaulted on payments so maybe it won't be too bad. A quick trawl on the internet reveals that I score 'good'. So far, so good.

I make some enquiries about a bank loan. Looks like my own bank is my best bet. They won't give me a definite answer right now, on the phone, but they say that, in principle, I should be able to borrow up to £12,000, repayable over three years. *Yes!*

I decide not to go for the full amount, knowing that I'm about to quit my job. The last thing I need is to default on repayments and ruin my credit score for the future. I fill in the online form for a loan of 10,000.

At this point, I suppose I should wait for confirmation that I've been accepted for the loan, but I'm on a roll now, so I don't intend to do so.

I check the time: 2.30p.m. It's nearly time for the school/nursery run; I won't be able to do any more today. Never mind, house-hunting starts in earnest tomorrow!

It's been a good day's work.

***

Two days have now elapsed since I applied for the bank loan; I don't yet have confirmation that it will be forthcoming but I'm pressing on regardless. I've looked at six properties so far, but they have all been unsuitable or too expensive. Let's hope today's efforts will be more fruitful.

The first place I look at today is currently unoccupied. It's a three-bedroomed semi: big enough for our needs, but unfurnished, which is less than ideal as I have absolutely nothing to put in it. The interior décor is really tired, but the landlord is, according to the letting agent, planning to redecorate before a new tenant moves in. The rent they are asking is a bit cheaper than anything else remotely suitable that I've seen. All in all, it's probably as good a compromise as I'm going to find.

The biggest issue is that I really want to move in as soon as possible but allowing time for the redecoration means it's not going to be available for at least four or five weeks. I make an offer: I'll do the redecoration myself, in due course, if they can knock a bit off the rent and can let me move in within a week. A phone call to the landlord results in a rent reduction of £100 per month and agreement that we can move in as soon as all the formalities are completed.

We are finally there!

***

Not quite! The following day, I learn that while my credit checks have all been satisfactory, the agent requires one, or preferably two references from previous landlords. This is a problem: the previous house was rented in James's name, and although I was contributing to the rent, there is nothing official to verify that. A phone call to James reveals him to be distinctly unhelpful, pointing out that it was my choice to walk out, and having made my bed, I will just have to lie in it. His parting shot is to remind me that there is no way he will be paying any maintenance for the kids, and that I will have to take him to court if I want to contest that. Like I've got the sort of money to get involved in a court case!

Bastard!

I've come too far, now, to fall at the last hurdle; I call the agent and explain the situation – or at least, as much of the situation as they need to know – and see if there's a way through this.

After an anxious wait while they talk to the landlord, the agent calls me back. There is, indeed, a solution, but it's a painful one: if I can pay six months' rent in advance, they can dispense with the need for references.

Six months! That will take most of my bank loan, all in one go … even assuming I do, indeed, get the bank loan in the first place.

With no other option available to me, though, I agree.

I hope to Christ that loan comes through …

Chapter 8

Two weeks later

'A fresh start'

We're in!

The house is barely more than an empty shell right now – we have no furniture to speak of, and as I already mentioned, it needs redecorating – but we're going to make it *home*.

The absolute basics are in place: there are curtains – old, but functional – at the windows, and most of the rooms have reasonably decent carpets. The kitchen has all the appliances we need: cooker, washing machine, dishwasher, fridge. There is, unfortunately, no crockery or cutlery, but Mum has lent us enough to get started.

The biggest problem is lack of furniture. The girls are sleeping on Mum's folding camp beds, while Liam and I are using inflatable camping mattresses which we have had for years. We have a separate dining room but no dining table or chairs. However, there's a reasonably sized breakfast bar in the kitchen, and I picked up a couple of bar stools from a nearby charity shop. We can only eat at the breakfast bar two at a time, but we're getting by.

Our big luxury is a twenty-eight-inch colour TV, given to me by a friend when she upgraded to a bigger model. With four beanbags, picked up cheaply online, we can all lounge in front of the TV together, on those rare occasions when there's time to do so.

It's a pretty austere way of living, but the kids love it! To them it's a huge adventure; it's a bit like the wonder and excitement of your first camping trip. Not sure how long the novelty will last, but for now, we're enjoying life together as a family in our makeshift new home.

Perhaps the biggest surprise – in a good way – is that none of them are showing any obvious signs of missing their father. But maybe I shouldn't be surprised: he never really devoted much time to them or showed them any love; in fact, recently in particular, he was often quite aggressive towards them. I'm more certain than ever, now, that for all the sacrifices we are having to make, I made the right decision in leaving James.

***

We've been in the house for around six weeks now, when the most amazing stroke of good fortune arrives.

My phone rings; it's my friend, Sarah. She works at the care home. We haven't seen each other since I left, but we've spoken on the phone a few times, and she's aware of my situation.

'Oh, hi Sarah … lovely to hear from you. How are things with you?'

'Oh, good thanks. More to the point how are things with *you*?'

'Well, we're in the new house, but it's all a bit spartan. No furniture to speak of, but we're managing. I had to blow most of my bank loan on paying six months' rent up-front, so money's tight, but hopefully my benefits will be coming through soon.'

'Well, at least you're out of that relationship now.'

'Uh, huh … I might have some new problems to deal with, but that part, at least, is like a huge weight off my shoulders. And the best part of all is that the kids seem happy.'

'No regrets, then?'

'No regrets,' I agree.

'That's great,' says Sarah. 'Look, it's lovely to catch up, but my main reason for calling was that I may be able to help with at least one of the things you're dealing with.'

I'm intrigued. 'Oh … er, what's that then?'

'You know Steve applied for that job in Australia?'

'Oh, yes … you told me about it. What's the score?'

'Well, he's got it. It means a big increase in salary and it's just the career move he was looking for.'

'Oh, that's great news, Sarah. Give him my congratulations.'

'I will … it's a great opportunity, but it does mean we'll have to move to Australia for the job.'

'Well, I guess I won't be seeing you for a while then.'

'Well, probably more than "a while" … we've decided to make it a permanent move. We're emigrating.'

'Wow … how exciting!'

'It is. We're going to sell up here and start a new life out there.'

'That's fantastic … I'm so happy for you.'

'Anyway,' says Sarah, 'that's what I was getting to. We're not taking any of our furniture with us, so we'd like you to take any of it that you can use.'

I'm momentarily stunned. 'But you have such nice things … I couldn't possibly afford—'

She interrupts me. 'We don't want any money for it. If we go to a house clearance company, we'll get next to nothing for it anyway. We'd far rather give it to a friend who needs it.'

I still can't quite take it in. 'Oh, Sarah … that's just … I don't know what to say …'

'Well, don't say anything then,' she laughs. 'Why don't you come round and put a sticker on everything you want to take? Steve's going up to London for a couple of days this week to sort out all the emigration paperwork, so we can have a coffee and a nice, long girls' chat.'

'Oh my God, Sarah, that's just … I can't believe it.'

'Just glad to be able to help. Can you make Thursday?'

'Yes … Thursday is fine. I'll come round straight after dropping the kids at school and nursery.'

'Great … see you then.' She hangs up.

Maybe my fortunes are finally starting to look up.

Chapter 9

One year later

'Liam starts school'

Monday, and it's Liam's first day at school. Our first stop, however, is to drop Grace off at nursery. Liam is uncharacteristically quiet in the car on the way over there, in marked contrast to his sisters who are chattering and giggling the whole time. Once we've deposited Grace at nursery, Megan also falls silent; it's a rather strange atmosphere.

I park the car and walk up to the school gates with the children; Megan immediately spots one of her friends and makes to rush off.

'Megs!' I call. 'Wait ... don't forget your bag.'

'Oh yes.' She swivels around and relieves me of her school bag.

Then, eager to catch up with her friend, she lunges again.

'Hey,' I cry, 'haven't you forgotten something else?' I bend down, place the tip of my forefinger against my cheek, and pucker up.

She rushes back, giggling, and gives me a perfunctory peck on the cheek.

'Have a good day,' I call, but as she skips away, my words are swallowed up by the cacophony of cries from dozens of excited children exchanging tales of what they've been up to over the weekend.

As the older children file into the building, the noise level gradually subsides. Before long, Liam and I find ourselves among the other reception class children due to start today, and their mums

… and in one or two cases, their dads. Now, virtually the only sound is the soft murmuring of conversation between a few of the parents who know each other because they already have older children at the school.

Just five minutes later, two teachers I know, and a couple of other staff members I don't recognise, emerge from the building.

'Look,' says Liam – the first word he has uttered since we arrived – 'there are Miss Steele and Miss Perkins.' He finally cracks a smile.

He knows the teachers from the induction sessions he attended the previous week; he told me they were both very nice.

Miss Steele stands by the door, beckoning, while the other staff members move among the little crowd, gently shepherding people towards the door.

As we reach the door, his new teacher bends down and places a hand on his shoulder. 'Hello, Liam … are you looking forward to your first day at school?'

He looks up at me, his expression pleading, but does not reply.

'Go on,' I say, encouraging him with a gentle push between his shoulder blades.

He finally shuffles through.

'He'll be fine,' Miss Steele assures me. 'Now, you know it's only a half day today, don't you?'

'Uh, huh.'

'The children will be ready to be picked up at 1.00p.m.'

'OK, thanks.' I move aside to let the next anxious mum deliver her child.

I linger for a few moments, gazing at the building, trying to imagine the emotions my beautiful little boy is experiencing. He's certainly not a shy child, but today, he seems so nervous, so vulnerable, so … small. But I have to let go.

With a sigh, I turn away and head for the car.

***

When I arrive to collect Liam at 12.55p.m. there are already a handful of other mums waiting. I exchange a few pleasantries with one of them; she seems as anxious as I am, as we discuss our respective children's attitudes towards starting school.

After a few minutes, the door opens, and Miss Steele appears with a little girl, encouraging her to identify her mother among the adults waiting outside. The child points and smiles; her teacher releases her into the arms of her grateful mother.

One by one, the children are issued from the classroom until, finally, Liam appears. He spots me immediately.

My previous anxiety about how the day would go proves to be completely unfounded. He bounds towards me, smiling broadly.

'How was it then?' I ask, gathering him up for a hug.

'It was brilliant!' he enthuses. 'I have two new best friends.'

I resist the temptation to point out that, technically, you can only have *one* best friend. I'm just pleased to see him so happy.

'You do? What are their names?'

'Leo and Katie.'

'But Katie's a girl's name.' I laugh. 'You said you don't like girls.'

'Well I didn't,' he replies, his expression earnest, 'but Katie's really nice … she's into "Star Wars".'

Well, there could hardly be a better qualification for 'best friend' status than that could there?

I'm so, so happy.

Chapter 10

'Planning for the future'

Liam is nicely settled in at school now, and it will be less than a year before Grace joins him. I need to start thinking about the future.

I quit my job at the care home some weeks ago and now I'm relying on benefits to get by; money is incredibly tight. I have no man in my life to help, and it will be years before I can go back to work full-time. When I do, though, I don't want to just drift from one low-paid job to another; I want a proper career. I want to give my kids a decent start in life.

I'm drawn towards the caring professions. I've always been a 'people' person. I could go back into the care home sector, but the money's just so poor. Maybe I could become a social worker, but I like working in a team and I wonder if this kind of work might be too solitary. I eventually decide to set my sights on nursing.

When I look into what's involved, I'm surprised to find that, to fully qualify as a nurse, you need to complete a four-year diploma. As if that wasn't enough, you need to be qualified to 'A' level or equivalent to even get a place on the diploma course. It would be a hell of a commitment, but at least, unlike a nine to five job, my study time would be reasonably flexible, and I could organise things around my regular commitments. By the time I'd have completed my six years of study and qualified as a nurse, it would only be another couple of years before both Liam and Grace would both be in high school, and able to make their own way to and from school. Then I could go to work full time.

The big sticking point is, as always, money. The prospect of trying to survive for another six years on benefits alone is a pretty scary prospect. However, as I investigate further, I discover that someone on low income or benefits may be eligible for a bursary to help fund full time education in healthcare related subjects. If I can secure one of these, then maybe, just maybe, I can make the numbers add up.

It's all starting to seem like a feasible plan, and if I *can* make it work, not only will I finally have a proper career, but I'll be doing work which is genuinely worthwhile … not only personally satisfying, but of value to society.

Chapter 11

Five years later

'The party … and an unexpected surprise'

I'm just about to start the final year of my diploma; it's been incredibly tough.

I managed to get the bursary I was seeking. Together with my benefits and the occasional bit of 'off the books' casual work, I was just about able to get by. I enrolled on an 'A' level course at college and secured three 'A' levels with good grades: more than enough to get me onto the nursing diploma course. I could never have imagined, though, just how hard it would be fitting in the studying around my commitments as a homemaker and mother. I had to get my mum and some friends to share the school run for me, and writing essays at 2a.m. became a regular occurrence. I was more or less permanently exhausted. But I stuck with it; I'm proud of myself for that.

And now, finally, the end is in sight.

I'm currently on a work placement at the local hospital. I'm loving it: the interaction with patients is so rewarding, and I've made some great friends. I'm more and more convinced that I've made the right career choice.

One of the nurses that I've become friends with is Sharon. She's recently separated from her husband, so she's happy to hang out with me and the other singletons. She's still on good terms with her ex, so when she organises a party for some of the staff nurses and student nurses, she also invites him and some of his friends along.

'Got to have a few men along,' she says, when she invites me, 'even if most of them are arseholes.'

She laughs at her own joke, but I have to say I agree with her.

When I mention the party to Mum, she has no hesitation in offering to look after the kids.

'Go on … enjoy yourself … you deserve it.'

She's such a dependable rock in my chaotic life.

***

It's not an especially big party, just five of us girls from the hospital and, by accident or design, five men, too – knowing Sharon it'll be the latter! To begin with, we girls are all chatting away in the living room, while the men congregate in the kitchen, next to where the drinks are laid out. However, as the evening wears on, and the booze starts to take effect, the two groups begin to mingle. Sharon disappeared ten minutes ago, ostensibly to get a drink, but she hasn't returned yet, so I guess she's talking to the men in the kitchen. Well, my glass is empty too now, so I'm also going for a top up.

When I go through to the kitchen, I see that Sharon has cornered one of the guys – I don't know him – and skilfully separated him from the rest of the group. As I move towards the drinks table, I see three heads swivel in unison in my direction. I recognise the lustful glint in their eyes. It's a long time since any man has looked at me like that, but then it's a long time since I've bothered to attend properly to my hair and makeup and shimmy into a figure-hugging dress whose hem finishes halfway up my thighs. *Guess I must still have it when I try!*

The guy talking to Sharon casts only a fleeting glance at me, before pretending he hasn't noticed me at all and returning his attention to Sharon.

Two of the guys shuffle back from the table so as to give me access to the drinks, but one of them is a little bolder.

'Sorry we've been monopolising the drinks … what can I get you?'

'Thank you,' I say, smiling, 'I'll have a glass of white wine.'

He pours two glasses and hands one to me, subtly positioning himself between me and the other three guys.

'Cheers!' he says offering his glass for a clink.

A bit pushy, I think, but he's not a bad looking guy, and when he smiles, there's an engaging twinkle in his vibrant, blue eyes.

We clink glasses and he offers me his hand to shake. His touch is confident and firm, but he avoids the finger-crushing grip which some guys feel obliged to employ – presumably to reinforce their macho credentials.

'I'm Adam ... pleased to meet you, er ...?'

'Oh ... Madeleine ... likewise.'

'Madeleine? Oh, Sharon's told me all about you.'

I'm completely thrown by this remark. But then a creeping realisation takes hold. Sharon never told me the name of her ex, but ... *oh my god this is going to be awkward.*

I try to compose myself. 'Oh, then you must Sharon's ...'

'Oh, yes ... we were married, but that's all over now. We're still friends though ... otherwise I wouldn't be here, would I?'

I smile, weakly. 'No, I guess not.'

I really need to extricate myself from this situation, but he's on a roll now.

'Shall we take our drinks through to the living room and sit down for a while? My legs are killing me after standing for so long.'

Before I have a chance to reply, he turns and places his hand in the small of my back, shepherding me gently towards the door.

By the time we sit down on the sofa, my initial panic is starting to subside. What does it really matter if he's Sharon's ex? They're separated now. It's a long time since any man paid me such attention, and he *is* quite attractive, if a bit over-confident. I decide to relax and enjoy some male company for a change.

***

Two hours have passed and several more glasses of wine been consumed. As he has relaxed into our conversation, he's become much less pushy, perhaps no longer feeling the need to assert himself. He's quite an interesting guy, and very easy to talk to. He's now attentive without being over-the-top and he really *listens* to what I have to say.

I like him.

Suddenly, we reach one of those moments which so often occur at social gatherings. You know, when the first guest or guests decide to leave, and it seems to trigger a chain reaction in which everyone else quickly follows.

'Oh, seems like we might be last to go,' I giggle, now distinctly tipsy.

He eases back from me – only now do I realise that our bodies have edged closer and closer together to the point where we are gently pressed against each other. I also back off slightly.

'Yes,' he says 'don't want to outstay our welcome. Look, it's been lovely to meet you, Madeleine. Perhaps I could see you again sometime?'

'Yes,' I reply, a little too eagerly, the wine having considerably lowered my inhibitions, 'I'd like that.'

He smiles and withdraws from his pocket a business card. 'Call me. I'm free most evenings.'

I slip the card into my bag. 'I will … right now though, I need to call a cab.'

***

In the cab, on the way home, I take a look at Adam's business card.

Blackford Garden Furniture

Adam Blackford – Managing Director.

Strangely, in all that time we were talking, he never mentioned what he did for a living. Sounds like he's the boss of this company.

Is all this too good to be true? A single, attractive man, who's interesting to talk to, attentive, and with a good job?

Doesn't sound like my sort of luck but maybe … just maybe …

Chapter 12

'Parents' evening'

Liam is ten now, and it's parents' evening. I have learned, through past experience, to approach these events with a certain degree of trepidation.

'Well …' says his form teacher. How can the tone of voice carried in just that one word, portend so much bad news?

'Well,' she says again, as though she couldn't quite muster up the courage to spit out whatever it was she wanted to say the first time, 'I always like to start with the positive things.'

I nod. 'Hmm … OK.'

'Well,' – third time now – 'he's very keen on all kinds of sports … especially football. And he shows a real aptitude for such activities.'

'And the more … "academic" stuff?' I prompt.

Her face falls. 'Well,' – *for Christ's sake, stop saying 'well', will you?* – 'I'm afraid he just doesn't seem to have much interest in the traditional subjects … Maths, English, Geography, and so on.'

I sigh. *Tell me something I don't know.* 'And his behaviour in class?'

'Well,' – *I will strangle you if you start one more sentence with that word* – 'he is rather cheeky … actually, a bit naughty to be honest.'

This all sounds remarkably like what I was told at the last parents' evening; clearly none of my stern admonishments at home have had the slightest effect. But his teacher, perhaps picking up on my crestfallen expression, does have some positive news.

She leans forward, making a steeple with her fingers. 'The thing is, Miss Fisher, although the traditional subjects don't seem to interest him, I have no doubt that he's a very intelligent boy.'

'How do you mean?' I say, intrigued.

'Well,' – I decide to give her a stay of execution on the 'well' thing, as she's evidently about to say something good about my son – 'just last week, I was giving a geography lesson and showing a film about the destruction of the Amazon rainforests.'

O...K, I think, *What does this have to do with my delinquent son's behaviour?* I bite my lip and wait.

'Right in the middle of the film, my computer completely froze up. I tried all the usual stuff … switching it off and on and so on but it was no good. I called I.T. but they said it would be at least a couple of hours before they could get to it, so I apologised to the children and said we'd have to leave it until another day.'

I'm getting impatient now. 'So, what exactly does this have to do with Liam?'

'I was just getting to that,' she says, raising a forefinger to underline the importance of what she is about to tell me. 'Liam asked if he could have a look at my computer to see if he could figure out what was wrong. Obviously, I wasn't expecting a ten-year-old to be able to solve the problem, but I was happy to let him look at it while I went to sort out some alternative material for the rest of the lesson.'

'And …?' I ask.

She spread her hands and raised her eyebrows. 'He fixed it! Took him about three minutes.'

'Well,' – *oh Christ, I'm doing it now!* – 'I know he is good with computers and techy things in general. I got him a PlayStation when he was only eight. Couldn't figure out how to set it up myself but he did it, no problem.'

She nodded, sagely, 'That's the thing you see … he's a bright child, but that's only evident when he's dealing with something that matches his interests and talents.'

I felt a warm wave wash over me. At least his teacher could appreciate that my son was much more than just a naughty, cheeky little boy.

She continued, 'We'll obviously do our best to get him more engaged with his other schoolwork, and you have a big part to play in that, too, but we should encourage his interest in computers and technology … and sport. Who knows? He could have a future career in one of these fields.'

I come away from parents' evening confused and conflicted. Is my son a waster, or a genius in the making? He's too young for me to be sure right now, but I guess time will tell.

Chapter 13

'A new man in my life ... and a father figure for Liam'

It is a couple of weeks after the party before I call Adam. He seems more than pleased when I do and immediately invites me out for dinner.

That first date confirms my initial impression: he is interesting, funny, and attentive.

It turns out that, in spite of running his own business, he's living with his mum. When he and Sharon split, she got the house, in exchange for relinquishing her part-ownership of the business. I would have invited him back to mine for a coffee but as *my* mum is there, looking after the children, that would have been a bit awkward, too.

As it is, he just drives me home and walks me up to the front door. As we say goodnight we exchange a brief kiss on each cheek, but we don't immediately let go of each other. Our eyes meet in one of those 'should I, shouldn't I?' moments which lasts for a second or two.

Oh fuck this, I think, *someone's got to make the first move.* I put my hand behind his neck and pull him gently towards me, parting my lips and planting them on his. That's all the encouragement he needs: his tongue insinuates itself between my lips and I feel his hand slide down to my backside, pulling me towards him. I feel his burgeoning erection pressing against my body, as our tongues entwine.

The clinch lasts for what seems like an age … but a very pleasant age. When, at last, we move apart, breathless and flushed, he looks into my eyes, his gaze lingering.

'Can I see you again?' he whispers, eventually.

I nod, smiling. 'Call me.' I withdraw from my bag a slip of paper, scribbling my number on it and handing it to him. 'Weekends are best for me. I'm pretty wiped out most weekdays … and evenings.'

As he steps into his car and prepares to drive off, we exchange a little wave. I stay there on the doorstep until his car has disappeared from view around the corner.

Is this the start of something special? I'm way too jaded and world-weary to have any starry-eyed expectations, but if I can have a nice time with a man who makes me feel good, then I'll be happy.

***

We see each other a lot over the coming weeks, and it's not long before I decide to subject my new man to the acid test: my children.

In my experience, most men run a mile once they come face to face with the reality of a relationship in which the object of their desires has kids in tow. Time to find out …

Megan is thirteen, Liam eleven, and Grace ten. They all like animals: the girls love the small and fluffy ones such as Bush Babies, while Liam is fascinated by the weird, creepy, and scaly creatures like snakes, lizards, and spiders.

I invite Adam to join me and the children for a trip to the zoo. If he passes this test, maybe he really *is* a keeper.

When we arrive at the zoo, the first thing I do is give strict instructions to the kids to stay together and not to run off out of sight. The first thing *they* do is scatter in all directions. We eventually find the girls cooing over a pen full of lop-eared rabbits, while Liam seems entranced by the behaviour of some weird-looking monkeys, licking one another's genitals.

Once we get everyone back together again, the kids are duly admonished for running off like that. We warn them that any repeat performance will result in withdrawal of the previous promise of ice creams after lunch. This seems to be a reasonably successful tactic as they all stay at least within sight after that.

When we stop for lunch, I make my mental assessment of how Adam is doing in this most important of tests. Well, he definitely looks a lot less comfortable than when it's just the two of us together, but he's making the effort. I guess he realises that the children and I come as a job lot; if he wants me, then the kids come as part of the deal.

The rest of the day goes OK. Adam is starting to look more comfortable interacting with the children, especially Liam. He seems a little less so with the girls, but maybe that will come in time. Overall, I decide to score him about seven out of ten: not too bad for a single guy who's never had children himself and certainly not a deal-breaker for our relationship.

***

Over the next couple of months, the impressions I formed at that first visit to the zoo start to crystalise. Adam never really does bond with the girls as well as I'd hoped he might, and to be honest, they don't really gel all that well with him. It's not enough of a problem to seriously spoil our relationship – just a bit disappointing.

Liam, on the other hand, absolutely loves him. Adam is happy to take him to see football matches and buy him replicas of the local team's latest kit. He also takes a lot of interest in the technology stuff which Liam is so good at and will play video games with him for hours on end. The fact that Adam gets on so well with Liam goes some way to compensate for his cooler relationship with the girls.

He and I are still good; we're sleeping together now … when we can. It's a bit awkward, though, when he's still living with his mum, and we both have busy lives.

All in all, though, things are going OK. I decide to risk taking the relationship to the next level.

***

It's 10.30p.m. The children are all settled in bed, and I'm enjoying a late dinner with Adam.

'That was delicious,' he says, as he finishes the small Greek salad which I prepared as a starter.

'Glad you liked it,' I smile, as I hold out my wine glass for him to top up. 'Shame we always have to eat so late by the time we're all finished for the day, and the kids are settled.'

'Mmm,' he murmurs, pouring my wine and then topping up his own glass. 'Never mind, though.'

'Well, actually, I sort of *do* mind. Don't *you* get a bit fed up with us having to just snatch time together when we can?'

His brow furrows and he inclines his head slightly. 'I guess ... but what's the alternative?'

'Why don't you move in with me?'

His eyes widen in surprise, and he sets down his glass so abruptly that a little of the wine slops over the rim. He swiftly blots it up with his paper napkin.

'Are you serious?' he asks.

'Well, why not? You don't have a place of your own and I have enough space here.'

He seems temporarily lost for words; when he does find his voice, all he can manage is, 'I don't know ... it's just a bit of a surprise.'

Really? I think. *Has it honestly never crossed your mind?*

'I mean, what about Mum?' he says.

'What about her?' I demand, a little irritated now.

'Well, I've always been there for her. I'm not sure how ...' His words tail off.

I breathe deeply in an effort to contain my frustration. 'Look, all I'm saying is that we both have busy lives and as things stand it's just not easy to find time to spend together. You're forty-six years old ... you're not going to live with your mum forever, are you?'

He doesn't reply.

'Look,' I say, 'Your mum managed OK when you were living with Sharon. It's only because Sharon got the house when you split that you moved back in with your mum. Otherwise, she'd still be on her own anyway, wouldn't she?'

His face creases in a doubtful frown. 'I suppose so, but ... well, she's that much older now.'

And hardly likely to get any younger, I think. *If you don't do it now, you never will.* I bite my tongue; I don't think pushing him any harder right now is going to help. Maybe he just needs a little time to think. *Time to back off.*

'OK,' I say, 'well, just have a think about it ... no rush.'

He nods, slowly, relief washing over his features. 'Yes, I will.'

'Ready for your main course?' I say, keen to lighten the mood.

As I go through to the kitchen, it strikes me what a strange contradiction this man is. When we first met, he was confident, pushy even, as he tried to win me over, yet now that we are established in a relationship, he seems reticent, almost nervous, much of the time. The only time he seems truly relaxed is when he's with Liam. Well, for that, at least, I'm grateful. My son doesn't make friends easily and it's good that he has gelled so well with Adam.

I've prepared a moussaka for our main course.

'Smells great,' says Adam, as I set the plates down on the table.

'Hope it tastes good too,' I reply.

And, apart from confirming that it does, he says very little else during the entire course of the rest of the meal.

Chapter 14

Four years later

'The teenager'

I'm a staff nurse at the local private hospital now. I had originally planned to join the NHS when I qualified, but when I saw that the Nuffield private hospital had vacancies, I jumped at the chance to work in a smaller, hopefully less frantic hospital.

Well, it's smaller, yes, but I was wrong about the 'less frantic' bit: it's incredibly busy. Nevertheless, I'm enjoying the work: I'm working with a good team of people and the interaction with patients is so satisfying.

Adam and I are still together. He never did move in with me, but we're doing OK. We're happy enough together and he's still so good with Liam. I guess you could say we've settled into a sort of comfortable rut.

Liam is at high school now; he's fourteen. He's become a bit of a recluse, spending many hours in his room on his own, playing video games or interacting with who knows who on social media. He's also always tinkering with his computer, opening it up to install extra memory chips or something – it all means nothing to me.

Imagine my surprise then, when, one evening, he announces that he has a girlfriend.

'What's her name?' I ask, delighted that there is finally a bit more social interaction in his life.

'Ava,' he replies. 'She's really nice.'

'Why don't you bring her round here?' I suggest, keen to see what sort of girl could have prized Liam's attention from his computers and video games. 'I'd love to meet her.'

'OK,' he grunts, 'would Friday afternoon be OK?'

'Of course ... she can join us for tea.'

'Alright ... I'll ask her.'

***

Ava isn't exactly what I expected. Thick black hair, with a fringe which almost covers her eyes: very heavy, dark eye makeup; large hoops dangling from her pierced ears. I have to assume that she doesn't go to school done up like that! Nevertheless, she's a pretty enough girl – underneath all the slap – and quite polite, if a bit quiet.

When we've finished eating, Liam says, 'OK if we go up to my room now?'

'Yes, that's fine ... Megan and Grace can help me clear up.' They both shoot me withering glances but don't object. They're probably just bursting to get Liam out of earshot so that they can compare notes on his new acquisition.

Sure enough, as soon as Liam and Ava have gone upstairs the girls are chatting and giggling as they discuss the new girlfriend's hair, makeup, and clothes ... and speculate about how many boys she might have been with. I chastise them for being so disrespectful, but I'm secretly rather enjoying their conspiratorial whispering.

***

It's around two hours later that Liam and Ava come downstairs, both looking a little flushed; heaven knows what they've been up to.

'I'm going to walk Ava home,' announces Liam.

Megan and Grace exchange a stifled giggle; I shoot them both a disapproving glance.

'OK,' I say, 'how long will you be?'

'Oh ... about forty minutes ... she only lives about a mile away.'

His voice sounds sort of different ... slightly slurred perhaps?

'Thank you for tea, Miss Fisher,' says Ava.

'You're welcome ... nice to meet you.'

As soon as they step through the front door, Megan adopts her best impression of her brother's voice. 'I'm going to walk Ava home,' she says. 'Oooh … *what* a gentleman.'

The two of them dissolve into gales of laughter.

'For heaven's sake, leave him alone,' I scold.

They return their attention to the TV programme they'd been watching.

I take the opportunity, while Liam's out, to go and check his room. There was definitely something a little odd about his manner and his voice when he came down. I suppose I shouldn't be snooping really, but I *do* need to collect his dirty laundry which, as usual, he has neglected to bring down himself.

As I push the door open, I am confronted with the usual mess: clothes and shoes strewn across the floor, his games console still switched on, and several dirty plates left over from snacks he has had in his room. The covers on the bed are rumpled and creased. I sigh as I start picking up some of the debris. And then I freeze …

Picking up Liam's blue sweater from the floor reveals an empty vodka bottle. I've never let him have alcohol in his room and, as far as I know, he's barely ever touched the stuff.

When I go back down to the living room, I send Megan and Grace upstairs and tell them to get ready for bed; I want to have a stern talk with Liam on his own when he gets in. Megan, in particular, complains that it's too early to go to bed, but I'm in no mood to argue. They both recognise the signs and eventually comply.

The forty minutes which Liam suggested he would need to walk Ava home turns out to be over an hour, but that's not what's been bothering me.

'What,' I say, holding the empty vodka bottle aloft, 'is this?'

Stupid question, I suppose, as it is, self-evidently, an empty vodka bottle. Now, most times Liam would respond to such a question by pointing out the obvious, but this time he's clearly read my mood.

'Oh … er … well, I can explain.'

I set down the bottle on the table and fold my arms. 'OK … I'm all ears.'

'It wasn't my idea … it's just that Ava's mum always has vodka in the house, and she doesn't mind Ava having a bit from time to time.'

'And how old is Ava?'

'Fifteen … she's a year older than me, but all my friends who are fourteen are allowed to have a bit of alcohol.'

'Well, you're *my* son, and you're not allowed alcohol. How much did you drink?'

'Oh, only a little bit … the bottle was only about a third full to start with, and Ava drank more than me.'

I'm not sure whether to believe him or not. Those big blue eyes are so convincing, but …. oh, I don't know.

'Look,' I say, 'don't ever try to deceive me like that again. Perhaps when you're fifteen you can have some alcohol but not now … understand?'

He nods. 'It won't happen again.'

If only that were true …

Chapter 15

'Cementing the relationship'

It looks like Adam and I are in it for the long term; we've been together almost five years now. Things aren't perfect – are they ever, in *any* relationship? – but we're comfortable with each other's company, we rarely argue, and he can still make me laugh. The sex isn't bad either!

The one thing which still bothers me is how relatively distant he still is with the girls; I sometimes wonder whether it has something to do with the fact that they're not his. And yet, he's so good with Liam. But his relationship with Liam seems almost like best mates rather than stepfather/son. I could see the two of them sharing a pint down the pub if Liam were a bit older. Probably not a good idea given how things evolve … but more later on that subject.

There's something else: the kids are growing up fast; they're all teenagers now, and I find myself missing that unique mother/child bond that goes with caring for a younger child. Would having another child simultaneously satisfy that maternal instinct and cement my relationship with Adam? I'm thirty-eight years old now, and the clock is ticking; if we're going to do it, best not leave it too long.

I've been thinking about all this a lot lately; it's time to talk it over with Adam.

***

It's Friday evening. The kids are all settled down for the night and we're enjoying a late dinner at my place. Adam has decided to stay over. He does that much more often these days, having discovered that his Mum manages just fine when he's away for a day or two from time to time. Maybe he'll eventually come around to the idea of moving in with me properly … but that's not the subject I want to discuss with him tonight.

Adam leans forward to top up my wine. 'That was great … why don't you settle down on the sofa while I clear up?'

He makes to push his chair back and stand up, but I place my hand on his wrist, gently restraining him. 'In a minute … first, there's something I'd like to talk over with you.'

He sits back down, a slight furrow creasing his brow as he tilts his head slightly. 'O…K,' he says, warily, 'what about?'

No point skirting all around the issue. I figure that if I come straight out with it, I'll be able to tell from his initial reaction what he really thinks. 'What do you think about us having a baby together?'

His eyes widen in surprise … but within seconds, his expression transforms into a broad smile. 'Are you serious?'

'Of course I am,' I laugh, 'otherwise I wouldn't have said it, would I?'

'I think it's a wonderful idea,' he says.

Really? I think. *Just like that*? This wasn't the reaction I was expecting. I thought he'd be much more cautious about making such a commitment.

He clasps my hand between both of his. 'There's so much we'd need to work out … like, where would the baby sleep? Would you need to give up work? Should I move in? Maybe we should find a bigger house?'

Well, implicit in that last question was the assumption that he *would* finally move in with me, I guess.

I could never have expected such an enthusiastic response to my suggestion.

'I guess that's a "yes" then,' I laugh.

We spend the next hour, and another half bottle of wine, talking over all the possibilities. Clearing up the dinner things can wait until the morning.

Chapter 16

'The habit begins'

Liam has invited Ava round. This has become a regular occurrence … and so has the drinking. They have become quite adept at hiding the evidence but it's plain to see that they are always tipsy when they emerge from Liam's room, and I can often smell the alcohol on their breath.

I've had several discussions with Liam on the subject, but he's fifteen now and has a mind of his own. He insists that he and Ava only drink in moderation, and that this is the norm for all their friends of a similar age. I'm concerned though.

Grace has gone to bed and Megan is up in her room. I'm watching TV on my own while Liam and Ava are still in his room. I check the clock: 10.10p.m. I know Ava is supposed to be home by 10.30p.m. but she's often late leaving, and her mother usually seems pretty relaxed about it. However, they both have school in the morning and it's getting late. I am just contemplating going to knock on Liam's door when I hear movement upstairs.

As his door opens, I hear their laughter, interspersed with various random bangs and thuds as they stumble towards the top of the stairs. Then suddenly an urgent cry.

'Ava … be careful … hold on to—'

A high-pitched scream accompanies the thunder of something heavy tumbling down the stairs, followed by a final loud thud as Ava spills onto the floor. Then dead silence for a second or two before Liam comes careering down the stairs, almost falling over himself.

I leap to my feet. Liam and I reach the body spreadeagled on the floor at exactly the same moment. Her eyes are closed and there is no movement.

'Ava … Ava …' cries Liam, 'are you OK?'

No response.

He looks at me in desperation. 'Mum … is she alright?'

My nurse's training kicks in. 'Liam … move back … let me check her over.'

He shuffles backwards on his bottom, leaning his back against the wall.

She is breathing normally – thank God for that at least. I pull back her eyelids – her eyes look normal, but I need to check their reaction to light. 'Liam, go and get me a torch from the understairs cupboard.'

But, before he returns with the torch, her eyelids flicker and she begins to focus. Within a few seconds she is making proper eye contact with me.

'Wh-what happened?' she stammers, starting to pull herself into a sitting position. The stink of alcohol on her breath is overwhelming.

I gently restrain her. 'Keep still for a moment.' She eases back down. 'You fell down the stairs.'

'Oh … yes … lost my footing.'

'We need to check whether anything's broken. Most important are your neck and back … any pain there?'

She pauses for a moment as though mentally assessing whether there is. 'No … nothing.'

'You sure?'

'Uh, huh – I'm fine.'

'OK, well let's sit you up then.'

I help her gently to a sitting position. She shows no sign of any discomfort, so I'm pretty sure there's no serious damage. Before long she's on her feet, and although she's unsteady – that'll be the alcohol – there seems to be no damage other than some bruises on her knee and elbow.

Liam, who has remained mostly silent for the last ten minutes or so, finally finds his voice. 'Thanks Mum … I'll walk Ava home now.'

I shake my head. 'I don't think either of you are in any fit state to walk to Ava's house. I'll drive her home.'

'But Mum—'

'No "buts". I'll drive her home, and you get to bed … you've got school in the morning. We'll talk about this tomorrow.'

***

Ava's mother, whom I've never met before, seems remarkably relaxed about the whole thing, as though such incidents are a regular occurrence – maybe they are. As I drive home, I mull over the situation. Who's leading who here? As far as I can tell, it always seems to be Ava who brings the booze round. Apparently, her mother is a heavy drinker and there's always vodka in the house for Ava to take whenever she likes. I've never caught Liam bringing alcohol home and, to be honest, I don't think he ever has enough money to be buying it.

No, it seems quite clear, now, that Ava is a bad influence on my son. The question is, what can I do about it?

Chapter 17

'Trying for a baby'

After falling pregnant so easily and unexpectedly with Grace, I kind of assumed that it would happen easily again this time. Not so: we've been trying for several months now and still no luck. Could the problem be with Adam? We decide to go for a series of tests – for both Adam and me; today, we are due to see the doctor to discuss the results.

'Well,' says Doctor Badawi, looking up from the sheet of paper on the desk in front of him, 'the good news, Mr Blackford, is that your sperm count is normal, and the sperm themselves are of good quality.'

'So no problems on my side then?' says Adam. He looks relieved.

'Not as far as I can see,' confirms Doctor Badawi.

I'm pleased, of course, but does that mean there's some problem with me? Hard to believe, considering how easily I've conceived in the past.

'So what about me?' I ask, with some trepidation.

The doctor removes his reading glasses and looks me directly in the eyes. 'I'm pleased to say, Miss Fisher, that everything with your reproductive system looks perfectly normal.'

I feel a strange, hollow, lightness in my stomach; relief mixed with confusion.

'So what could be wrong then, Doctor?'

'Well, probably nothing … how long have you been trying for a baby?'

'Well, about five months.'

He gives an indulgent smile. 'That's really very little time at all … many couples try for years before they are successful.'

'But,' I say, 'in the past I have fallen pregnant so easily … once when I was actually on the pill!'

'Hmm … how long ago was that?'

'Oh, about thirteen years.'

He places both elbows on the table, leaning forward and interlacing his fingers. 'Thirteen years is a long time in a woman's reproductive timetable.' He pauses, donning his reading glasses and checking his notes. 'You are now … let me see … thirty-eight years old. Correct?'

I nod. 'Uh huh.'

'Well, you probably still have plenty of time left to conceive but you must understand you will not be anywhere near as fertile as you were thirteen years ago.'

A melancholy realisation settles upon me. *My God! I'm actually on borrowed time now.*

The doctor is still talking, but his words blend to form a distant, unintelligible miasma of sound. I'm not sure for how long I drifted off, but when I tune back in, he's moved on.

'Now, as I said, there are various drugs which can increase your fertility, but I would suggest you try a little longer before resorting to those. You are still a relatively young woman.'

But old enough to be on the slippery slope, I think, still reeling from the realisation that time is starting to run out.

Adam, who has been silent for most of the conversation, puts his arm around my shoulders. 'Come on, let's go home and talk about it. At least we know there's nothing really wrong.'

I nod, miserably.

'Thank you, Doctor,' he says. 'We'll be in touch again soon.'

***

Once I've come to terms with the fact that the end of my fertile years may be in sight, I'm ready for a sensible discussion with Adam. We decide to carry on trying for another couple of months and, if it doesn't happen by then, ask the doctor about the fertility drugs.

But then a small miracle occurs: my next period is late. I wait a full week after it was due, and still nothing. I can't contain myself any longer before taking a test.

The test is positive. *Thank God!*

I have my first scan at eight weeks; everything looks good. It's early days of course, but I'm feeling wonderful. All my anxiety about impending infertility has been swept away and I'm looking forward to strengthening our relationship with the birth of our child.

But just two weeks after the scan, I sense that something is wrong. It's hard to explain exactly *how,* but somehow, I just *know* that something isn't right. I arrange for another scan. Adam comes with me.

The nurse is bright and breezy as she sets up the equipment, her manner clearly intended to reassure ... but I'm not feeling reassured.

'Now then,' she says, as she starts to interpret the fuzzy image on the screen for me, 'let's see ... ah yes, here's the baby's head and here's ...' Her voice tails off and her brow wrinkles in a frown.

A hollow dread eviscerates my stomach. 'What ... what is it?'

'I ... er ... there's something I'd just like the doctor to see. Can you give me a minute or two?'

Adam is on his feet now. 'What is it, Nurse? Is something wrong?'

'Just wait a moment, sir ... I'll be back very soon.' She hurries from the room.

As I crane my neck to see the image on the screen, the creeping doubt morphs into a horrific certainty. There is no movement – just a static image, devoid of life.

Adam clutches my hand. 'Don't worry, Mads ... I'm sure everything's OK.'

But it isn't.

When the doctor arrives, his face gives nothing away, but within seconds of his first glance at the screen, he instructs the nurse to usher Adam out of the room. The message could hardly be clearer.

He spends several minutes manipulating the equipment and traversing my belly with his stethoscope. At length he lets go of the instrument and allows it to hang, limp and lifeless from his neck.

A metaphor?

When he makes eye contact his expression is grave. 'I'm sorry Miss Fisher, but I'm afraid there is no heartbeat.'

I can't honestly say I'm shocked because I already knew before he said it. I guess 'numb' is the best way to describe how I feel.

'So, she's dead,' I murmur. Don't know why I said 'she' when, at this early stage, I can't possibly know the gender of my unborn child … and yet somehow, I *do* know. My baby girl is dead.

'I'm afraid so,' says the doctor placing his hand gently on mine.

I try to compose myself enough to speak coherently.

'H-how long do you think …?'

'Impossible to say for sure … several days at least.'

'But why … why would …?'

'Also, impossible to say, at this stage. There could be any number of reasons.'

My mind is now a maelstrom of wild and disconnected thoughts. *Is it my fault? Did I eat the wrong things? Sleep in the wrong position? If I had come in for a check-up earlier, could things have been different?* I just can't process it all.

The doctor interrupts my frantic, internal questioning. 'Would you like a little time alone with your partner, Miss Fisher?'

I nod, dumbly.

Time seems to stand still after the doctor leaves the room. I honestly have no idea how many minutes have elapsed before he re-enters the room, accompanied by Adam, whose face is a mask of sorrow.

He rushes over and hugs me. 'I'm so sorry, Mads,' he whispers.

'I'll give you some space, now,' says the doctor, quietly. 'Just ring when you're ready. We need to discuss what happens next, but I think it will be best to leave that until tomorrow … give you time to come to terms with your loss.'

With that, he leaves the room, leaving Adam and me to grieve on our own.

I have never before known such crushing emptiness inside.

***

Adam takes the following day off work so that we can both see the doctor together. The raw edge of grief has softened a little but, in truth, I'm barely any more composed than I was the previous day.

'Firstly,' says the doctor, adopting a soft and caring tone, 'let me offer my heartfelt condolences for your loss.'

Adam and I both nod but remain silent.

'You are probably wondering why this happened, and the truth is that we will probably never know for sure. It's relatively rare for the foetus to fail at this stage of pregnancy but ...'

I drift off for a moment, or maybe longer. My *foetus* has *failed* – such impersonal terms. No, my *baby* has *died*.

The doctor is still talking when I come back to the here and now.

'... and since you have already given birth to three healthy babies there is no reason to suppose you won't be able to successfully conceive again.'

Adam squeezes my hand. 'That's good news, Mads, isn't it?'

I nod, weakly and without conviction.

The doctor continues. 'However, we have some more immediate issues to consider and—'

I interrupt him. 'Yes ... what happens now?'

'Well, if we let nature take its course, you will probably go into labour naturally within the next three weeks and the foetus will be expelled.'

You mean my dead baby.

He continues, 'However, there are a number of medical risks associated with that course of action, not to mention the unnecessary anxiety you may suffer during that period. I would suggest it would be better to undergo a termination procedure as soon as possible.'

I exchange a glance with Adam; we both nod, silently. There is no point prolonging the agony. The decision is made, there and then.

Chapter 18

'A career plan for Liam'

Two months have elapsed since I lost the baby. We are doing our best to move on and are, once again, trying for a baby. My immediate concern, though, is Liam: he and Ava are drinking heavily again, and my hope that their relationship would quickly fizzle out has not come about. However, she's a year older than Liam and will soon be leaving school, probably to go to college. Maybe that will cause them to drift apart.

I'm also concerned about his attitude towards his education. It's becoming increasingly clear that he's not taking his schoolwork anywhere near as seriously as he should. I've been thinking about that conversation I had with his primary school teacher years ago. He's an intelligent boy, but it only shows when he's engaged with something that really interests him. I've seen something which *might* just capture his imagination.

***

Liam looks decidedly disinterested when I say that I want to have a serious discussion with him about his career prospects, but he dutifully sits down to hear what I have to say.

'Muuum,' he says, drawing out the word to turn it into a complaint, 'it's another couple of years yet before I leave school. Do we really even need to be thinking about this right now?'

'Yes … we do. Your grades in just about every subject except maths are going down and down.'

He shrugs. 'Well, maths is quite easy – you just have to work stuff out – but every other subject is boring: it's all about remembering a load of facts and figures.'

'Well, I think it's a bit more than that, Liam.'

'No ... it *isn't*,' he insists. 'Geography's all about remembering capital cities and flags and stuff, history's about remembering kings and queens and battles and dates, and as for—'

I raise my hand, palm-outward, and cut him off. 'Stop!' I take a deep breath and pause before continuing – I don't want to turn this into an argument. 'Look, I know a lot of this stuff doesn't interest you, but I also know you are far brighter than your grades would suggest.'

He gives me a puzzled frown. 'So what are you saying?'

'What I'm saying is that when you apply yourself you can do really well. Just look at how good you are with computers and the internet. And the way you take things apart to see how they work is amazing.'

At last, I see a spark of interest in his eyes; I think he's realised that this chat is not going to be just a routine bollocking about his grades after all.

'Well, yeah ... I guess ... but that sort of stuff is interesting.'

'Exactly! That's my point ... when you apply yourself to something that interests you, you show that there's a brain in there.' I reach over and tap the side of his head, which elicits a reluctant smile.

His brow crinkles and he pouts his lips. 'So where, exactly, are you going with this, Mum?'

'Look, when you *do* leave school—'

'Oh Muuum ... not that again.'

'Listen ... please.' I take another deep breath. 'When you *do* leave school, wouldn't it be good to do something that really interests you, rather than get some low-paid job which bores you to tears?'

'I guess ...' he says.

'Good ... So what do you know about "ethical hacking"?'

He shoots me a quizzical look, before shaking his head. 'Never heard of it. What is it?'

'It's a possible career route which you might find really interesting and pays really well.'

He leans forward, his interest seemingly piqued. 'Like what, exactly?'

'You know how much crime is online now, don't you?'

'Well, yeah … if you know what you're doing it's far easier to rip people off online than go and steal stuff from a house or a business.'

I'm a little disturbed that he acknowledges that so readily; I hope to Christ *he* hasn't been doing anything like that. I let the thought go for now; I don't want to spoil things when, at last, I seem to have got his interest.

'Yes,' I say, 'so as criminals turn more and more to cyber-crime, so the police need to turn to technology to be able to combat them. They need more tech-savvy people to fight the bad guys online.'

Now I see the realisation of where I am going dawn in his eyes.

'So you can get a job with the police, working at a computer to fight the criminals?'

'You can,' I say, flipping open the cover of the iPad which I have alongside me.

I call up the university website which I have been exploring and hand the device to him. He is silent for a couple of minutes as he studies it.

When he finally looks up at me, he is more animated than I have seen him for ages. 'That's really cool!' he declares. 'An actual degree course specifically on "ethical hacking" … even the name sounds cool!'

My heart leaps: *I've got him!*

'It's good, huh? It could lead to a really well-paid job with the police, doing what you enjoy and you're good at.'

'It does sound good, Mum, but surely I don't need to be thinking about it just yet?'

'Well maybe you do … take a look at the qualifications required for entry onto the course. You'd need "A" levels with good grades in maths and at least one science subject. And to get onto the "A" level course at college you'd first need several decent GCSEs. Now I don't doubt you'll be OK with maths, but you'd need to get good grades in a range of subjects to get on the "A" level course.'

As my words start to sink in, he nods slowly. 'I guess you're right.'

'Look, I thought you'd be interested, so I've already got this for you to read.' I hand him a copy of the ethical hacking course prospectus which I had already procured. 'Take your time … think about it and then figure out what you're going to do about schoolwork over your final couple of years.'

'I will … thanks, Mum.'

'And Liam … one more thing.'

'What's that?'

'If you *are* going to have a serious stab at getting some decent GCSE's, it's going to take a bit more time studying and a bit less time sitting in your room with Ava, drinking.'

'Oh, Mum … that's not fair. I don't drink that much.'

'Just saying, Liam … it's up to you'

I just hope he makes the right choices now.

Chapter 19

Four months later

'A bombshell'

Adam is in Spain; he spends a lot of time in Spain of late. One of his mates, Mike Roberts, has bought a villa near Marbella on the Costa del Sol, where he now lives, more or less permanently. There are, apparently, no less than seven world-class golf courses in the vicinity. The weather there is much kinder, during the autumn and winter months, than in England, so Adam is taking maximum advantage of Mike's open invitation to go over there and play as often as he likes.

Adam has suggested I might like to come over with him, but that's just not practical while the kids are at school, and somehow the dates that he can go there never seem to coincide with school holidays.

I'm not really sure how he manages to keep running his business while spending so much time away, but the money still seems to be coming in, and in fact, we've just put down a deposit to rent a larger, four-bedroomed property, so I suppose I can't really complain.

Anyway, I have some news for him now: in spite of all his time away, he has been back home often enough to get me pregnant again!

After the trauma of the miscarriage, and the veiled hints from the doctor that I shouldn't get my hopes up too much just yet, it's finally happened. Adam will be so, so happy; I need to get in touch and give him the good news.

For some reason, though, he's just not answering his mobile, and in spite of my having left a couple of voicemails he hasn't responded. OK, well, somewhere in his desk, tucked into a corner of the living room, there's probably a landline number for the villa. I decide to try that.

A brief rummage through his desk drawer results in my finding his address book: a bit of a throwback in the modern era of smartphones and the like, but he's always kept one and, hopefully, it will, on this occasion, prove its worth. I thumb through the pages, wondering where to look for the number I seek. Nothing under 'S' for 'Spain or 'Spanish', nothing under 'V' for 'villa'. I try 'R' for 'Roberts'. Bingo! There's Mike's mobile number, and underneath two landline numbers: one for his English home, which he still has, and one for his villa in Spain.

I call the number. On the third ring, a heavily accented, female voice responds. '*Hola ... diga me.*'

This rather throws me. 'Oh, sorry,' I say, 'do you speak English?'

'Si ... a leetle ... how can I help you?'

'I think I may have the wrong number. I wanted to speak to Adam Blackford.'

'Oh no ... you have correct number. Adam ees *fuera de casa* – out – at the moment. He plays the golf with 'is *amigo*, Mike. 'Oo is thees calling?'

What the fuck is going on here?

'My name is Madeleine ... and may I ask who I am talking to?'

'I am Rocío – per'aps Adam mention my name?'

A creeping dread begins to descend on me. 'No, I don't think he has. So how do you know Adam?'

'Oh, I am 'is *novia* – how you say? – girlfriend.'

A leaden boulder descends in my gut as the creeping doubt solidifies into a chilling certainty. The air is sucked from my lungs, and my legs will no longer support me. I stagger backwards, just managing to clutch the arm of a chair and slumping down into it. I can't find any words.

''Alo ... are you steell there?'

I finally find my voice. 'Yes,' I gasp, 'I'm still here.'

'Are you OK ... you don't sound good.'

'No, I am not feeling good. Has Adam told you about me?'

'No ... I don't think so ... what ees your name again?'

'Madeleine … Adam and I have been partners for six years, and right now, I am carrying his baby.'

The line goes silent for several seconds. When she speaks again her voice is faltering.

'I don't understand … thees ees not possible. 'E tell me I am only one. And you are *embarazada* – with baby?'

I ignore her question. 'How long have you been with him?'

'I am weeth Adam almost two years … I am weeth him all the time he ees in Spain … thees make no sense …'

My initial shock is now turning to a simmering anger. *Even while we were trying for a baby, even while I suffered the miscarriage, even when I fell pregnant again, he was fucking this Spanish bitch. The absolute bastard!*

I need to get off the phone … I need to think. 'You're right … it makes no sense. Can you tell him to call me when he gets in? He knows my number.'

'But how—?'

I hang up.

***

By the time Adam phones me, some two hours later, I have made up my mind. I listen to all his pathetic excuses before giving him my bottom line in no uncertain terms.

'It stops right now … today … or we're through. You get your sorry arse on a plane and get back here tomorrow. You never, ever see your Spanish whore again; you never, ever see your golfing buddy Mike Roberts again; and you never, ever go back to Spain.'

'But Mads … I need a bit of time to explain to—'

I cut him off sharply. 'No "buts". It's me or her.'

'Well of course it's you … you know—'

'I don't know anything anymore. All the time we were trying for a baby, you were fucking her. All that talk about moving into a bigger house together … and meanwhile you had your love nest in Spain, aided and abetted by that bastard Mike Roberts.'

'Mike's not all—'

'Shut up! Don't you dare try to make excuses for him. He knew full well what you were doing and even helped you do it. That was a direct slap in the face to *me*. If I should ever have the misfortune to see his ugly face again, he'll get more than a slap in the face … a kick in the balls more like.'

Adam finally stops his whining explanations and falls silent.

'So … do we understand each other?' I demand.

'Yeah …' comes the weak response, 'I'm sorry, Mads.'

'So are you going to be here tomorrow, or are we finished?'

'I'll be there,' he murmurs.

Chapter 20

'Leopard spots'

Adam and I somehow weather the storm. When he gets back from Spain, the day after I discovered the affair, he is contrite. In spite of all the furious invective I hurl at him, he makes no attempt to fight back, no attempt to defend himself. He just accepts that he's screwed up badly, accepts all my demands, and swears he'll never, ever, do anything like that again. It's like trying to land blows on a sponge; he just absorbs everything I have to throw at him, giving me nothing back to feed my rage. In the end, my anger is spent without ever provoking the furious row which I was prepared for. I'm not ready to forgive him but, eventually, I accept that we can move on.

We go ahead with the move into the bigger, four-bedroomed house. Now Megan, Liam, and Grace all have their own bedrooms, and we have made the study into a nursery for the new baby. Adam and I have our own space in the largest bedroom. I am now on maternity leave, and the birth of our baby is imminent.

***

No-one ever warned me just how out of practice the body gets at popping out babies when you're pushing forty and it's thirteen years since the last time! Compared with the relatively easy time I had giving birth to Grace, this time it is hell: a fifteen-hour labour followed by an excruciatingly painful birth. But it's worth it.

As I hold Amelia in my arms, her little mouth latched onto my nipple, I feel her suckling begin to subside as she is finally satiated. In just a few more minutes, she is fast asleep. I ease her away from my breast and stand up, as carefully as possible, anxious not to wake her. As I lay her gently in her cot, she makes an assortment of gurgling and snuffling noises, but she does not wake.

As she lies there, settling once more, I wonder at this little miracle in front of me: her perfect features, her delicate little nose, her tiny fingers. It's been so long that I had almost forgotten just how small and vulnerable a new baby appears. The surge of love I feel as I lay a light blanket over her is impossible to put into words. Only another mother can begin to understand.

Finally, I tear my gaze away from my beautiful baby and close the curtains, drawing a veil of semi-darkness across the room. Hopefully she will sleep for a few hours now.

With Amelia settled down, I decide to make myself a cup of tea and relax for twenty minutes or so in front of the TV before starting on the inevitable round of household chores vying for my attention. As I gaze out of the kitchen window, waiting for the kettle to boil, I hear a single high-pitched beep from somewhere close.

As I glance around, the source of the unexpected sound becomes clear: Adam's 'work' phone is lying on the worktop. He has two mobiles: one for business use, which he takes with him to work, and one for private use which he sometimes leaves at home. He must have accidentally taken the wrong one to work this morning. Perhaps I should let him know, in case any important calls or messages come in.

I tap the screen which lights up with the first part of a WhatsApp message. An icy shiver crawls down my spine.

From Rocío

Thanks for great time yesterday. See you at flat Friday as we arrange. I get ready to give you very special ...

My knees begin to buckle and threaten to give way completely. I grab the edge of the worktop for support and ease myself down onto one of the bar stools. My brain can hardly process what my eyes are telling it. *He's still seeing her ... in spite of everything, it's still going on. But surely, she's in Spain ... far away. Or is she?*

I try to open up the message, but the phone is PIN protected, and I don't know the number. I take a deep breath and try to compose myself. OK, so what can I work out from this fragment of a message?

Firstly, there is no way Adam could have been in Spain yesterday: he set off for work in the morning as usual and was home by 7.00p.m. But did he even go to work at all? He's the boss ... he can come and go as he likes. Could he have met his Spanish bitch here in England? Could she have been here for some time, messaging him on his work phone, which I normally don't get to see?

And what about this arrangement to see her at 'the flat' on Friday? What flat? The enormity of the situation is gradually dawning on me. I have to assume he has actually brought her over here and put her up in a flat where he can see her any time he likes. His own personal fucking ... fucking pad.

A lot of things start to make sense now. When he was seeing her in Spain, he seemed to be able to keep his business going at the same time as spending vast amounts of time away from attending to it in person. Lately he's been spending long hours at the factory with hardly any time off ... or at least that's what I'd thought. But I guess a leopard doesn't change its spots.

My world is collapsing around me ... again. I feel sick to my stomach.

***

Adam arrives home at around 6.30p.m. Fortunately, Megan is round at a friend's house this evening. I have made sure Amelia is well fed and settled down, and I've told Liam and Grace to stay in their rooms while Adam and I have a private chat. They're more likely to be eavesdropping from the top of the stairs but I really don't care anymore.

'Good day?' I enquire, as he comes forward and gives me a perfunctory peck on the cheek.

'Oh, OK I guess,' is his cryptic reply. 'How was yours?'

'Interesting,' I say.

He has clearly failed to pick up on my tone of voice and doesn't even wait for a reply before flipping on the TV and easing himself into his armchair.

'Did you realise you left this behind this morning?' I say, extending my hand to offer him the phone.

'Huh?' he replies, absent-mindedly, giving only a cursory glance at the device I am holding. 'Oh that's OK, I don't really need my private phone when I'm at work.'

My anger starts to build. He's so bloody smug in his assumption that he's got it all sewn up.

'You need this one though … otherwise how will you keep in touch with your girlfriend?'

He snaps his head towards me, his jaw dropping and forehead crinkling as he takes the phone from me. He appears to freeze as he taps the screen and registers the message displayed there. I reach down and take the TV remote control, plunging the room into silence as he continues to stare, dumbstruck, at the phone.

Several seconds elapse before he raises his eyes to meet mine. 'I … I don't know quite what to say. I—'

Is that the best you can come up with, you spineless piece of shit? My anger finally bubbles over.

'I'll bet you don't, you lying, cheating bastard.'

'Mads … I—'

But I'm in full flow now. 'How long has it been going on this time? Did it ever even stop?'

He looks at me, helplessly. He has no answer for me, and to be honest, I don't even want one.

'And what "very special" thing does she have planned for Friday? A blowjob? Sitting on your face? A bit of sadomasochism? Just what is it you're looking for, Adam?'

'Maddie, she's really not—'

'Oh, no … don't you dare tell me what she is or what she isn't. It's what *you* are that concerns me.' I take one long, deep breath. 'We're finished, Adam.'

His expression is like that of a pathetic, wounded puppy. 'No … Mads … we need to talk about this.'

'I'm done talking … you've had your chances, and you've blown them. Get out of the house … and get out of my life. You'll find two suitcases outside, on the pathway alongside the house … your clothes are in those. If you want to come back and collect anything else, just let me know. I'll make sure that Amelia and I are out somewhere. But don't leave it too long, I'll be changing the locks in a few days' time.'

I could tell, from the expression on his face, that he knew it was useless to argue.

Suddenly, a familiar voice sounds from behind me. 'Mum …
you can't just—'

I whirl around to see Liam standing at the bottom of the stairs.
'Don't you tell me what I can and can't do … did you *know* what he
was up to?'

'No, of course not, but … well …'

Fucking men … even my own son. I've had enough. 'Get back to
your room!' I yell.

He looks imploringly at Adam, but Adam knows the situation is
irretrievable. 'Bye buddy … maybe we can keep in touch?'

With that, he turns and steps through the front door.

Chapter 21

Six months later

'The aftermath'

Neither Megan nor Grace was fazed by my split with Adam. To be honest, neither of them had really taken to him in the first place, and when they learned what he had been doing, they were fully supportive of my decision. As Grace succinctly put it, 'It's just us again now, Mum. We were OK before, and we'll be OK again.'

I can't tell you how much that support from my daughters meant to me.

Liam, however, did not react well to the split. He had looked up to Adam who, in turn, had always found time for my son, almost as if he were his own. Even when I explained exactly what had happened, Liam felt I should have given him another chance. Well, to hell with that … I think I gave him enough chances.

As for me … well, I guess I'm pretty much back to square one. There is no longer any man in my life, I have four children to care for, including a young baby, I can't go back to work yet, and the rent on the new house is more expensive. Money's incredibly tight once again. Megan – now seventeen – is working and contributing a bit towards the expenses, and I'm claiming all the benefits I can, but it's still a struggle to make ends meet. Fortunately, I managed to save a bit while Adam was contributing to our costs, although that won't last long at the rate we're burning through it. As always, Mum is there as a backstop, ready to lend me some money if needed. However, I'm going to do my damndest to try to avoid calling on her help.

There is, however, something which is bothering me even more than money: it's Liam. His girlfriend, Ava, has turned sixteen and left high school to go to college. It's quite a distance from the school where Liam still goes, and they have just sort of drifted apart. In many ways, I'm pleased about this: I always felt she was a bad influence on Liam, always turning up with a bottle of vodka and encouraging his worsening drinking habit. But Liam has gone into a dark place since Ava has moved on. He seems to have few, if any, friends and spends more and more time ensconced in his room, playing video games or immersed in social media. I'm not sure how much is due to his split with Ava and how much due to Adam's departure. Maybe there are other factors, too – who knows? Liam doesn't share much with me these days. Whatever the reason, it's not good.

I had hoped that the drinking might stop, or at least reduce, once Ava was off the scene, but it hasn't. He hides it well; there is never an empty bottle, or any other evidence left in his room - but there are clues. Sometimes it's just a tell-tale change in his demeanour: subtle, and probably not noticeable to others, but I notice it – I'm his mother. Sometimes it's more apparent: the distinctive smell of alcohol on his breath; his sisters pick this up in an instant. And then there are the occasions when it's blindingly obvious: when he's stumbling around, on the point of falling over.

I don't know where he gets the booze from; I hardly have any in the house these days. If he's buying it somewhere, I have no idea how he's paying for it. The only money he gets from me is a meagre allowance which would never run to buying alcohol; I couldn't afford to give him more even if I wanted to. He has a Saturday job in the local newsagent, but that pays only a pittance. I'm starting to worry about what the hell he may be doing to fund his habit.

I decide it's time for a heart-to-heart.

***

Having chosen my moment, I decide to start on something less confrontational than the drinking.

'So … how are you feeling about the GCSEs coming up?'

I can tell by the way he narrows his eyes and tilts his head that he knows this is just an opening gambit.

'OK, I guess … think I'll be fine on maths and science … probably OK on English, too. Why are you asking me about this?'

'Well, why wouldn't I? You need to get good grades to get onto the "A" level course at college.'

He casts his eyes downwards, apparently lost for a reply.

I give it a few seconds before continuing. 'You are still keen to do your "A" levels aren't you?'

He still avoids eye contact. 'Yeah … I guess.'

'You guess? What about the ethical hacking course? You're still up for that aren't you?'

He finally drags his gaze up to meet mine. 'Yeah … sounds like a way into a pretty cool job.'

'Well, you won't get it unless you get your qualifications.'

He looks away again. 'I know.'

I give it a few more seconds, but he says nothing more. *Time to get to the nub of the matter.*

'What's holding you back, Liam? Is it the drink?'

He jerks his head up sharply. 'What do you mean?'

I sigh. 'I think you know what I mean.'

He looks away again, avoiding my gaze. 'Well, I don't drink much now that Ava's not around.'

'Oh, come on, Liam … do you honestly think I can't tell?'

Now he looks me directly in the eye. 'Well, what if I do have a drink from time to time … what does it matter?'

'I'd say it matters quite a bit if it stops you getting the grades you need.'

'And who says it's going to?' he retorts, starting to raise his voice now.

I try to lower the temperature before things get out of hand. 'Only you really know whether it's affecting your schoolwork.'

'Well, it isn't,' he insists.

I decide to change tack. 'OK, well that's good, then. Where do you get your drinks from?'

'I buy them,' he mutters, 'just like everyone else does.'

'But where do you get the money? Alcohol isn't cheap.'

His eyes dart from side to side, like some sort of cornered animal. 'Does it matter?' is his feeble response.

Now I'm starting to get pissed off by his evasive manner. 'Yes, it matters,' I hiss. 'Are you doing something illegal, Liam?'

Now he actually laughs in my face – which doesn't improve my mood one bit.

'Well? Are you?'

'Of course not … well apart from lying about my age, I suppose, but everyone does that.'

I let the casual reference to underage purchase of alcohol pass; he knows full well that's not what I'm getting at.

'Well, what then?' I yell, the frustration now taking over from the calm I had been trying to maintain. 'Where are you getting the money from?'

'If you must know …' he says, 'poker.'

Of all the possible answers I was envisaging, that wasn't one of them. I am dumbstruck for a second or two before responding. 'Poker? But how … where?'

'I get together with a few of my friends after school a couple of times each week and we play a few hands.'

'So that's why you're late getting home sometimes?'

He nods. 'We only play for about an hour each time though.'

'But you're playing for money?'

'Uh, huh … I usually make about fifty pounds each time we play.'

'Fifty pounds?' I exclaim, incredulous. 'But where the hell do these boys get that sort of money to throw away?'

He shrugs. 'Dunno … not my problem, is it?'

I'm still struggling to process the revelations which are unfolding. 'And what happens when you lose?'

He gives a knowing smile. 'I hardly ever do … I'm good at it.'

It seems his reticence to divulge how he has been funding his habit has now given way to a kind of pride at how he's been able to do it. I'm still fishing for answers though.

'Where do you get together for these poker games?'

'It varies, but most times it's in the changing room for the football pitch – it's usually deserted after normal school hours.'

Now I am completely knocked sideways. 'On school premises … you're actually gambling on school premises? I can hardly believe you'd do anything so stupid. They'll expel you if they find out.'

His eyes blaze fiercely now. 'So what? I've only got a few more months to go before I leave, anyway.'

'So what? So what? Even if you get the grades you need in your GCSEs, do you think they'll accept you on the college course if they know you've been expelled for gambling?'

I've pushed him too far now. 'Just fuck off and leave me alone, will you. I'm almost sixteen now. I'm old enough to decide what I do with my life, and I don't need your lecturing and moralising. You're not exactly a perfect role model of stable family life yourself, are you?'

'What the fuck do you mean by that?' I blaze.

'First Dad, then Adam … you can't even hold down a relationship.'

That really hurts … completely knocks the wind out of my sails.

'Liam … that's not fair … you know I've always done my best to …' My words peter out, my energy spent.

'Go fuck yourself … leave me alone!' He storms off to his room.

I'm left on my own, drained and deflated. *Well, that didn't exactly go according to plan, did it?*

Chapter 22

'Sophie'

We didn't speak again about our row over Liam's gambling and drinking: it was abundantly clear that he had no intention of engaging with me on these subjects. Against the odds, however, Liam's GCSE results were good enough to get him into college. He failed history and geography and only scraped a pass in French, but his maths and science grades were good, and English wasn't too bad either. Thankfully, his gambling was never discovered by the school, so that didn't scupper his chances of a place at college.

Now, he's three months into his 'A' level course and – thank heavens – he seems to be applying himself reasonably diligently. He's still drinking, though – the signs are obvious – and I don't know where he gets the money from. He's split up with his poker buddies from school – or at least, I think he has. He has managed to find a part-time job for Saturdays and three evenings during the week, as shift supervisor at a trampoline park. Does that pay enough to fund his habit? I just don't know; Liam has become so secretive of late.

***

I'm back working at the hospital now, so Friday evening is the first opportunity to really relax. It's just after 10.00p.m. and I'm curled up on the sofa watching TV, having just got Amelia settled down for the night. Grace has supposedly gone to bed too, although I suspect she's probably trawling through social media on her phone rather than asleep. Liam has been working at the trampoline park this evening, but he should be home any time now; the park closes at 9.30p.m. Megan is out clubbing with some friends; goodness knows when she'll be back, but I won't go to bed until I know she's safely home.

I hear muffled voices outside the front door; one sounds like Liam, but the other is higher pitched … a girl's voice. Who could that be? Moments later, I hear the sound of a key in the lock and the door being opened. I sit up and turn towards the door from the hallway to see Liam coming in, followed by an attractive girl wearing a pink track suit and white trainers. Long, blonde hair, tasteful makeup – enough to enhance her natural good looks but nothing over-the-top.

'Hi Mum,' says Liam, standing aside and encouraging the newcomer to step forward, 'this is my friend, Sophie.'

'Hello,' she says, raising her hand and giving a little wave, 'nice to meet you.'

Well, this was the last thing I was expecting; by 'friend' does he mean *girlfriend*? As far as I knew, he had not had any girls in his life since Ava had moved on more than a year ago. But, as I've already mentioned, he has become so secretive lately.

I suddenly realise I must be gawping like some sort of bewildered goldfish. I finally pull myself together and find my voice.

'Er, sorry,' I say, casting an accusing look in Liam's direction, 'I wasn't expecting any visitors this evening.' I stand up and offer her my hand. 'Anyway, pleased to meet you, Sophie.'

'Likewise,' she says, responding with a tentative handshake.

Liam breaks the awkward silence which follows. 'Is it OK if Sophie stays for a little while? I don't have college tomorrow, and I'm not working at the park until the afternoon, so I don't have to get up early.'

'Er … well, yes, of course, but how will she get home?'

'Oh,' she interjects, 'I can walk … I live quite close.'

'Well, you shouldn't be out on your own after dark, Sophie.'

'Oh, I can walk her home,' says Liam. 'Don't worry, Mum.'

'Well, OK then.'

'OK, if we go up to my room, then?'

'Er, well, yes … but don't leave it too late.'

'We won't. Don't bother to wait up,' says Liam, leading his new friend towards the stairs.

Well, if this is 'meet my mum' evening, there is clearly not going to be a lot of conversation with Mum.

Only now do I notice he is holding a plastic carrier bag containing what looks, from the shape, like a heavy bottle. By the time I have processed this disturbing observation, it's too late to tell him I'm waiting up, anyway, for Megan.

***

The following morning, Liam doesn't emerge from his room until almost 11a.m. I make him some breakfast and wait until he's finished it before quizzing him about last night and his new friend.

'So what time did you walk Sophie home last night?'

'Oh, not sure exactly ... I think it was about twelve-thirty. You were asleep on the sofa ... I didn't want to disturb you, so I just turned the TV off and laid a blanket over you.'

I shake my head. 'Megan was out last night ... she got home just before two and you were still out then. I tried to stay awake until you got home but I guess I must have dropped off before you got home.'

He avoids my searching stare. 'Oh ... well, like I said, I wasn't exactly sure of the time. Anyway, what does it matter ... there's no harm done, is there?'

I exhale a long, slow breath. 'No, I guess not ... but I worry about you when I don't know where you are or what you're doing.'

'Muuum, I'm seventeen ... I can look after myself.'

'I suppose so,' I sigh. 'Anyway, tell me all about Sophie. How long have you known her?'

'About two months ... she works at the trampoline park.'

That appears to be all the information he is going to offer up; I prompt him for a little more. 'So are you two ... you know ... going out together?'

'Oh Muuum, we're friends ... that's all.'

He's clearly not ready for more questions just now. That's OK; even if they are just friends, that's a step forward from the solitary and secretive life he's been leading of late.

'Well, she seems very nice.' I say. *Not that I can tell much from my five-minute acquaintance with her.* 'Why don't you invite her over for lunch on Sunday?'

He rolls his eyes. 'Well, maybe ... I'll see what she says.'

'That'd be really nice ... we could—'

He cuts me off. 'Anyway, I need to go ... I need to be at work by twelve-thirty.'

With that, he gets up and makes for the front door, grabbing his coat from the stand in the hallway and shrugging into it. 'See you later.'

Moments later he is gone.

Well, maybe this Sophie will be good for him. Perhaps she'll get him out a bit more and get him to reduce his drinking. *Talking of which ... was that a bottle of booze he took up to his room last night?*

I decide to go and take a look in his room. I know I shouldn't snoop, but I worry about him. I'm somewhat surprised at the scene which meets my eyes. The bed has been made, there are no heaps of clothes strewn across the floor, and no dirty cups or dishes adorning his desk or bedside cabinet. Maybe Sophie is a good influence on Liam.

What's even more promising, as I scan the room carefully, is that there is no sign of a bottle or glasses to be seen. Mind you, Liam is, as I have previously mentioned, very good at covering his tracks.

I go down to the kitchen and take a look in the recycling bin: mostly plastic bottles and tubs; the only glass items are a marmalade jar and a bottle which had contained the fruit cordial which Amelia likes. Things are looking good, but I'm still not completely convinced.

I don a pair of rubber gloves and delve below the top layer in the bin. And there it is: my heart sinks as my eyes settle on the empty vodka bottle. Well, I did say he's good at covering his tracks. Did they actually consume an entire bottle last night?

All my positive thoughts begin to crumble into dust.

Chapter 23

Two months later

'The driving test'

Liam and Sophie are officially an item now, and it seems she is, after all, a good influence on him. He's still drinking too much – there's no doubt about that – but Sophie has been doing her best to get him to cut down a bit. He seems more outgoing and less secretive lately, and Sophie is encouraging him to get out and socialise a bit. I like her; in many ways she reminds me of my own middle daughter, Grace.

This morning, she and I are in the house on our own; Liam is taking his driving test.

'Oh, God,' says Sophie, 'I'm so nervous … do you think he'll pass?'

'He'll be fine,' I reply, placing a reassuring arm around her shoulders. 'He's a good driver.'

'I know,' she says, 'but … well, anything can go wrong on the day.'

'Come on,' I say giving her shoulder a little squeeze, 'I'm sure he'll be OK. Want a cup of tea?'

She smiles. 'Thanks.'

Liam has a huge incentive to pass, because I have promised him that when he passes his test, I'll help him to get his first car. I've told him it will only be a basic runabout – I can't afford anything fancy – but I remember the excitement I felt when I got my first car. It's all about the sense of independence and freedom a car provides, regardless of how basic it might be. Sophie doesn't have a car herself, so she's looking forward to it almost as such as Liam.

What Sophie doesn't know is that I've actually gone ahead and bought him a car; it's sitting in the garage right now. It's a nice little Toyota Aygo, white, and in great condition. It was rather more expensive than I'd had in mind, but I've managed to scrape together £4,000 for a deposit to keep the monthly repayments just about affordable. I hope to Christ my confidence that he will pass is not misplaced.

The kettle has boiled, so I pour us each a cup of tea.

Sophie takes a sip before setting down the cup and nervously checking her watch. 'Should be finished by now if they're running to time,' she says.

'Relax,' I say, 'they might be running a bit late ... we'll know soon enough.'

'I know, but—'

She's interrupted by the sound of a car pulling up outside. We go to the window to see Liam stepping out of the driving school car. All thoughts of the tea now forgotten, we rush to the front door. I'm now as nervous as Sophie is.

'Well?' I blurt.

His expression gives nothing away, at first, but then a slow smile spreads across his face, and he raises both hands in a double 'thumbs up'.

Sophie rushes to him and gives him a hug.

'Well done,' I say, when she lets go of him. 'Well, in that case ...'

I grab the handle of the up-and-over door to the garage and swing it open to reveal the nose of the little Toyota, glinting in the morning sun which now streams in.

There is a moment of stunned silence before it dawns on them both what is happening.

Sophie gives a squeal of delight. 'It's *lovely*,' she gasps, clapping her hands together.

'Thanks, Mum,' says Liam, uncharacteristically coming to me for a hug. 'You're the best.'

It's one of the happiest moments in my life.

Chapter 24

One month later

'An unexpected shock'

It's my day off; Liam is due to take a maths test at 10a.m. this morning, but he's not even out of bed yet. I glance at the clock: 9.21a.m. If he leaves it any longer, he'll never get there in time.

I go to his room and tap on the door. 'Liam, come on ... you'll be late for your test.'

No reply, so I push the door open. He's still in bed, fast asleep. A gentle shake of his shoulder elicits nothing more than an incoherent grunt as he nestles deeper into the pillow.

I shake him again, more forcefully now. 'Liam ... come on, get up.'

Finally, he comes to, blinking at me, evidently disoriented. 'Mum,' he murmurs, pushing my hand away, 'what's the matter?'

'You need to get up ... you've only got three quarters of an hour before your maths test.'

'Oh, that ... I'm not going.'

'What ... what do you mean, you're not going?'

'I'm dropping out of college.'

The impact in the pit of my stomach feels almost like a physical blow to my guts; I have no words. Absently, I drag the chair from the corner of the room to his bedside and sink into it.

'Are you serious, Liam? Dropping out of college?'

He turns away from me and pulls the duvet close around his neck. 'Can we talk about it later?'

My shock and surprise morph into anger. I grab his shoulder and pull him towards me. 'We'll talk about it right now.'

He rolls over and props himself up un one elbow, finally making eye contact. 'Honestly Mum, I'm just not enjoying it at all. The only subjects I'm any good at are maths and science; everything else is boring.'

'Maybe it is, but you need to get your qualifications before you'll be able to apply for the ethical hacking course.'

He averts his gaze. 'Well, I'm not so sure about that course either now to be honest.'

My shoulders slump; I exhale a long, slow sigh. 'But … but you were so keen. Why …?' My words tail off.

'I'm not sure I'm cut out for the police.'

'Why not?' I demand, exasperated with his cryptic responses. If you get into that line of work, you'll be working with computers and the internet … just the kind of thing you like … and you'd be good at it.'

'Oh Mum, by the time I get my 'A' levels and my degree it'll be another five years, and even then, there's no guarantee I'll get that kind of work. I need to be earning more money right now.'

'Why? Is it to buy more booze?'

As soon as I hear my own words, I regret saying them, but the words, once uttered, can't be withdrawn.

'For fuck's sake! Won't you ever stop going on about my drinking? I'm almost eighteen years old; it's up to me how much I drink.'

I try to retrieve the situation, which is threatening to spiral out of control. 'I know … I didn't mean … Look I can help if you need a bit more money.'

He expels a sigh through pursed lips; his tone softening when he replies. 'Mum … you've got enough on your plate without handing out money to me. At my age, I should be earning enough money to look after myself *and* contribute something towards running the household.'

The moment of tension seems to have passed. 'Oh Liam, your future is the most important thing: I can get by without a contribution from you.'

'Well my mind's made up,' he says. 'Luke has offered me a full-time job at the park.'

Luke, I should explain, is the manager of the trampoline park. He and I went out together a few times in the past, but it didn't really work out. Maybe he thinks offering a full-time job to my son might help to rekindle some kind of relationship between us. Well, that's not going to happen.

'Oh, Liam … are you really sure this is what you want? It's hardly the start of a long-term career plan, is it?'

He leans over and gives me a hug. 'It's not forever, Mum … but it's OK for now. There'll be time enough to think about the future.'

And that, apparently, is that. All my hopes for Liam's career plan dashed, and with more money in his pocket, a risk that his alcohol habit may escalate.

What have I done wrong?

Chapter 25

Six months later

'Can things get any worse?'

In spite of several more conversations which I have with Liam, he will not be dissuaded from his decision to drop out of college and go to work full-time at the trampoline park. Naturally, I am hugely disappointed, but I have to accept that he is no longer a child, and old enough to make his own choices. At least he seems to have been applying himself diligently enough to his new job, even if it's not a career with long-term prospects.

He's still drinking too much, but Sophie seems to be helping him to cut down a bit, as far as I can tell, anyway. She's a really nice girl.

Maybe things are starting to settle down a bit, even if not exactly as I would have liked.

But then the next hurdle presents itself …

***

Saturday morning: I'm busy in the kitchen preparing breakfast, when I hear the letterbox flap clang as today's post arrives. I rinse my hands and wipe them with a tea-towel before going to collect the post. Sifting through the half-dozen envelopes, I can see that three are junk mail, two are bills – I'll leave those until last – and one is unidentified. I'll start with that one.

As I tear open the envelope and scan the letter inside, my heart sinks. It's from the letting agent. My landlord wants his house back; I have two months to get out.

***

Saturday evening: I should be relaxing after a particularly gruelling week at work, but the spectre of potential homelessness looms large in my mind. With just two months to relocate, I need to move fast to find a new home, so my Saturday evening is spent scouring the internet. It turns out that there's a severe shortage of suitable rental properties in the area and the rents are sky high. As I close down my laptop and slump back on the sofa, the phone rings.

The voice on the line is halting and tremulous. 'Madeleine … it's Mum.'

'Hi, Mum … is everything alright? You sound a bit upset.'

There is a moment's silence, and when she does reply there is a catch in her voice. 'It's your father.'

I haven't seen or heard from my father in a very long time; he walked out on Mum years ago. This can't be good news.

'Dad? What's happened?'

She stifles a sob. 'He's had a heart attack.'

'A heart attack … is he OK?'

'I'm afraid not; he passed away this afternoon.'

Chapter 26

'A change of luck?'

The news of Dad's death hits me far harder than I could have imagined. Even though he has not been a part of my life for years, he was still my father. And Mum has been clearly badly affected, too. She is clearly in no fit state to handle all the funeral arrangements and so on; I am going to have to take care of that stuff.

The timing could hardly be worse – not that there's really *any* good time to die, is there? I have less than two months to find somewhere for us to live, and now I have this to contend with this as well.

By the time the funeral has taken place and all that is left of Dad is a plastic urn full of ashes sitting on my kitchen windowsill, I have less than six weeks left to find a new home.

***

It's just two weeks since Dad's funeral and it looks like our fortunes have finally turned: we have managed to find a decent four-bedroomed house in the local area which is available to move into immediately.

It isn't ideal: the rent is even more expensive than I had been paying, and that was already a struggle. Also, two of the bedrooms are very small. In compensation, though, the kitchen is a really good size, with room for a table and chairs, so it would be perfectly feasible to turn the separate dining room into an additional bedroom. A further factor to consider is that our space requirements have reduced a bit now, as Megan has recently flown the nest and found herself an apartment locally. We aren't likely to find anything else in the short time we have left, so I sign up; I'll worry about the rent later.

After some negotiation, it is decided that Grace and I will each have one of the larger bedrooms while Liam will have the re-purposed dining room. Amelia is persuaded to sleep in one of the smaller bedrooms with the offer that she can have exclusive use of the other small bedroom alongside to use as a playroom. This suits all of us because we can cram all her toys, and the associated myriad tiny plastic bits and pieces that kids seem to like at that age, in there and shut the door. No need, any longer, to enter her bedroom on tippy toes to avoid a painful encounter between stockinged feet and a sharp, unyielding, plastic princess's crown or Lego piece.

***

We've been in for six weeks now and are pretty much settled.

We've just finished breakfast; Grace is helping me clear up. Liam had to go in to work early, so I haven't even seen him this morning. Apparently, it's the monthly maintenance day at the trampoline park when everyone has to go in early to do a couple of hours cleaning and routine maintenance of equipment before the park opens to the public. I don't know if he's had any breakfast; judging by the fact there are no dirty dishes or cups adorning the kitchen worktops, probably not.

I glance up at the clock: 7.50a.m. I have a busy day ahead. Firstly, I need to get Amelia, who's now three, ready for nursery. After I've dropped her off there, I have a job interview at 9.30a.m. I love my job as a nurse, and I have no intention of leaving it, but money is so tight that I've been looking for some weekend work to supplement my income. Today's interview is for a senior carer at a local care home, to cover one shift per week every Sunday. I'm loath to give up some of my precious weekends but needs must.

This afternoon I also need to do the weekly supermarket shop, and then, before I know it, it will be time to collect Amelia. Somewhere amongst that lot, I need to squeeze in a bit of lunch; it'll probably end up being just a sandwich on the go.

I leave Grace to finish off clearing up in the kitchen while I go to get Amelia ready.

***

The interview goes well; the job is mine if I can start immediately: this coming Sunday. That doesn't give me much time to organise childcare for Amelia, but I guess Mum will always help if I need her. I accept the job.

By the time I've grabbed a sandwich and done the shopping, it's time to collect Amelia. As usual, she greets me with a big smile, and a hug, proudly presenting me with today's painting; the googly-eyed, straw-haired, toothy image staring back at me is apparently a portrait of me! Oh my God, how I love my little girl.

We get home around 3.45p.m. To my surprise, Liam is already home, lounging on the sofa, feet up.

'Well, hello … what are you doing home so early?' I enquire.

'I've been fired,' is his blunt reply.

'What?' I exclaim, his words slamming into me like a blow to the solar plexus.

'I've been fired,' he repeats. His voice is slightly slurred.

I turn to Amelia. 'Why don't you go up to your room and play?' I reach into my bag and retrieve a small pack of sweets. 'Here, as you've been such a good girl, you can have these.'

Her little face lights up as she takes the sweets and bounds towards the stairs.

I turn back to Liam. 'So what happened then?'

'I dunno … Luke was just being an arsehole today.'

Well, I can relate to that … he often behaved like one when I was dating him … but he wouldn't fire Liam for no reason.

'Come on Liam, there has to be a reason he fired you.'

He folds his arms, defensively, across his chest. 'He said I was drunk.'

'And were you?'

'I'd had a few drinks, sure, but I wasn't really "drunk".'

'What on earth were you doing, drinking in the early morning before going to work?'

'Well, mostly it was the night before, but I did just have a couple in the morning.'

Only then do I spot the half empty tumbler and the completely empty bottle on the side table alongside him.

'And you're still drinking now, I see.'

'Yeah, well he pissed me off so much, I needed a drink when I got home.'

I slump down into an armchair, allowing my coat and bag to fall to the floor. 'Oh, Liam, what have you done?'

'It's no big deal ... I can get another job.'

'Not if you carry on like this,' I sigh. 'Look, why don't you go and sleep it off? I'll call Luke and see if he can be persuaded to change his mind.'

'No need, Mum,' he mumbles, '... I don't need that bastard.' He's almost on the point of passing out, now.

'Come on ... let's get you to bed.'

I take his arm and help him to his room.

***

'Luke? It's Madeleine.'

'Oh, hello Mads,' comes the familiar, gravelly voice, 'I guessed I might be hearing from you.'

'I've just heard what happened.'

'Well, I expect you've heard Liam's *version* of what happened.'

'Oh, come on Luke, I know he can be difficult at times but he's a good boy at heart.'

The sigh at the other end of the line is clearly audible. 'What did he tell you, Madeleine?'

'Well, only that you thought he was too drunk to work and fired him without giving him another chance.'

I'm not sure if I was supposed to hear the suppressed, ironic, laugh, but I did. 'Another chance? Did he tell you how many chances he's already blown?'

A wave of confusion courses through me. *Oh no! What hasn't Liam told me?* 'What do you mean?' I say, almost afraid to hear the answer.

'This is at least the fourth time I've had to send him home for coming into work drunk.'

'Oh ...' I murmur, 'he never told me that.'

'No ... I don't suppose he did. And did he tell you how he got the bruise on his hip today?'

'What bruise?' I demand, alarmed now.

'You know the "Devil's Dive" ride at the park?'

'Yes, of course … it's the one where you jump from a high platform into a deep pit full of foam balls.'

'Right, well this morning, Liam was doing the routine safety check on the security of the handrail and barriers round the platform at the top. He was so bloody pissed that he forgot to put on his safety harness, and he managed to fall.'

My hand flew to my mouth, stifling a gasp. 'But that platform must be around twenty feet high.'

'It is. Fortunately though, the foam pit extends some distance either side of the actual drop zone, so Liam just managed to land inside the edge of it. The foam balls broke his fall, but he still managed to whack his hip against the perimeter fence as he bounced sideways. Nothing's broken, but he must have one hell of a bruise by now.'

I'm stunned, quite literally lost for words for a few moments. Eventually, I find my voice. 'How do you know nothing's broken?'

'I took him to A&E myself. They X-rayed him.'

'Oh …' is all the reply I can muster.

'Look, Mads … I've given him all the chances I can. He's become a danger to himself, the other staff, and the customers. I can't risk keeping him on any longer.'

I'm still struggling to process the revelations unfolding before me; my throat is now as dry as sand. I swallow hard, trying to moisten my mouth enough to speak.

'OK, Luke … I understand. I need to talk to him. I need to …' My voice tails off.

'Can I make a suggestion, Mads?'

'Uh?' My mind is elsewhere now. 'Er … yes… what's that?'

'I think he might need professional help. It's gone beyond just heavy drinking now.'

'I don't know … I don't know what to think … I can't talk any more right now.'

'OK … just think about it will you?'

'Er … yes … bye Luke.'

'Bye Mads … take care.'

When I hang up, my mind is in turmoil. Liam and I need to have a serious talk.

Chapter 27

Two months later

'A family Christmas'

Liam and I had a long, heart-to-heart chat following his losing his job. It was a real wake-up call for him. Once he'd had time to think about what he'd done and how close he'd come to permanently disabling, or even killing himself, he seemed to realise he needed to fundamentally change. He promised me he would cut down on his drinking and seriously buckle down to finding another job. Sophie was also doing her bit to encourage him to change his ways. She's such a good influence in his life, and to me, she seems almost like one of the family.

Against the odds, Liam did, indeed, succeed in finding another job, within just a few weeks of his sacking from the trampoline park. He had originally applied for a job on the tills at a local supermarket, but, amazingly, by the time his interview concluded, he had been offered a post as duty manager. How exactly he had explained his sacking from his last job, and how he had convinced them of his suitability for this one was a bit of a mystery to me, but, for all his faults, there was no doubt that my son had always been able to talk a good talk when he needed to. I was proud of him.

As for me, I've started my Sunday job at the care home. The arrangements for childcare were always going to be tricky, but with help from friends and my lovely mum, I've been managing. And God knows, the extra money is certainly welcome.

***

Boxing Day: 26th December. We had previously decided to have the big Christmas lunch today rather than on Christmas day so that Sophie could join us – she was to be with her own parents on Christmas day.

Sophie comes over early and helps me all morning with preparing the meal; I don't know what I would have done without her. I'm not sure what my own kids are doing while there is cooking to be done but they all show up quickly enough when I yell that lunch is almost ready!

It is, however, worth all the hard work: to have almost my whole family seated around the table spending some quality time together is a rare treat. I say 'almost' because Grace has gone off on an overseas trip with her boyfriend; they are visiting Thailand, New Zealand, and Australia. *How come I never got an opportunity to do anything like that when I was their age?* Anyway, having Sophie there helps to fill the gap.

What makes a lovely Christmas lunch even better is that everyone behaves impeccably. Liam, to my surprise, drinks only fruit juice at the table and there are no silly arguments or anything like that.

And yet, there is something going on with Liam: something I can't quite put my finger on. Usually, when he's with Sophie, he's quite upbeat and outgoing – by his standards, anyway. But today, at lunch he is more subdued and withdrawn than I would have expected.

Well, whatever is troubling Liam, overall, lunch is a big success.

Once everyone has finished their desserts, Liam announces that he and Sophie are going to his room 'for a chat', whatever that means.

'Is that OK?' asks Sophie. 'I can help with the clearing up first.'

'No, that's OK, Sophie, you've already done more than enough. Megan can help me clear up.'

Megan shoots me a petulant glance but does not protest. Sophie and Liam duly headed off to his room.

***

It's 9.00p.m. by the time I finally slump down in front of the TV, having got Amelia settled down for the night. Megan has gone home now, so I'm on my own with only the remote control for company.

As I trawl through the programme guide, I am confronted by the usual array of re-heated Christmas movies and comedy repeats that the mainstream channels serve up at this time of year. I settle for one of the few comedy shows I haven't seen before.

I soon find my attention drifting off. There was definitely something not quite right between Liam and Sophie today, but I have no idea what it was.

We had previously arranged, with her parents' agreement, that Sophie would stay the night. Neither her parents nor I are, any longer, trying to impose restrictions on their sleeping arrangements. Christ, when I think of what I used to get up to at their age, it would have been hypocritical to say the least. Heavens – I was only a couple of years older than them when I became pregnant with Megan! All I ask is that they are careful.

Anyway, as Sophie is still going to be here in the morning, I'll maybe get a chance to see whether the atmosphere between the two of them has lightened.

I try to focus my attention back on the TV, but the nagging doubt keeps gnawing away at the edges of my mind. By 10.00p.m. I give up and go to bed.

***

As usual, I'm the first one up the next morning. I need a cup of tea before I tackle the day ahead. I fill the kettle and switch it on but also fill the filter coffee machine sufficiently to make two cups – Liam and Sophie will surely be wanting coffee soon. I flip the power switch on, and after a short while, the gurgling and glurping noises start. The first whiffs of the uplifting aroma begin to suffuse the air.

As I prop myself against the kitchen worktop, I happen to glance at the washing machine and notice that the power light is blinking; that's the sign that it's finished a cycle and is waiting to be unloaded. That's odd – I didn't put a load in last night. I go over to the machine and open the door. It looks like one of Liam's duvet covers inside; it's damp. *Why on earth would he have put that in to wash last night? Oh well – might as well hang it up while I'm waiting for Liam and Sophie to surface.*

I reach inside and start pulling the contents out. As I do so, a shower of small pieces of some sort of solid matter spray from the drum. Some of them land on the floor and some splatter all over me.

What the ...?

I stand up, brushing the debris from the front of my sweater and jeans; some of it sticks to my hands. I gaze at the squidgy fragments in disgust, trying to identify just what this stuff is. As I squint at it closely, a creeping realisation dawns. The bile rises in my throat, and it is all I can do to stop myself throwing up. The item I am examining is a small piece of partly digested broccoli. Also stuck to my hand is what looks like a small piece of Yorkshire pudding. As I kneel down and survey the mess on the floor, any shreds of doubt are erased: I am looking at the partly digested contents of someone's stomach.

Bloody Liam! In spite of his unusually civil behaviour the previous day, I could cheerfully strangle him right now.

First though, I need to deal with this mess. I'm already covered in this disgusting stuff, so I decide to tackle the mess on the floor while I'm still dirty. I gather up the duvet cover and sheet, folding it all inwards to try to trap as much of the solid matter as possible. I take them out into the garden, shaking them vigorously to get rid of all the bits before taking them back inside and dumping them into a laundry basket. Next, I set about clearing up all the pieces on the floor and those few bits still inside the washing machine drum, before putting the original load back in the machine and setting it for another wash cycle. Finally, once the machine is running, I mop the kitchen floor.

Only now do I head towards the bathroom for a shower and a change of clothes.

***

Once I'm clean and presentable again, I take a peek through Amelia's door; she's still fast asleep, so I head back downstairs.

There's still no sign of Liam or Sophie, so I sit down to have some breakfast on my own. Just as I'm about to take my first spoonful of cereal, Sophie appears, carrying her overnight bag. She looks awful: her eyes look puffy and red, in contrast to the rest of her face, which is deathly pale.

I try not to show my shock at her appearance. 'Good morning, Sophie. Can I get you some breakfast?'

'No thank you,' she murmurs, 'to be honest I'm not feeling very well.'

'Oh … sorry to hear that. Can I get you anything?'

'No … really. I'll be fine in a while, but I don't want anything to eat.'

'Coffee, or tea then?'

'No thanks … in any case, I should be getting home now.'

'Well, OK then … if you're sure. Er, isn't Liam coming down to say goodbye?'

'Oh, he's not dressed yet … we've already said our goodbyes.' *Was that a sob she stifled?* 'Thank you for a lovely lunch yesterday, Miss Fisher.'

'Hey, what's with the "Miss Fisher" bit?' I say, getting up from the table to give her a hug. 'I've told you before … call me Madeleine.'

She manages a wan smile. 'OK … bye, then.'

With that, she heads for the front door, giving me a little wave as she steps outside.

No sooner do I step back into the kitchen, than Liam appears, looking barely any better than Sophie had. I don't feel inclined to exercise the same degree of restraint as I had with Sophie.

'Well, I see you've finally surfaced; you look awful.'

He shrugs, uttering an unintelligible grunt.

'What the hell were you doing puking all over your bedclothes like that and shoving it all into the washing machine without clearing the mess off them first? Do you realise how long it took me to—?'

'Mum!' he barks, cutting me off mid-sentence.

'What?' I demand.

'It wasn't me.'

'What do you mean?'

'It was Sophie who was sick.'

'Oh,' I say, the wind somewhat taken from my sails.

'It was me who put the things in the machine, but to be honest I was so drunk I didn't really know what I was doing. Sophie was even worse. I'm sorry.' As he raises those big blue eyes, full of remorse, my anger begins to evaporate.

'But you weren't drinking at all over lunch, and Sophie doesn't normally drink all that much. What happened?'

His lip begins to quiver, his brow creasing up. And then the dam breaks; he bursts into tears, rushing forward and enveloping me in a hug.

'What? What is it, Liam?' I say, pulling him to me.

'She's found someone else, Mum,' he gasps, each desperate sob racking his body. 'She's dumped me.'

Chapter 28

'The vegetable knife'

I'm working between Christmas and New Year, and with the reduced staffing level at the hospital over the holiday period, I've been absolutely working my butt off trying to cover everything. Now it's Friday evening, around 8.00p.m. and I'm completely exhausted. And I still have a morning shift to work tomorrow, Saturday.

Amelia is staying over at her dad's tonight, Grace is in Thailand, and Liam is ensconced in his room playing on his PlayStation, so I'm on my own. I decide to have a bath, go to bed early, and watch a bit of TV in bed. But I just can't focus on the TV programme; my mind keeps wandering off towards Liam.

In the few days since Sophie has left, Liam has completely withdrawn into his shell. I know he's been calling and texting her, but he won't talk to me about it. I think it really must be over between them. Sophie was such a good influence on Liam, and it breaks my heart to see how their split has dragged him down. He's reverted right back to his old ways: disappearing into his room for hours on end and being withdrawn and secretive when he does emerge. I want to help him, but what can I do?

My mind goes round and round in circles, the sound from the TV becoming nothing more than formless background noise. Eventually, exhaustion starts to take over from anxiety, and my eyelids begin to flutter.

When I next surface from that halfway house between sleep and wakefulness it's around 10.00p.m. The TV is still on, but the programme I was watching has finished. With a weary sigh, I turn off the TV and the bedside lamp, rolling over onto my side and pulling up the duvet snugly around my neck, before surrendering to sleep's warm embrace.

***

'Mum … Mum … MUM!' The panicked cries pierce my consciousness, dragging me, in an instant, from that dark comfortable place I was occupying to a state of full wakefulness.

Disoriented, I sit up in bed, trying to figure out what the hell is going on.

'MUUUM!' comes the frantic cry again. It's Liam's voice – *what the hell is he up to this time?*

Cursing out loud, I haul myself out of bed and pull on my dressing gown, making my way down the stairs. Liam's room is directly below mine, and when I reach the bottom of the stairs, I can see that his door is slightly ajar; maybe that's why his shouts sounded so loud.

I've already started remonstrating with him for disturbing my sleep before I even push the door fully open, but when I do so, my words are frozen in my throat, and the air is sucked from my lungs. I can't breathe.

Liam is sitting on the edge of the bed wearing just shorts and a tee shirt. Nothing unusual in that: it's a warm room. No, what has hit me like a hammer blow to my guts is the sight of a knife, buried right up to the hilt in his leg. It's my favourite vegetable knife; aqua blue handle; I use it every day. The blood is streaming down his leg, soaking into the thick pile of the rug alongside his bed, forming a rapidly expanding, deep red circle. And then the smell hits me: the familiar metallic, coppery tang of blood.

After what feels like an age but is probably no more than a second or so, I tear my gaze from the bloody scene and raise it to look into his frightened eyes. He's been speaking, but so far, I haven't registered a word he's said. Finally, I start to focus; he has his phone to his ear; he's calling an ambulance.

As he lets his phone drop onto the bed, I see him start to reach down towards the knife protruding from his leg.

'Liam … don't touch it … don't move!' I yell.

As I emerge from my initial state of shock, my nurse's training is starting to kick in. If that knife has gone through an artery – and judging by the amount of blood issuing from the wound, it may have done – then removing it would be the worst possible thing to do. He could bleed out in minutes.

I sit down on the bed beside him, putting my arm around his shoulders. 'Keep very still … we have to leave the knife where it is until we can get you to hospital.'

He turns and looks at me, nodding weakly. He's starting to shiver now, even though the room is warm; that will be the shock setting in. I take off my dressing gown and drape it around his shoulders, all the time re-iterating that he must keep still.

'You did this to yourself, Liam? Why?'

He shakes his head, his face a mask of sorrow and confusion. 'I don't know, Mum … it's just Sophie, my job, everything. I just don't know what to …' He starts sobbing.

'OK … OK … we can talk about it later. Just keep still … everything's going to be OK.'

Will it? Will it be OK? Will he be able to walk again? Will he even make it to the hospital? Where's that damned ambulance?

Finally, I see the flashing blue lights, lots of them, piercing the thin fabric of the curtains. I ease myself gently away from Liam, urging him, once more, to keep very still while I go to the door to let the paramedics in. *Oh Christ, there are police here too.*

Within seconds there are people everywhere and the entire house seems to be in chaos. While the paramedics attend to Liam, the police question me in the living room. It's a stabbing, after all, and they need to ascertain what happened. *Am I actually a suspect?* I answer their questions as best I can, or at least I think so – I'm so shaken up I don't really know what I have said.

Finally, they seem to have finished with me, and I can go and talk to the paramedics. Liam is now sitting in a wheelchair talking to another policeman. My eyes are immediately drawn to the aqua blue handle of my vegetable knife still protruding from his leg.

One of the paramedics updates me on Liam's situation. They have checked his vital signs, stemmed the bleeding with a tourniquet, and stabilised his condition, but they need to get him to hospital and into an operating theatre as soon as possible.

The policeman seems to have finished talking to Liam, so I go and grab my son's hand. 'It's going to be OK, Liam. They're going to get you straight to hospital.'

'We have to go right now,' interrupts the paramedic.

'Wait, I need to get dressed.'

'There's no time for that, Miss Fisher. Look, when we get him to hospital he'll be going straight to theatre, and then he'll be asleep for some time. There's nothing you can do tonight. Try to get some sleep, and then you can come and see him tomorrow. Phone the hospital tomorrow morning and they should be able to let you know how he is and when you can come and see him.'

'Where are you taking him?'

'St. Raphael's – they have a specialist wing for trauma of this nature.'

St. Raphael's Hospital is some thirty miles distant, but I have to trust that these people know what is best for my son.

Reluctantly, I let go of Liam's hand. 'I'll come and see you tomorrow. Everything's going to be OK.'

He gives a silent nod, looking lost and confused as they wheel him away, with me following until they get him into the ambulance. As the ambulance sets off, and I step back inside the house, I see the police officer who questioned me talking to his colleague who had spoken to Liam.

'We'll be off now, too, Miss Fisher. Your son has explained what happened … we'll be in touch if we need to ask you any further questions. Try to get some sleep now.'

As I shut the front door behind them, the house descends into silence – a deathly silence – in sharp contrast to the bedlam which had reigned just minutes earlier.

I go back into Liam's room. The blood has gone sticky and lumpy; the formerly white, deep-pile rug is now almost entirely deep red in colour. The blood is on the divan base too, and the bed cover is covered in bloody handprints. The whole thing looks and smells like a murder scene. I'm just standing there, looking at it, my brain still unable to take it all in.

Suddenly, I feel sick – really sick. The surge of nausea breaks the trance. When I glance at Liam's bedside clock, I'm astonished to see that I've been standing there – just standing there – for almost half an hour. I need to try to get some sleep. I flick off the light and shut the door on the horrific scene: I can't deal with this right now.

***

As you might imagine, sleep just won't come. The image of Liam is indelibly imprinted on my mind; every time I close my eyes, that's all I can see: a young face, scared and helpless.

My boy – what has happened to my boy?

This feels like the longest night of my life. The coppery smell of blood lingers in my nostrils, and time just refuses to move on. The whole scene just hangs there in my mind, never shifting its focus. It's like some sort of portent of a long and difficult road ahead.

I just have no idea of how long, or how difficult, that road might be.

Chapter 29

'The morning after the night before'

The night stretches before me like an eternity. My mind is whirling in circles as I try to make some sense of what has just happened: a maelstrom of disconnected thoughts. Was this really all about Liam's split with Sophie? Perhaps his feelings for her were far deeper than I had appreciated. Was this his way of crying out to her to come back? But then I remember his words: *'I don't know, Mum ... it's just Sophie, my job, everything ...'* Maybe the split with Sophie was more like a catalyst, a trigger which caused all the things troubling him to culminate in a crisis. In truth, I'm not sure even *he* would be able to rationalise quite what he was doing and why. But it wasn't rational, was it? It was surely an *emotional* response. We have to talk about it – get him to let it all out. What sort of mother am I if I can't help him through this? But there'll be time enough for all that later; right now, it's his physical condition which is my immediate concern.

I shudder as I recall the sight of the knife, buried to the hilt in his shin, the sight – and smell – of the slick river of blood coursing down his leg and soaking into the rug. As a nurse, I'm well used to the sight of traumatic injuries; normally it doesn't faze me one bit. But when it's my own son, bleeding out in front of me, it's a very different proposition.

I glance at the glowing red digits of my bedside clock: 5.17a.m. The time has advanced by just eleven minutes since I last checked. I have not slept at all, and to be honest I'm not likely to now. I decide to phone the hospital. Whether I'll be able to get much information at this time of the morning, I don't know, but I have to do *something* other than just lie here tormenting myself.

The nurse's tone is calm and reassuring, but as a nurse myself, I know that doesn't necessarily mean anything: we're trained to deal with worried relatives in such a manner. 'Your son is out of surgery and in Recovery now. He's doing fine.'

Well, that doesn't tell me a lot; I have a million questions, which I start firing at the nurse. 'But what did the surgery involve? How long did it take? Is he going to be OK? Will he—'

She gently interrupts me. 'Whoa there … look, I understand you are a nurse yourself, Miss Fisher?'

'Yes.'

'Then would you like to speak to Mr Derwent, the surgeon?'

'He's still there?'

'Yes, he was called in around 1.00a.m. to operate on your son. He only finished around an hour ago. He's about to go home, but I'm sure he could spare a few minutes to talk to you.'

My heart leaps. 'Then, yes … if he's available, that would be great.'

'Hold on … I'll fetch him.'

After a couple of minutes, a deep male voice comes on the line. 'Miss Fisher?'

'Yes … how is he?'

'Well, I'm pleased to tell you that the surgery went well. The injury was severe, but I believe, given time, your son should make a full recovery.'

The wave of relief which courses through my body feels almost physical in its intensity. 'Thank God … and thank *you* … I can't thank you enough.'

'Much of the credit goes to you, Miss Fisher. The blade of the knife was within a millimetre or so of an artery; your quick thinking in making sure the knife was not disturbed was critical. If the knife had been carelessly removed it could easily have severed the artery. Had that happened, the outcome could have been very different.'

My stomach lurches. In spite of the calm tone of voice, I know what those words 'the outcome could have been very different' mean.

The surgeon continues, 'The blade of the knife penetrated almost right through his lower leg; the point very nearly emerged from the back of his leg – the calf area. The surgery was extensive.'

My stomach clenches, and the breath catches in my throat as I picture the injury in my mind's eye.

The surgeon is still talking; I think I missed some of his words, but as I tune back in, I hear him say, '... he lost a lot of blood, but we've given him a transfusion of three pints, and all his vital signs are normal now.'

'Oh, thank you ... thank you again for saving my son.'

'That's my job ... I'm just pleased it all went well. Now I'm going to leave him in the capable hands of the Recovery staff here and go home to catch up on missed sleep.'

'Yes ... of course. Er ... when can I see him?'

'Well, he's asleep at the moment, and we will need to keep him sedated a while longer. He'll probably still be asleep for quite a few more hours. I suggest you call again around mid-afternoon to check.'

'I will ... thank you again.'

'You're welcome. Now, why don't you try to get some sleep yourself. I don't imagine you got much last night.'

I force a small smile, which is, of course, lost on the surgeon at the other end of the line. 'I'll do that ... thank you again.'

What to do now? Bizarrely, given what has just happened, my first thought is that I might be late for work if I don't get a move on.

***

Matron's face is a mask of puzzlement and concern when I arrive at work. 'Madeleine, are you alright? You look awful.'

Clearly my best efforts with my hair and makeup have been pretty ineffective; it's the dark circles under my eyes which were hardest to conceal.

'Thanks,' I say, doing my best to force a smile.

'No, really ... what's wrong?'

While I have no particular desire to share all my domestic problems with everyone at work – and be in no doubt, once Matron knows, the entire hospital will know shortly afterwards – I can't hide this one. 'Can we go into the office?' I say.

She ushers me in. Ten minutes later, I have told her everything, or at least everything she needs to know, about last night's incident. I stop short of going into chapter and verse about the background.

'Oh, heavens, Madeleine, what on earth are you doing here?'

'Well, he's still asleep at the moment, and I know we're short-staffed today.'

Her round face crinkles in a frown and her eyebrows knot. 'Your family comes first. How much sleep did *you* get last night?'

'Not much,' I admit. 'Well, probably none, to be honest.'

'Go home, get some sleep, and then go and see your son.'

'But what about—?'

'No "buts" … we'll manage OK.'

'Are you sure? I mean—'

'Go!' she says, flipping the back of her hand towards me.

***

I stare at the closed door of Liam's room. As my gaze settles on the handle, all thoughts of sleep flee my mind in an instant. I have to deal with this. It's just blood, after all, and I'm a nurse. I've trained in A&E, attended operations, and worked in dermatology for years.

I take a deep breath and open the door, flipping on the light switch. My legs start to buckle as I hang on to the open door for support. My nurse's training counts for nothing now. This is not an accident and it's not the result of an operation. Most of all, this is not just a *patient*: it's my *son*.

I take a few seconds to try to pull myself together; the moment passes, and I go to the window, pulling back the curtains.

As the sunlight streams into the room, the true horror of the scene reveals itself.

There are trails of blood from the door, the spots shining bright, standing proud, looking almost like rubies scattered on the floor. I lift my eyes toward the rug. The blood has soaked deep into the pile and turned brown in colour. The base of the bed is also heavily stained the same sinister brown colour. Handprints on the sheets remind me starkly just where all this blood has come from. Liam's keys are on the floor in the corner.

Where do I start?

I gather up the bedclothes and, in a daze, stumble towards the back door, turning the key with one hand while trying to hold the bulky pile of bed linen in the other. The incinerator in the garden still contains the charred remnants of the garden refuse which was the last thing disposed of there. I bundle the ruined sheets and duvet on top of them.

Returning to Liam's room I roll up the rug; the blood has soaked right through to the underside. I swallow deeply as I rise unsteadily to my feet and head out to the garden. There isn't enough room to jam the rug into the incinerator, so I dump it on the ground alongside.

I go back into the kitchen and make up a bucket of hot water and cleaning fluid, grabbing a scrubbing brush before returning to Liam's room to deal with the mess on the floor.

An hour later I am done; the last bucket of dirty water which I tip into the toilet is, like the first, a deep pink colour. As I flush the toilet for the second time, the water in the pan finally runs clear; it seems symbolic, somehow, of a cleansing – partially, at least – of my troubled mind.

I return to Liam's room to survey the scene; only the heavily stained bed base remains as witness to the previous night's events. I'll have to get rid of it … but that will have to wait for now.

And then it hits me: I am absolutely exhausted. I can hardly stand.

I check the clock: 10.57a.m. It will be hours yet before I can see Liam. I need to sleep.

***

The synthesised tones of 'Livin' la Vida Loca' dimly pierce the blackness which envelops me. I shut them out. Seconds later they start again – somehow, more insistent this time. I try to make sense of what's happening. It's such a familiar tune … it's … my ringtone!

Suddenly, I snap awake, fumbling for my phone as I register the time on my bedside clock: 3.51. Is that a.m. or p.m.? I'm completely disoriented. As my grasping fingers finally find my phone, I notice that daylight is streaming through the gaps around my curtains: it's the afternoon.

I hit the green button.

'Is that Madeleine Fisher?'

'Yes, that's me,' I say, propping myself up on one elbow and rubbing my eyes.

'My name is Stella … Recovery Nurse at St Raphael's Hospital. I'm calling about your son Liam.'

'Yes … yes … how is he?'

'He's doing well. He's awake now, though still very woozy. Given the extensive nature of the surgery he has undergone, and the fact that he's still somewhat disoriented, we're going to keep him in Recovery for a bit longer.'

'Can I come and see him now?'

'Well, we don't normally allow visitors into Recovery, but I understand you are a staff nurse yourself … is that right?'

'Yes.'

'Then you will be aware of protocols in Recovery, so I think we can make an exception in this case.'

'Thank you. I'll be there in about an hour.'

I jump out of bed and go to the bathroom for a pee and to splash my face with water. I don't bother with my usual morning routine, so after just fifteen minutes, bereft of makeup and with my hair unkempt, I am on my way. I haven't eaten anything for at least eighteen hours.

**

'Hi Mum,' croaks Liam, as his eyelids stop fluttering, and he finally focuses on my face.

'How are you?' I say, leaning forward to kiss his brow – a gesture which would normally have him shushing me away, but he seems too weak to protest right now.

'I'm OK … just feel a bit … vague.'

I look for space to sit on the bed, but there is a cage under the bedclothes to protect his leg from any sort of pressure; it takes up most of the width of the bed. I glance around for a chair, but there is none to be seen; this is, after all, Recovery, where visitors are not normally allowed. I remain standing.

'Why did you do it, Liam?'

He breaks eye contact. 'Don't know really … after Sophie … after she dumped me, I felt so … shit. I just needed to … oh, I don't know. Funny thing is … it didn't even hurt all that much. Hurts more now, actually.'

I know full well, that after surgery like this, he'll be dosed up to the eyeballs with powerful painkillers, so God knows how he'll be when he comes off the meds.

He's mumbling now. 'Think I must … going to … got to see if … tired.' His eyelids flutter again, before closing completely.

'Liam?' I whisper, gently nudging his shoulder, but he's asleep now.

The nurse, who has been hovering in the background, comes over. 'Probably best to leave him to sleep, now.'

I nod, giving him another little kiss on the forehead before turning away from the bed.

'I've been asked to return this to you,' says the nurse, holding forth my vegetable knife – aqua blue handle. It looks so familiar, so … *everyday* … but now, it holds such different connotations.

My legs threaten to buckle beneath me, but I manage to control the moment. 'Thanks,' I say taking the weapon – for that is how I now regard it – and putting it in my handbag.

What will I do with it? Throw it away? Keep it as a grotesque memento of this horrific situation? One thing's for sure: I will never again use it to peel or slice vegetables.

Chapter 30

'Realisation'

The following day, Sunday, I am feeling rather better, both mentally and physically. Knowing that Liam has come through the surgery without any major complications is a huge weight off my mind; I finally got a pretty solid night's sleep last night. It's 9.00a.m. now, and a call to St Raphael's reveals that Liam has been moved from Recovery to Fortman Ward. He is, apparently, much brighter now, the effects of the drugs having largely worn off. I can come and see him whenever I like. However, Mr Derwent – the surgeon – has come into the hospital today, and he would like to talk to me first. Neither Megan nor Amelia is due to return home until this afternoon, so I arrange to see Mr Derwent at 10.30a.m.

Neither of the girls knows yet what has happened, and I really don't know how to break the news to them. At least, if I've spoken to the surgeon and seen Liam again, I'll know more about his condition and recovery prognosis. That will, hopefully, put me in a better position to explain things. Even so, it's not a prospect I'm looking forward to.

***

Mr Derwent is a tall, slim man, probably in his mid-fifties, with greying hair, a strong, straight nose and sharply sculpted cheekbones. Actually, quite handsome; *almost certainly married,* I surmise, before any untoward thoughts might enter my head. Anyway, I'm here to talk about Liam.

The surgeon's voice is soft but deep in tone. 'As I explained to you on the phone, Miss Fisher, the surgery went well, and your son should, eventually, make a full recovery ... but it will take quite a bit of time.'

I nod, concentrating intently on what he is saying.

'Now,' he says, 'I understand you are a nurse. Are you familiar with a procedure called a fasciotomy?'

I dredge the deepest recesses of my mind, trying to recall the term from my training. It's there, but only dimly. 'I've heard of it, but I've never actually attended the procedure ... something to do with relieving pressure, isn't it?'

'Yes, that's right. In cases of trauma like this, there can be a severe build-up of pressure in the vicinity of the wound, which can, in turn, result in loss of blood circulation. If left untreated, the restricted blood circulation can be very serious, even leading to loss of the affected limb.'

Thank God I am sitting down. The wave of dread which courses through me is like a physical thing, eviscerating my entire body. The beads of perspiration which spring up on my forehead prickle my skin. The surgeon doesn't seem to notice.

'I had to make two deep incisions in his lower leg: one at the front and one at the back. For now, the wounds have been left open and he has a surgical pump attached to his leg to draw away the discharge which will inevitably continue for some time. Once we are satisfied that the discharge has slowed sufficiently and there is no infection, he will need skin grafts to close the incisions. As a nurse, you may be curious and wish to see the incisions yourself. If so, I should caution you that they are extensive, and very deep. I understand you are used to dealing with trauma injuries, but you may find that seeing your own son in this condition evokes a very different reaction from dealing with a patient whom you do not know.'

I recall the way my stomach lurched when I saw Liam sitting on the bed, the handle of the knife protruding and the blood streaming down his leg before soaking into the deep-pile rug. I swallow, involuntarily.

'Yes, I understand.'

'After the wounds are closed, he will be bed-bound for some days and then only able to get about in a wheelchair for a while after that. The next step will be to get him moving about on crutches, but it will be several more weeks before he can start to bear his own weight on the injured leg.'

The enormity of the long road to recovery stretching ahead starts to dawn.

'When do you think he'll be able to come home?'

The surgeon's brow crinkles in a thoughtful expression. 'Hard to say for sure; it depends on a several factors, but I would imagine that someone young and healthy like your son could possibly be discharged after around four weeks. He'll still be on crutches, though.'

My mind starts to race as I try to imagine the logistics, over at least a four-week period, of getting to and from work, getting Amelia to and from school, and visiting a hospital some thirty miles from home.

The surgeon seems to sense my dilemma. He pauses for several seconds, waiting for me to restore eye contact before continuing.

'Now then, this part is not within my field of expertise, but do you know what drove your son to such an extreme act of self-harm?'

It's the question I've been dreading, because in all honesty I'm not entirely sure.

'He's recently split from his girlfriend; he says that's what's behind it.'

The surgeon's expression is kindly, but I feel his eyes boring into me. 'You don't sound completely convinced.'

I spread my hands, helplessly. 'How can I know whether that's the whole story? Sophie dumping him definitely hit him very hard, but enough, on its own, to do *this*? I just don't know.'

'Kids of that age can be quite secretive,' he says, '…bottling up things which they don't necessarily share with their parents.'

Tell me something I don't know, I think.

'Look,' he continues, 'can I make a suggestion?'

I look up at him. 'Yes … of course.'

'I don't doubt that you and Liam will talk much more about this, and maybe it will all become clearer, but sometimes it's easier with a stranger.'

'What are you saying?'

'The hospital has two mental health specialists. Perhaps it would help if Liam spoke to one of them.'

'Maybe …' I murmur, not really sure if it would help or not.

'Talk it over with your son at some point, and if you both feel it might help, Matron can arrange an appointment.'

'OK … thank you.'

'Look, that's all from me at the moment. I'm guessing you're anxious to see your son, so why don't you do that now? I'll show you to the ward.'

My mind is whirling with all the things the surgeon has said, but he's right: at this moment I just want to see Liam.

***

'Hi Mum.' He's a different person from the boy I saw yesterday. He's fully alert and sitting up in bed. His voice is strong.

'How are you feeling today?' I ask.

'Well, it still hurts quite a bit, but I'm OK.'

I pull up a chair and sit down. 'That was one hell of a fright you gave us all.'

He casts his eyes aside. 'I'm sorry.'

'Do you want to talk about it?'

'Not really,' he says, still avoiding eye contact. 'Look, it's no big deal … I was drunk, I was upset about Sophie. I just needed to *do* something … I just sort of … lashed out, I suppose.'

'Liam, it *is* a big deal. Do you realise you could have *died*?'

'Well, I didn't, did I? Look, I know it was stupid … I was drunk and upset and not acting normally. Can we just leave it at that?'

I'm not about to push it further right there and then. The tone of his voice signals the anger burgeoning within him. The last thing I want to do is wind him up into a mood when he needs to be concentrating on his recovery.

'OK, we'll leave it for now, but don't ever scare me like that again.'

'I won't, Mum,' he says, the temperature easing a bit.

I change the subject. 'Have they spoken to you about what happens next in terms of your treatment and recovery?'

'Yeah … the surgeon explained it all to me. Looks like I'll be stuck in here for at least a few weeks.'

'Yes, he went through it all with me, too. Look, I'll come and see you as often as I can while you're in here, but it's tricky with work and the school run.'

'I know … I'll be fine,' he says, his manner conciliatory now.

'Is there anything I can get for you … books, magazines or anything?'

'Can you bring my laptop and my PlayStation?'

I smile. *Why on earth did I think he might want books or magazines? They're so yesterday to someone like Liam.*

'OK, I'll bring them over tomorrow evening.'

'Thanks, Mum.'

The mood has lightened considerably now, so we carry on chatting for almost an hour – about all manner of things but studiously avoiding the subjects of his drinking and his mental state. Those things can wait for now.

Chapter 31

'Amelia'

Grace is still in Thailand, so I have to break the news to her on the phone. She is a sensitive girl, and devoted to her brother, so it's no surprise that she's devastated. Her first thought is that she should come home straightaway, but when I point out that Liam will be in hospital for some weeks at least, and that there is really little she can do, she agrees that there isn't much point in doing so.

Megan, on the other hand, seems to take the news relatively calmly. She's concerned, naturally, but she doesn't seem as shocked as I would have expected. Had she had some inkling about her brother's mental state? How could she? Maybe I'm imagining it.

But what can I say to Amelia? She's just five years old; she can't possibly be expected to comprehend. I resort to a lie: I tell her Liam had jumped a fence on his way home and accidentally impaled himself. She seems pretty surprised that he could be so stupid but accepts the explanation. I make both her sisters, and Liam himself, swear they will back up this story. There will, of course, be a time, at some point in the future when she can know the truth, but I will be the one to decide when the time is right for that.

***

Liam is in hospital for the next four weeks. His recovery progresses pretty much as the surgeon suggested it would. But Amelia is just so sad and confused; she misses her big brother so much.

The two of us go to visit Liam together as often as possible, fitting around work and school commitments as best we can. She

121

struggles with the vastness of the hospital, its network of corridors, and the all-pervading smell of surgical procedures. She is always pleased to see her brother, but like most five-year-olds, her attention span is limited. Sometimes she will just sit in the corridor and chat to the staff about school, her friends and – most often – how she wants her ears pierced. She sits close enough that she can see me, but the glass between us means she can't overhear my conversation with Liam, so at least it allows some time for us to talk privately.

I'm pleased to find that he seems pretty upbeat for most of his time in hospital. He seems happy enough to spend hours on his PlayStation or surfing the web. More surprisingly, he seems to have struck up something of a relationship with some of his fellow patients in the ward, though most of them are not in for such a long time as Liam. For around ten days, there is a young man named Noah in the bed alongside him; he shares some of the same interests as Liam and, when he is ready for discharge, the two of them exchange contact details and resolve to stay in touch.

Most of the other patients on the ward, however, are much older. In the bed opposite, is an elderly gentleman named George, who, in spite of the age difference between them, seems to gel with Liam. He is apparently suffering from ulcers, which at times, cause him considerable pain. When he's feeling down, Liam will chat to him and try to lift his spirits.

George unfortunately passes away around two weeks before Liam is due to be discharged; it affects Liam deeply: the blackest day of his entire stay in hospital.

As the days pass, Amelia becomes increasingly bored with the repetitive nature of our visits. I try to find ways to break the routine. One day, after leaving the hospital we make a visit to the nearby viewing tower, a tourist attraction allowing a 360-degree view of the surrounding area. We take pictures, smile false smiles, and drink fizzy soft drinks – I resist the sparkling wine on offer as it feels tainted and improper while Liam is still in hospital. Amelia enjoys our outing, but I can tell she knows it's just a ploy to make the hospital visit more positive. My final – and most successful – tactic, aimed at lifting the mood of these hospital visits, is to cave in and allow her to get her ears pierced.

As the day for his discharge draws closer, Liam seems to put the darkness of George's death behind him, and his mood begins to brighten. As his mood continues to improve, so does mine. When I speak to the mental health specialist, Eileen, who has been working with Liam, I'm pleased and relieved to learn that she does not think Liam is suffering from clinical depression or any other persistent mental disorder. More likely the stabbing incident was a moment of madness triggered by the split with his girlfriend. As Eileen observes, a teenage love affair, especially if it's the first, can be far more intense than most adults realise.

As well as Eileen's positive assessment of Liam, there is something else which lifts my spirits as the day of his discharge grows closer: he has, as far as I can tell, not touched a drop of alcohol in four weeks. Luke, the trampoline park manager, was wrong: my son has *not* become addicted.

Chapter 32

'The long road to recovery'

Liam is due to come home today. Megan has offered to collect him so that I can take care of the school run. He's still on crutches; it's likely to be at least a couple of weeks before he can bear his weight unaided, and several more after that before he can begin to walk normally again. The good news, though, is that the surgeon is confident that he *will* be able to walk normally again – in time, perhaps even play football again. It will be a long road, but right now, I'll just be happy to have my son back. As the estimated time of his arrival approaches, Amelia and I keep stealing expectant glances out of the window.

Finally, the time has come: Megan's car pulls into the drive, and the two of us rush to the front door. By the time we step outside, Liam is levering himself out of the passenger seat, while Megan is holding his crutches for him. She passes them to him, and he hoists himself onto them in what has become a well-practiced manoeuvre.

He smiles as he looks up at the front of the house, which is decorated with balloons and a banner which reads 'Welcome Home Liam'. As he swings toward me on his crutches I step forward and envelop him in a hug, a gesture which he would no doubt have shrugged away from had he not needed to stay put to retain his balance. As it is, he just says, 'Hello Mum'.

When I finally let go of him, Amelia also rushes up for a hug. She's tall for her age but still has to stand on tiptoes to fling her arms around him.

The love in the air is palpable; Liam is *home*.

***

Liam has been home for two weeks now and is finally able to get around the house without his crutches. He can even walk, unaided, for short distances outside, though he is still noticeably limping.

Today, I am redressing his wounds: a long incision in the back of his calf, a large skin graft in his shin, and the site on his thigh from where the graft has been taken. He was supposed to have the wounds redressed at the local GP surgery, but refused to go, so the task has fallen to me. Anyway, the wounds, which looked horrendous immediately after his surgery, are healing nicely now, and probably won't need dressing at all after today's dressings come off.

'Thanks, Mum' he murmurs, as he rolls down the leg of his boxer shorts and levers himself to his feet.

As I watch him limping off towards his room, the questions which have been haunting me for weeks resurface in my head.

What is this boy capable of? Why are the lows so very low? Why didn't I see the signs? Am I a bad mum?

Our relationship is good, but his moods are very erratic these days. Sometimes we can chat and share things as though it is the most natural thing in the world; at other times, though, he becomes quite secretive, even irrational. Perhaps coming off all the medication he has been taking is a factor. He has been on quite a cocktail of drugs, including Librium, both for its calming effect and to help him withdraw from his previously heavy alcohol consumption. And that begs another question.

Will he stay off the alcohol now? He hasn't touched a drop, as far as I know, for well over a month, so maybe he'll be OK now. Maybe this horrific incident has shocked him into changing his ways. Maybe the darkest days are behind us.

Maybe ...

Chapter 33

'Regression'

Liam is back at work now. His employer has been incredibly tolerant; he had only spent a couple of weeks in his new job before having to take some six weeks off sick. I was the one who had had to explain the situation, resorting to the same fabricated story of a fictitious accident which I had given to Amelia. I felt as guilty as hell. To my surprise, they kept his job open for him.

He's still not right though; at home, he's still withdrawn and miserable much of the time. He's less and less inclined to share things with me, but it's as clear as day that he still hasn't come to terms with the break-up with Sophie. As Eileen, the mental health specialist at the hospital, had observed, a young person's first love affair can be much more intense than even their own parents will realise. He needs to get out more, move on, rebuild his life. Spending all his time within these four walls, online or playing video games just isn't healthy.

With this in mind, I take every opportunity to encourage him to rekindle the relationships with some of his former friends and socialise more.

Little by little, it starts to work. He is gradually rebuilding his social circle and going out in the evenings. He seems brighter in himself and even a little more open and sociable with me.

He's out with friends tonight, and as it's Friday evening, he'll probably not be home until quite late. Amelia's in bed now, and I'm exhausted after a hard week at work, so I decide to have an early night.

I usually watch a bit of TV in bed before settling down to sleep, but tonight I'm just too wrecked to even be bothered with that. I just want to sleep. I switch off the bedside lamp and allow my head to sink into the soft embrace of the pillow.

***

What's that noise? I am dimly aware of voices – male and female - just outside the house. They're loud ... *too* loud. *Is it an argument? No ... the shouting is interspersed with laughter.* I prop myself up on one elbow and blink through the haze of half-sleep at the clock on my bedside table: 2.35a.m. I've been asleep for over four hours.

The voices stop; a car door slams before I hear the engine revving loudly and a screech of tyres as the car speeds off up the road. *What the fuck?*

I'm furious now. If Liam wants to stay out late with his friends that's fine, but I'm not having him making a godawful racket at all hours, waking me up and disturbing the neighbours.

I lever myself out of bed and slip into my dressing gown, stomping angrily down the stairs. As I emerge into the hallway the front door opens, and Liam staggers unsteadily forward. In that moment, my worst fears are confirmed: he's as drunk as a skunk. My heart sinks like a stone.

'Oh ... you shtill up?' he says, voice heavily slurred. 'Iss a bit late issn't it?' He's swaying back and forth as though just about to lose his balance and keel over.

I grab his shoulders to steady him. 'Oh, Liam ... what have you done? You're supposed to be off the booze.'

His head retracts, eyes blinking and unfocused. 'Well, you said I should get out and scochall ... scochallise more, so thass what I'm doing.' A stupid grin spreads across his face.

My initial shock turns to anger. 'Don't you dare lay this on me, you—'

My words are cut short as his face contorts, and a stream of vomit erupts from his mouth hitting me squarely in the face and coursing down the front of my dressing gown. I recoil, involuntarily, and as I let go of his shoulders, his legs finally give way; he sinks to the floor.

'Sorry, Mum ... don't feel well,' he says, as he looks up at me with puppy-dog eyes.

No kidding, I think, as I try to wipe the stinking mess from my face with my sleeve.

There's clearly no point trying to reason with him while he's like this, so I set about helping him out of his ruined clothes, stripping him down to his boxer shorts – about the only item of clothing that is still intact. I shrug out of my soiled dressing gown, leaving it in a heap on the floor before hoisting Liam to his feet and draping his arm across my shoulders. With some difficulty we stagger through to his room – now bereft of all traces of the stabbing incident. I dump him unceremoniously on the bed and leave him to sleep it off. My next stop is the bathroom, where I have a quick shower and change into a clean nightdress.

Returning to the hallway, I gather up the pile of soiled clothing and make my way to the back door, dumping it all on the path outside. *I can't deal with these tonight.* The thing which can't be left until the morning, though, is the mess on the carpet. With a weary sigh, I grab a fresh roll of paper kitchen towel and go back to the hallway to scoop up all the solid matter on the carpet. I drop the filthy paper towels into a plastic bin liner before making up a bucketful of carpet cleaner and water to deal with the remaining stain on the carpet.

When I'm finally done, I glance at the clock: 4.17a.m. *So much for my early night.*

And then it dawns on me that, throughout the whole wretched incident, there has been no sign of Amelia. Was she completely oblivious of what was going on?

I trudge wearily up the stairs and take a peek in her room. Sure enough, fast asleep.

Bloody incredible!

Chapter 34

'A brush with the law'

Unfortunately, the incident on that fateful Friday night wasn't a one-off; it was just the start of an implosion.

Before long he is going out almost every evening, coming home late at night, drunk and usually miserable. He is getting up later and later; sometimes he is still in bed when I have to leave for work. He must frequently be late getting to work; how on earth is his employer putting up with all this?

It isn't long before I get my answer …

***

It's Monday; I have a day off, having worked two shifts over the weekend. Liam has, for once, set off for work on time, and I've just finished the school run. Time to do some shopping and run a few errands.

It's almost midday by the time I get home, and to my surprise, Liam is sprawled on the sofa engrossed in his PlayStation.

'Hi Mum,' he says, avoiding eye-contact.

What the fuck?

'Liam …' I say, conscious of the unintended menace in my own tone of voice, 'what's happened … why are you home?'

'It's OK … no big deal.'

'What the hell does that mean?' I can hear both the tone and volume of my own voice escalating.

'Like I said … it's OK.' He's still staring at his wretched PlayStation and not at me.

That's it! My anger boils over. I rush forward and sweep the device off his lap with a swipe of my arm. 'Look at me when I'm talking to you!'

That finally gets his attention. 'What the hell are you doing?' he yells.

I ignore the question. 'What's happened? What are you doing here at home?'

He finally raises his eyes to meet my gaze. His tone is sombre. 'I've been fired.'

I don't know why the strength drains from my legs in the way it does; I already knew what the answer would be. I guess I just needed to hear him say it out loud. I sink into the armchair opposite.

'Oh Liam … not again. Why? What was the reason?'

'Does it matter? I'm fired, right? No sweat … I'll get another job.'

'Yes, it matters. You can't just keep walking into a new job every time you get fired. Sooner or later, no-one will give you a job. Now, tell me … what happened?'

He expels a long, slow, sigh. 'OK … well, it started when I was a bit late getting into work in the mornings once or twice.'

'Once or twice?' I say, unable to keep the irony out of my voice.

'Alright … quite often. Anyway, they gave me what they called a "verbal warning".'

'When was this?' I demand.

'Oh, I don't know exactly … maybe a couple of months ago.'

'Why didn't you tell me at the time?'

'Didn't seem that important.'

Not important? For now, I resist the urge to remonstrate with him: I want the whole story.

'Then what?' I prompt.

'Well, then they noticed that the physical stocks of alcohol didn't exactly match up with the computerised records for those products.'

My stomach lurches as I start to process what this means. 'Oh Liam, you weren't stealing it were you?'

'No, of course not … well, only a little bit for my personal consumption. Trouble is … the boss caught me drinking some of their vodka on the premises.'

I can hardly believe it. 'You stole their vodka and actually drank it while you were at work?'

He looks up at me. 'Yeah … didn't think they'd miss it.'

'So is that why they fired you?'

'No, they said they'd give me another chance. They gave me what they called a "final written warning".'

I slumped forward, cupping my forehead between my hands. 'So what the hell happened today to tip them over the edge?'

'Looks like I forgot to lock up the shop on Saturday.'

'You did what?'

'Dunno … I don't remember leaving it open, but then again, I don't exactly remember locking up. S'pose I must have left it open.'

'So was it left unlocked all day Sunday?'

He shrugs. 'I guess so.'

'Oh, Liam … how could you be so careless?'

He pulls a 'how the heck do I know?' face but does not reply.

'Was any harm done?' I say, dreading the reply.

'Kind of … some stuff got stolen.'

'What? How much?'

'Mostly alcohol and ciggies.'

'How much, Liam?' I persist. 'How much was it worth?'

'Don't freak out, Mum … they're going to try to claim on their insurance.'

'For Christ's sake, Liam … how fucking much?'

He takes a deep breath before raising his eyes to meet mine. 'They reckon about ten grand.'

My stomach performs a somersault. 'Ten *thousand*?'

''fraid so.'

'Oh Christ! Are the police involved?'

'Uh, huh … they've already spoken to me.'

'And do they know you left the shop unlocked?'

'No … I told Gary, my boss – and the police – that I locked up properly, but now can't find the key. I said that maybe I accidentally dropped it outside the shop.'

Oh shit! So now my son is not only negligent, but he's lied to his boss and the police.

'And they believe that?'

'I think so … there's no CCTV at the front of the shop, and I've now thrown the key into the canal. How can they know that I'm not telling the truth?'

'Christ, Liam … lying to the police is a big deal.'

'Well, they seem to have accepted what I said, and Gary has backed me up, saying I'm an honest employee.'

'Even though he knows you have previously been guilty of stealing booze for yourself? That man must be a bloody saint.'

'Well, he likes me ... he didn't want to get me into any more trouble.'

'Christ, Liam ... you can't keep trading on people's goodwill while you're behaving like a total dickhead.'

He casts his eyes downward, apparently unwilling to try to defend himself.

'Anyway,' I continue, 'have the police finished with you now?'

'Seems like it ... I don't think I'm under suspicion of any involvement in the actual theft.'

An unbidden – and probably unworthy – thought crosses my mind. 'And you're *not* involved ... are you?'

His head jerks towards me. 'Muuum ... how could you even think that?'

'Sorry,' I say, realising that I have really hurt him now.

We sit in silence for several seconds before I continue.

'Well, to be honest, if the worst that happens to you is your losing your job, you'll have gotten off lightly, but what happens if the insurance won't pay up?'

He shrugs and spreads his hands, helplessly. 'Dunno.'

I guess that's tomorrow's problem, I think. *At least he's off the hook for now.*

Chapter 35

Three months later

'Emily'

The police never did follow up any further on Liam's possible involvement with the theft at the supermarket, and we've heard nothing more about the insurance claim made by his former employer. Liam has been beyond fortunate to have emerged from the incident unscathed, apart from the loss of his job.

It's September now, and autumn is drawing in. Liam has spent the summer socialising with friends, meeting girls, and drinking – drinking heavily. He doesn't have a proper job, so he's relying on benefits, plus what he can earn from informal 'off the books' work here and there. I don't know how he can afford this lifestyle, but I don't ask too many questions.

I'm rather preoccupied with something else right now, though. My late father's inheritance has finally come through, and with it, the promise of the dream of owning my own house. Grace is back from her travels now, so if she, Liam, and Amelia are each to have their own rooms, we need at least four bedrooms.

After some weeks of scouring the internet, I find an ideal house: 1930s, detached, four bedrooms, semi-rural location but still local. There's a small convenience store almost right next door and the village pub just a few doors on the other side. It's a bit too expensive to buy outright, even with Dad's substantial bequest to me, but by supplementing this with a modest mortgage it's feasible. It's perfect!

We move in October and quickly settle into our new home.

***

We have only been in the new house for a few weeks when Liam drops a bombshell. It's delivered quite casually on one of those rare occasions when we sit down for breakfast together.

'Umm … you remember Emily, Mum?'

'Emily?' I murmur, absently, as I add a little milk to my tea.

'You know … you met her when I brought her home one evening a few weeks ago.'

My brow wrinkles as I dredge up the memory. *Oh yes … that one.* I had assumed she was just one of the many girls Liam had casually dated over the summer.

'Oh yes … I remember. What about her?'

'Well, Emily and I are in a serious relationship.'

I set down my cup and snap to attention. 'You are? You haven't said anything about it before now.'

'Well, I didn't want to say anything until I was sure.'

'OK … well, I'm pleased for you.' And I am: this might be just what he needs to help him move on after his split with Sophie, who he obviously cared for much more than I had realised at the time.

'She's really nice, Mum … you'll like her.'

'Well, yes … I'd like to get to know her … you can bring her round here whenever you like.'

He breaks eye contact and dips his head a little … *uh, oh … I know that look. What's coming?*

'The thing is, it's not that easy for her to get out.'

'Why not?' I say, curious and apprehensive in equal measure.

'Well, she has to organise childcare before she can get out.'

'Childcare?' I splutter. 'She has a child?'

'Yes … a little boy called Jack. He's three.'

'Oh Liam … what are you getting into here?'

'It's OK, he's a nice little boy.'

'I don't doubt it, but …' My voice tails off; I'm really not sure what comes after the 'but'.

'Look, Mum … we've talked it over and we've agreed that the best way we can find time to be together is if I move into her flat.'

Whoa there! This is all too much, too fast, for me to process. I am literally dumbstruck.

It takes several seconds before I find my voice. 'Liam … isn't this all a bit sudden?'

'Not really … we've been talking about it for a while.'

Not with me, you haven't.

I try to stay calm and open-minded. He's an adult and can make his own decisions.

'Alright,' I say, forcing a smile, 'well a bit sudden for me, then.'

He reaches across the table and touches my hand. 'Sorry Mum … maybe I should have said something sooner.'

'OK … well now you have. So, tell me a bit more about Emily. Is she working? Wouldn't be easy for a single mum with a three-year-old.'

'No, she's a full-time mum, but she's getting a reasonable amount on benefits, and she's got a pretty nice council flat. Once we pool our benefits, we'll be fine. And I'm going to start looking for another job, too.'

'OK,' I say, giving his hand a little squeeze. 'Look, I'd like to get to know her. If childcare is a problem, she can bring her little boy round here when she comes to visit. I'll bet Amelia would like to take him under her wing.'

'That'd be great,' he says. 'It's going to be just fine.'

And maybe it will; perhaps being in a long-term relationship and sharing responsibility for looking after a child will engender that sense of responsibility that Liam has, so far, lacked. Maybe it will give him something worthwhile to focus on other than the booze.

Maybe …

Chapter 36

'The calm'

It's four months since Liam moved in with Emily, and thank God, it seems to have worked out OK. They seem happy together, and to my great surprise, Liam appears to relish being a stepdad to Emily's little boy, Jack. The one thing I don't really know is whether he's still drinking heavily.

Yesterday was Jack's fourth birthday; I couldn't get to his birthday party, as I was working, but Liam and Emily have arranged to bring him over to my house this morning so that I can see him and give him his birthday gift. They're due here right around now.

I hear Liam's car pull up outside before I hear the doorbell. When I open the door, I am confronted with Jack's smiling, chubby little face, all smiles and tousled blonde curls. He's right up at my eye level; Liam has lifted him up so that he can reach the doorbell.

'Hello auntie Maddie,' he chimes, his arms outstretched towards me.

I take him from Liam, enfolding him in a hug. 'Wow! You're getting too big and heavy for me now.'

I quickly set him down.

'Mummy says you might have another present for me,' he says, big, blue eyes wide and expectant.

'Does she now?' I laugh. 'Well, why don't you go and have a look in the living room? But if there is one, it could be hidden.'

'I'll find it,' he squeals, scampering past me.

By the time Liam, Emily, and I make it through to the living room, Jack is well into the search. He pops out from behind the curtain, still empty-handed, and casts his gaze around the room as he tries to decide where to try next. He decides to wriggle into the gap behind the sofa.

Within just a few seconds he emerges, triumphantly clutching a gift-wrapped parcel. 'Is it for me?' he cries.

'Well, who else has just had a birthday?' I say.

'YES!' he cries, tearing off the wrapping paper in a matter of seconds, to reveal a large set of Lego bricks.

I had been determined that whatever I bought him, it would encourage creative play and not be an electronic device with a screen. I've seen enough of what those wretched things can do.

'You know how to use them?' I say.

'Oh, auntie Maddie,' he says, his voice laden with disdain, 'of *course* I do. My friend Justin has Lego bricks … they're good fun.'

'Well,' interjects Emily, 'what do you say to auntie Maddie.'

'Thank you,' he chirps.

'You're welcome,' I reply. 'Now … what are you going to build?'

His little forehead crinkles for a few seconds as he considers the question before his face lights up. 'I'm going to build a spaceship.'

'Fabulous!' I say.

He opens the box and tips the entire contents on the floor.

'That should keep him busy for a while,' says Liam.

'Sit down … I'll make some coffee.' I say, heading off towards the kitchen.

When I return with coffee and biscuits, and a cup of tea for me, Liam is sitting on the floor, helping Jack build his spaceship.

'OK,' he says, '… now just do that bit the same on the other side of the spaceship.'

Jack nods, evidently ready to take over. Liam gets up and takes a seat next to Emily on the sofa. I take the armchair opposite.

And then we chat – about Jack's party, the school he will soon be going to, Liam's job search, and a host of other things. The time flies by.

***

An hour or so later, Jack presents his finished spaceship. He doesn't want to break it down yet, so Liam carefully transports it to his car in one piece and settles it on the back seat alongside where Jack is sitting in his child seat.

As I wave them off, watching the car disappear around the corner, I reflect on the scenario I have just witnessed. Emily, Liam, and Jack seem to make a lovely little family ... a *normal* family. They have a delightful little boy, and Liam seems, as far as I can tell, completely sober.

All in all, it's as much as – maybe more than – I could reasonably have hoped for.

Chapter 37

'The storm'

It's Saturday evening; Amelia is in bed, while Grace is out with her boyfriend; I'm watching TV on my own. It's a very wet evening; I can hear the rain battering against the window, even over the soundtrack of the TV. But then another sound intrudes: it's the doorbell.

When I open the door, I am confronted by the sight of a wet and bedraggled Liam, a large suitcase on the ground alongside him.

'What the ...?'

'Hello, Mum ... can I come in?'

I stand aside to let him in. 'What's happened ... what are you doing here?'

He stumbles forward, dragging the suitcase awkwardly across the threshold; I can smell the alcohol on his breath from four feet away. When he replies, his speech is heavily slurred.

'Itsch Emily ... sheesh thrown me out.'

'Oh Christ, Liam ... what happened?'

'Sheesh thrown me out,' he repeats.

'But why ... what have you done?'

'Nothing ... just had few drinksch.' As if to illustrate the point, he sways precariously for a moment before taking a sideways step to steady himself.

I glance at the suitcase. 'You need to stay here tonight?'

He nods. 'Not just tonight. She shays sheesh never letting me back in her flat again. Shays she doesn't want Jack living with a drunk.' Suddenly he raises his voice to a frighteningly loud pitch. 'Sheesh a fucking BITCH! Thatsh what she is ... a fucking BITCH!'

'LIAM,' I yell back, 'calm down … you'll wake Amelia.'

But it's too late. Even as I try to cool him down, Amelia appears in the doorway, bleary-eyed, in her pyjamas. 'What's going on?' she mumbles.

'It's nothing,' I lie. 'It's just that Liam needs to stay here tonight.'

She casts him a suspicious look. 'Well, he's not having *my* room.'

Liam's face crinkles in a puzzled frown. 'Why would I want *your* room little shister?'

I haven't yet had a chance to explain to him that, after he moved out, Amelia vacated her tiny bedroom and took over his larger room. She's clearly in no mood to give it up now.

'Because you're drunk and you're a … PIG.'

'AMELIA!' I scold, 'don't you dare speak to your brother like that. Go back to bed … Liam can have your old room.'

She glares at me before shifting her gaze to her brother and sticking her tongue out. Before I can remonstrate further, she scampers up the stairs. Liam seems totally bemused by the whole situation.

There's clearly no point trying to have a coherent conversation with Liam until he's sobered up. 'Come on,' I say, 'let's get you dried off and into bed. We'll talk more in the morning.'

***

The following day, Amelia is due to go to the zoo with her friend, Hannah. Hannah's mum has offered to take them both; she's picking Amelia up at 9.00a.m. Grace is staying over at her boyfriend's place, so I should have some time alone with Liam to find out just what the hell is going on.

It's after 10.00a.m. before he surfaces. When he does, his demeanour has totally changed: gone is the belligerence, to be replaced by a morose introspection. We exchange few words until I sit across the table from him at breakfast.

'So what's the score, Liam? Is this just a row which will blow over, or has she really called time on the relationship?'

He says nothing, but just keeps his gaze cast downwards, absently stirring his coffee.

'Liam?' I press. 'Talk to me.'

Reluctantly, he raises his eyes to meet mine. 'She's serious, Mum … we're done.'

I sigh. 'And yet you seemed so happy with Emily … and you're so good with little Jack.'

'I was … I was happy, but every time I have a few drinks, Emily gets so angry with me.'

'So why don't you cut down a bit?'

He averted his eyes again. 'I've tried, but … well, I just can't seem to do it.'

'But when you were in hospital, you never touched a drop.'

He expelled a long, slow breath. 'Sorry Mum, but I'm afraid I did … my friends used to bring some in for me, disguised in soft drink bottles.'

I feel the anger flare within me like some uncontrollable volcanic eruption. What the hell were his so-called 'friends' thinking of? How was this helping him? Somehow, I manage to avoid boiling over.

'Oh, Liam … why didn't you tell me?'

He shrugs. 'Didn't want to upset you.'

'Christ Liam … I'm your *mum*. You know I would do anything to try to help you.'

'I know,' he says, his tone soft and doleful. 'But I thought I could keep it under control without help. Anyway, Emily used to get so upset with me she gave me an ultimatum: stop drinking or we would be finished.'

'But she's already thrown you out … without giving you a chance.'

'Not really … that was weeks ago. She's given me plenty of chances since then, but …'

I finish his sentence for him. '… but you didn't take them.'

He looks up at me with those doleful blue eyes. 'I did try … really.'

'Obviously not hard enough.'

'I'm sorry, Mum.'

'It's no good apologising to me … it's your own life you're ruining.'

His voice catches in his throat; a tear begins to well from the corner of his eye. 'I know … what can I do?'

'Look,' I say, placing my hands on his shoulders, 'she's a lovely girl, she loves you, and so does little Jack.'

He raises his gaze to meet mine, nodding slowly.

'So get yourself together, quit the booze, show her you've changed. Maybe … just maybe … she'll take you back.'

'You think so?' he murmurs, his tone laden with doubt.

'I don't know … but isn't it worth trying?'

He nods, stifling a sob. 'I'll do it … thanks for listening, Mum.' With that, he hauls himself to his feet and heads off towards his room – or more accurately, his little sister's old room.

Will he do it? Will he sort out his life? Is he even capable of doing so?

I just don't know…

Chapter 38

Three months later

'A fresh start?'

It seems that the break-up with Emily may have been just the shock that Liam needed. He says he's drinking much less, and certainly it looks that way from his general demeanour. What's more he's managed to get a job, working in an out-of-town fast-food outlet. It's hardly the start of a career, but at least he's starting to take some responsibility for his life. There's no sign that Emily is likely to take him back, though, and as far as I know, he hasn't even seen her since they split. But his new job has allowed him to make new friends and given him some social events to attend. What's more, living and working away from the town centre has surely helped mitigate the temptation of the many bars he used to frequent. He's working long hours and is clearly tired in the evenings, so he usually tends to retreat to his room and go to bed quite early.

All in all, I think he's headed in the right direction.

***

It's only a few weeks until Christmas, and the inevitable round of works Christmas parties has begun; Liam tells me he's meeting the rest of his workmates in town for a meal and 'a few drinks'. It's good to see him socialising more, but those last three words fill me with trepidation.

'Well, have a good time,' I say, trying not to let my voice betray my apprehension, 'but don't drink too much, will you?'

'Oh Muuum … don't fuss. You know I don't drink so much these days.'

'I know, but … well, just saying …'

He smiles. 'Don't worry … I'll be fine.'

'What sort of time will you be home?' I say, realising I'm really starting to sound like an over -protective mother hen now.

He shakes his head slowly, shooting me an indulgent look. 'Probably late … I think we're going round to Matt's place afterwards for coffee and a bit of music. Don't wait up.'

I have no idea who 'Matt' is, or where he lives, but I realise I have to let it go now. 'OK … well, see you in the morning then.'

He gives me a peck on the cheek, grabs his jacket from the coat stand by the door and, moments later, he is gone.

***

By the time I've got Amelia settled down for the night, it's around 10.00p.m. Grace is in her room, watching TV or glued to her phone. I'm feeling pretty tired, and there's clearly no point in waiting up for Liam … heaven knows what time he'll get in. I decide to go to bed and read for a while.

What is it about trying to read in bed? I've only covered a few pages when I realise that I'm dozing. I shake my head and retrace my steps to the last bit I remember reading. Before I know it, my eyes are flickering, and I've lost track again. Once again, I determinedly shake myself back to full wakefulness and press on.

It seems as though no time at all has passed when I sense the book slipping from my grasp and wake abruptly.

It's time to admit defeat.

I close the book and place it on the bedside table, checking the clock which is there: the glowing digits show 11.13p.m. I imagine it will be some time yet before Liam gets home, but I'm shattered; I switch off the bedside lamp, ease myself into the pillow, and pull the duvet up around my neck. Some minutes pass and then …

What the fuck? Moments ago, I couldn't keep my eyes open. Now, when I settle down to sleep, I'm wide awake. I check the clock again: 11.26p.m. *This is bloody ridiculous!* I try, once more, to will myself to sleep. It doesn't work.

144

And so, for the next several hours, I lie there, exhausted but wide awake, now getting anxious about how I'll get through the coming day without at least a few hours of decent sleep.

Finally, it happens: I hear the front door slam, followed by muffled voices. One is Liam's, but is that a female voice too? I'm past caring; I'm just happy he's home.

***

I don't remember another single thing until I'm awakened by the soft glow of the morning light seeping through the curtains. My throat is parched, and I need a pee. I haul myself to a sitting position, rubbing my eyes before taking a few sips of water and reluctantly swinging my legs over the side of the bed and rising to my feet. After a trip to the bathroom to relieve myself and splash my face with water, I decide to go downstairs and make myself a cup of tea. On the way, I steal a peek through the open door of Liam's bedroom; he's not there, and the bed looks unslept in. I feel a flutter of anxiety in the pit of my stomach. What about the lounge? The door is slightly ajar; I push it fully open. What confronts me elicits a strange mixture of relief and surprise.

Liam is lying on the sofa, his arm draped around a girl whose denim-clad leg hangs over the edge of the narrow space, her foot reaching the floor. They are both fast asleep.

I don't recognise the girl, but then I can't really see her face properly. She's slim – she'd have to be to fit on the sofa with Liam – long, dark hair, dressed in skinny jeans and a stretchy pink top, clothes which show off her enviable figure. I don't know what they have been up to, but at least they're both fully clothed and, thankfully, Amelia won't have found them – she's still asleep in her room. I tiptoe out of the room, closing the door quietly and move through to the kitchen to make my tea.

I decide to take my tea back up to the bedroom rather than risk a potentially awkward encounter with the two of them when they eventually wake up. As I settle back into bed and take a sip of my tea, I wonder just who the mystery guest is. A new girlfriend? Maybe just a workmate who was too tired or too nervous about making her way home in the small hours of the morning? I can't imagine Liam would have been in any fit state to drive her home. Well, I guess Liam will tell me in his own time. Right now, I'm just hoping they'll wake up and vacate the sofa before Amelia finds them and starts asking a whole heap of awkward questions.

They do; around forty minutes later, I can hear sounds of movement downstairs accompanied by the sound of quiet voices. Then, just a few minutes later, I hear the front door close, much more gently this time, followed by silence. I imagine Liam is going to drop her home.

I wonder whether this might be the start of a new chapter in Liam's life.

Chapter 39

'Sienna'

It turns out that the mystery girl on the sofa was much more than just a co-worker. Her name is Sienna, and Liam had already been seeing her for several weeks before the night of the Christmas party.

It wasn't long before Liam introduced her to me properly; I took to her immediately. A lovely girl with an agreeable, laid-back manner, softly spoken yet confident. In spite of the age difference, we soon became great friends.

Sienna was good for Liam. As their relationship developed, she prized him away from his computers and towards other, healthier pursuits. Bowling, eating out, and long walks with her beloved Spaniel, Jasper. They seemed so happy together.

And yet, there were times – usually towards the end of a day or evening that they had spent together – when the atmosphere between them was not quite right. I couldn't put my finger on what was wrong, but there was definitely something awry. I had to know what was going on, but whenever I tentatively approached the subject with Liam, he quickly clammed up. Maybe, though, Sienna might talk to me …

***

It's Friday. Liam's at work, but Sienna and I have both booked a day off to go shopping together. Liam absolutely detests shopping, so he has no problem at all leaving us girls to it.

It's 1.30p.m. We've been shopping all morning and are now laden with numerous carrier bags. Sienna has bought two pairs of ultra-skinny jeans, some cowboy-style boots, and a lovely, fitted jacket. My haul includes a cashmere sweater, some slingback shoes and a couple of skirts for the coming summer.

'Shall we head back to the car now?' I say. 'My feet are killing me.'

'Mine too,' laughs Sienna. 'In any case, I don't think we can carry any more.'

'Want to stop off for a spot of lunch first?' I suggest.

'Oh, good idea … I'm starving.' Not for the first time, I wonder at this girl's voracious appetite and how on earth she maintains her super-slim figure. *Oh well … she's young, I suppose.*

'OK, how about Lorenzo's? It's on the way to the car park.'

'Sounds good.'

An hour later, we have finished our lunch and rested our tortured feet. We're chatting over tea and coffee now.

'Er, Sienna,' I venture, 'I've been wanting to ask you something.'

'Oh? What's that?' she says, inclining her head, and drawing her eyebrows together enquiringly.

'It's about you and Liam … you're so good together, and yet …' I pause as I try to find the right words.

She rescues me. 'Oh,' she says, her expression serious now, 'you've noticed, then.'

I don't know how to respond. 'It's just that …' I struggle to frame the question.

She raises her hand to save me further discomfort. 'I knew you'd realise something was wrong, sooner or later.' She lowers her gaze, breaking eye contact.

'Can you tell me about it?' I venture.

Taking a deep breath, she re-engages my gaze. 'It's his drinking.'

My heart skips a beat. *Oh no … not again!*

'But I thought … I thought he'd cut right back on the drink.'

'Uh, uh …' she mutters, shaking her head, 'he hides it well, but he's drinking more than ever. He's usually already had a few drinks before he shows up for work in the mornings, and sometimes he even brings a bottle into work When we take Jasper for a walk, he often brings a bottle in his rucksack. In all honesty, I don't think he often goes more than a couple of hours without a drink.' She gives a despairing shake of her head, casting her gaze downward again.

Stunned, I slump back in my chair, literally lost for words. Sienna reaches over and places her hand on mine. 'Don't get me wrong, Madeleine. I love him ... I really do, and we have such fun together when he's sober. But these days, he rarely *is* sober; when he's drunk, he's a different person: surly, self-centred, even aggressive.' She stifles a sob. 'The truth is, I just don't know what to do.'

This is my worst nightmare come true. He finally gets a steady job and a relationship with just the loveliest girl he could hope to meet, and he's in danger of throwing it all away. This has to stop before he ruins his life completely.

'Try not to worry, Sienna. He loves you ... I know he does. Liam himself is the only one who can turn this around, but I believe he cares for you enough to do it.'

'You think so?' she whispers, her eyes brimming with tears.

'I do,' I say, giving her hand a squeeze. 'I'll have a serious talk with him tomorrow. Maybe we can help him to help himself ... together ... you and I.'

I hope I'm right ...

Chapter 40

'Realisation'

It's Saturday morning. Liam's not working today; it's time …

Breakfast on a Saturday is one of the few occasions when Liam, Grace, Amelia, and I can all sit together at the same time. This morning, as soon we're finished, Amelia scampers off to her room. Grace starts to clear up the breakfast things and Liam pulls back his chair as he makes to leave.

I place a gentle restraining hand on his arm. 'Can you hang on a bit?' I say. 'I want to talk to you.'

The expression on his face as he turns towards me telegraphs clearly that he knows it's something serious.

Grace instantly picks up on the mood – she's a very perceptive girl. 'Er, shall I …?' she inclines her head towards the plates she is holding.

'It's OK … you can leave those. I'll finish off.'

She doesn't need any further explanation. She lays the plates down on the table and heads up the stairs to her room.

'What's up?' enquires Liam, his face a mask of apprehension.

'I had a chat with Sienna yesterday.'

'So? You went shopping together, didn't you?'

'You want to know what we talked about?'

'Girls' stuff, I suppose,' he says, squirming uncomfortably in his chair.

No point in dancing around the subject, so I dive straight in. 'She told me about your drinking.'

His face fell. 'Oh … well, I suppose it is still a bit too much.'

I feel a surge of anger at his complacent attitude. 'A bit too much?' I say, hearing the tone and volume of my own voice starting to escalate. 'You're drinking before work; you're even drinking *at* work. Before you know it, you'll lose your job *again.*' I can tell by the startled look which sweeps across his eyes that I've struck a nerve. 'What? What is it?'

He looks away. 'I already have.'

'What? What do you mean?'

'They fired me yesterday.'

My anger starts to dissipate, to be replaced by a weary resignation. 'Oh, Liam ... was it for drinking?'

He nods, miserably.

I can't bring myself to yell at him; he looks so utterly dejected already. My tone softens as I change tack. 'Does Sienna know?'

'Not yet,' he murmurs.

'You know you're going to lose her, too, if you don't change your ways, don't you?'

That does it: he erupts into a flood of tears. All my anger has gone; I am just consumed with love and pity for my son.

'It's OK,' I say, knowing that it absolutely isn't.

As the tears start to subside, he finally opens up. 'I've tried, Mum ... I really have. But each time I stop drinking for more than half a day or so I start to feel ... sort of ill.'

'Ill ... how do you mean?'

'My hands start to shake ... I can't pick up a cup of coffee without spilling it. Sometimes I get these ... sort of ... oh, I don't know ... cramps ... my arms and legs seize up or go all jerky. It scares the shit out of Sienna. Honestly, it's horrible, Mum.' His lip begins to tremble.

A dead weight descends in my stomach, my heart flutters uncontrollably and the breath is sucked from my lungs. Tremors, seizures: these are classic alcohol withdrawal symptoms. There can be no denying it any longer: *my son is an alcoholic.*

I rise from my chair, leaning over to envelop him in a hug. 'You need help, Liam ... professional help.'

'I know,' he whispers, descending into a fit of sobbing, his shoulders heaving with each ragged breath. 'Can you help me? I don't want to lose her.'

'Of course I'll help you, Liam ... and Sienna will too. Together we can do this.'

I am cursing myself for being in denial for so long, but finally, this feels like a turning point: I've accepted that my son is an alcoholic, and he's accepted that he needs professional help. And importantly, Sienna seems willing to stick with him while he tries to quit his destructive addiction. *I hope we are all strong enough to stay the course.*

Chapter 41

'The battle begins'

With very little idea of how to go about tackling Liam's addiction, we decide to start with the GP. For our first visit, Liam and I go together. The doctor is very sympathetic and understanding but makes it clear that he can't be the one to support Liam all the way through the difficult journey that lies ahead, and neither is such help available elsewhere within the NHS. We need a private addiction specialist. When, however, the doctor warns us of the likely costs involved, my heart sinks like a stone.

'Doctor Parsons, we just don't have that sort of money. I'm on a nurse's salary and Liam doesn't have a job at all.'

'Don't worry,' he says, his tone reassuring, 'there's an alternative. Have you heard of "CLASP"?'

Liam and I glance at each other blankly and shake our heads.

'It stands for "Charitable Local Addiction Support Programme". As the name suggests, it's a local charity that supports people in the grip of addiction … usually alcohol or drugs. It's free of charge, funded by donations and benefitting from the kindness of some doctors, nurses, and addiction specialists who give up some of their time for free. They're fantastic people, and as long as you're really ready to do what it takes to quit, Liam, they can help you.'

My spirits are immediately lifted: at last, a lifeline.

'That sounds perfect, Doctor. Don't you think so, Liam?'

He looks a little doubtful but nevertheless nods in agreement.

'So shall I refer you for an initial meeting?' says the doctor.

'Yes,' I reply, eagerly, 'we'll work with whatever date they can fit us in.'

The doctor draws his eyebrows together in a half-frown. 'I'm afraid it won't be "us", Miss Fisher. They like to have their first meeting with the patient on his or her own.'

'But why?' I ask, genuinely puzzled.

'I believe it's so that they can gauge the addict's understanding of the severity of their condition and their commitment to doing what it takes to quit.'

'But,' I protest, 'wouldn't it be better if—'

Liam cuts me off, placing his hand on my arm. 'It's OK, Mum … I get it … and I'm up for it.' He turns to the doctor. 'Yes … please refer me … I'm fine with coming on my own.'

And so … Liam has taken his first tentative step towards fixing his life.

***

It's 5.30pm on a Tuesday and I'm home from work as early as I can manage. Liam was scheduled for his first meeting with CLASP today, and I'm desperate to learn how it went.

When I enter the lounge, I find him sitting on the sofa studying some sort of brochure.

'Well,' I say, 'how did the meeting go?'

'It was good … they asked me loads of questions, but we've got a definite plan now.'

My heart soars at his positive response. 'That's fantastic … I want to hear all about it, but first I need a cup of tea. You want one?'

'You sit down and put your feet up … I'll make it,' he replies.

Was that Liam – my son – actually offering to make me a cup of tea? Crikey, whatever they've said to him has certainly had some sort of positive effect.

Minutes later he brings two cups of tea, and we settle down to talk.

'OK,' he begins, 'the first thing is that they want to know just how much I'm drinking. I've given them a bit of an idea, but they say that's not good enough; apparently people like – he hesitates – well, most people, actually … underestimate when asked to guess. So they want me to keep a drink diary for two weeks. Every time I have a drink I have to write it down.'

'Seems like a good idea,' I say.

'It is … because, as they explained, if you try to cut down too quickly, that's what causes withdrawal symptoms like the seizures I was getting when I tried to quit before.'

'So why do they need to know what you're currently drinking?'

'Well, apparently that will decide how quickly I should cut down. I have to do it gradually and keep going with the diary so they can keep track of my progress and advise when to move to the next stage each time.'

'Makes sense,' I agree, 'but …'

'But what?'

'It's just that … oh, nothing.'

'Are you worried that I won't be honest with what I write down?'

I give a wry smile. 'I'm sorry, Liam. I didn't mean to …'

'Don't worry, Mum. It's a reasonable thing to question. They've already drummed it into me that if I don't do it properly then my chances of quitting will be much lower. I'll only be hurting myself.'

I place my hand on his. 'They're right … only *you* can make this work.'

'I know … and I'm determined that I will.'

With the elephant in the room dealt with, the mood lightens.

'So essentially, the plan is to keep accurate records of your consumption and cut it down gradually. Anything else?'

'Yes, I have to attend a group session once a week with others who are in a similar situation, and we each have to share details of what progress we're making and what setbacks we've faced. They say knowing what issues others are dealing with helps you to stick to the plan.'

'Sort of "strength in numbers" I suppose.'

'I guess so,' he muses.

I take a sip of my tea and grimace – it's gone cold while I've been listening to Liam. 'So when do you start?'

'Right now … today. Look,' he says, holding out a printed sheet of paper, 'I've already started the diary with the couple of drinks I had before going to the meeting today.'

I take the sheet and scan it:

9.30 a. m. – Vodka 100ml
10.00 a.m. – Vodka 100ml

I smile. 'Good start. So … anything else to tell me?'

He tips his head to one side, stroking his chin. 'Don't think so right now. I expect there'll be plenty more as time goes on.'

You can bet on that, I think. I'm no expert on alcoholism, but I know enough to know it isn't going to be easy.

Right now, though, I'm just pleased we've made a start.

Chapter 42

'The first hurdle'

The results of Liam's initial assessment, based on his diary entries, are not good. His average consumption is around thirty-five units per day, occasionally exceeding forty units. Considering the maximum recommended safe level is only fourteen units *per week,* this is alarming news. Liam has been warned that it would be extremely dangerous to come down from such a high level of consumption too quickly. The reduction programme must be slow and steady.

How on earth had I not realised he was drinking so much?

In spite of the magnitude of the task ahead, the people at CLASP are not fazed by it, and neither, to my surprise and relief, is Liam. They have given him a chart, enabling him to easily check the unit value of every drink he takes, and set him weekly targets. So far, he is diligently keeping his records, checking them against his targets, and attending his weekly meetings.

Sienna is beside him, supporting him every step of the way. I can see how much that means to him and how much happier she seems, too.

Things are going well, until …

***

It's now exactly three months since Liam started on his recovery programme, and his progress is pretty much on target. His relationship with Sienna is blossoming again, and tonight they have gone out for a nice, romantic meal together. They aren't expecting to be late, so I decide to stay up until they get back.

I'm curled up on the sofa, reading a book recommended to me by a friend; it's a good story but, even so, my eyelids are beginning to droop. I glance at the clock: 11.55p.m. *They should be back by now.* I'm debating whether to give Liam a call, but he'd probably chide me for being a fusspot. Maybe I should just go to bed and stop worrying.

My deliberations are interrupted by the sound of a key in the lock of the front door. *They're back.*

As soon as they enter the room it's immediately obvious from the looks on their faces that something is not right.

'What's the matter?' I enquire, closing my book and laying it on the coffee table.

'I crashed the car,' replies Liam.

'What? Are you both OK?' I spring to my feet scanning for any signs of injury; I can't see any.

Sienna intervenes. 'We're both OK, but Liam's ...'

She seems tongue-tied now. My first reaction of relief quickly gives way to suspicion.

'Liam, what happened? What have you done?'

'Look, it's no big deal, Mum.'

Uh, oh ... when Liam says, 'it's no big deal', it's usually a very big deal.

'What happened?' I repeat.

'Well, the road was wet, and I guess I must have taken a corner a bit too fast.'

'So what happened?' I say for the third time.

'I skidded into a parked car.'

'Oh Liam, how bad's the damage to your car ... and the other one?'

'Well, the engine stopped when I hit the other car, and then it wouldn't start.'

'So how did you get home?'

He casts his gaze downward, avoiding the question.

'Liam?' I press, the tone of my voice hardening.

Sienna rescues him. 'The police gave us a lift back.'

'The police?' I cry. 'How did they get involved?'

'Well,' said Sienna, 'what happened was—'

I cut her off, my anger bubbling over now. 'Liam can answer me, thank you.' She shrinks back, her eyes widening at my unintendedly sharp tone.

Liam raises his head slowly. 'The impact with the other car set its alarm off and the owner came out of his house. He wouldn't let us leave until he'd called the police.'

For the first time, I detect a slight slur in his voice. 'Have you been drinking?' I snap.

'We only intended to have a glass of wine each with our meal, but …'

Now I'm furious with having to drag every bit of information out of him.

'But what?'

'Well, as we finished our meal and were about to go, we bumped into some of the others from work, so we stayed to have a drink with them.' He hung his head again. 'I guess we had a few too many.'

'Oh, Liam … you absolute idiot.'

Sienna tries to defend him. 'It really wasn't all his fault, Miss Fisher …' – *so now I'm 'Miss Fisher', rather than 'Madeleine', am I?* – 'they were egging him on.'

I turn on her. 'So couldn't he have just said "no"? Couldn't you both have just left before getting bloody plastered?'

'I did try to tell him … honestly … but …' She begins to cry.

I realise my anger was misdirected. 'I'm sorry … it's not your fault, Sienna. He's a grown man, who should be able to make his own decisions. You've done everything you can to help him.'

I turn back to Liam.

'So what's the situation now, Liam? What happens next?'

'OK,' he sighs, 'well. I've exchanged insurance details with the other guy … his car looks as though it's still driveable until it can be repaired properly. Mine's had to be trailered to a garage; the insurance will be in touch with them soon, but I think it'll be off the road for a while.'

'And what about the police?' I prompt. 'Did they breathalyse you?'

He nods, miserably. 'Turns out I was quite a bit over the limit. I'm going to have to go to court at some point, when they'll decide on my penalty.'

Could it be any worse? Of course it could: at least neither he nor Sienna have been physically injured.

All my anger drains away as I survey my son's haggard and dejected face. I have been standing throughout out whole exchange, but now I sink back, mentally exhausted, into the sofa.

'Why don't you go to bed and sleep it off?' I say. 'I'll take Sienna home.'

He slinks off to his room without uttering another word.

The short journey to Sienna's house passes in near-silence. It's clear that she's devastated by tonight's incident, but I sense that it's something more than that.

Could this be the beginning of the end for Liam and Sienna?

Chapter 43

'The wilderness months'

The events of the night when Liam crashed his car mark the beginning of a new and dangerous chapter in his life.

His encounter with the Magistrates' Court results in his being disqualified from driving for a period of twelve months. In any case, it turns out that the damage to his car is more extensive than originally thought: the cost to repair it would be more than the car was worth. The insurance company declare it a write-off.

With no job and no transport, he no longer has any structure in his life. He begins playing on his PlayStation again, and this soon becomes a regular activity. Before long, he is playing well into the night, often shouting out loud as he engages in his online battles, his headphones rendering him oblivious to the disturbance he is causing. It turns out that many of the unseen players he interacts with are based in the USA, and over time, more and more of the nighttime hours are consumed. So then he ends up sleeping for much of the day.

It soon becomes clear that the pattern his life is descending into is resulting in his alcohol reduction programme faltering badly. He keeps the alcohol diary going for a while, but I know he's drinking far more than he records; I'm quite sure that he's drinking heavily at night without recording any of it. He starts missing his weekly meetings with CLASP, using his lack of transport as an excuse. I have offered to pay for taxis or even drive him myself, but more often than not, he will find a reason not to go. Even on the increasingly infrequent occasions when he does attend the meetings, he is often so drunk that he either makes a fool of himself or can barely remember what happened at the meeting. In the end, he is taken off the programme. As they reasonably point out, CLASP is a charity, and they need to concentrate their limited resources on people who are determined and serious about beating their addictions.

As far as I know, Liam has no income other than his benefits, so I try to limit his alcohol consumption to only what I will pay for, but somehow, he's always able to lay his hands on more. It turns out that friends often come over and drop off additional booze when I'm out. And God knows what other measures he is resorting to in order to fuel his habit.

Throughout this period, he is seeing less and less of Sienna, and my fears for the future of their relationship intensify.

Chapter 44

'The first fit'

It's 6a.m. and I feel like shit. I barely had more than an hour or two's sleep last night, partly due to the noise from Liam's usual nocturnal activities, but in truth, more because I'm so worried about him. He's settled into such a negative rut, and I just don't know where we go next to help him break out of it. As I lie in the darkness, the whole situation swirls around in my mind like some impenetrable sandstorm, formless and all-enveloping.

I can't dwell on things any longer right now though: I have to get Amelia to school and myself to work. To be honest, although I'm exhausted, it's almost a relief to have the distraction of the daily routine prise me away from my dark, brooding thoughts.

With a weary sigh, I prop myself up on one elbow and lever myself out of bed. I head for the bathroom and take a pee, before washing my hands and splashing my face with water. I turn on the light above the mirror, blinking as I register the haggard, sleep-deprived face staring back at me. *This is going to take a serious amount of makeup to sort out.* I turn off the light and return to the more agreeable dim glow of the early morning natural light seeping through the curtains in my bedroom.

As is usual, on a school/work day, I'm going to go down to the kitchen and make myself a cup of tea before getting ready for the day ahead. I go out to the hallway, where the light is even dimmer, feeling along the wall with my hand to help guide me to the top of the stairs. As my bleary eyes acclimatise to the semi-darkness, I notice a strange, mottled pattern of shadows on the wall. It must be cast by the wisteria which climbs the wall and is now starting to encroach on the window. *Must get that trimmed soon*, I remind myself.

Curious as to why I hadn't noticed the shadows before, I reach out and run my fingers over them. Instead of the smooth, painted surface of the wall I feel a strange irregularly textured surface. Then I notice that the mottled shadows are not showing on the back of my hand. *What the ...?* My heart skips a beat as I try to process what this means. I reach for the light switch; it takes a moment for me to register what I am seeing, but when it does, a cold wave of dread envelops me.

Blood ... lots of it. Dried blood in random smears and smudges all over the wall, interspersed with bloody handprints. Instantly, my senses are assailed by a vivid flashback to my blue-handled vegetable knife, buried to the hilt in my son's leg, blood coursing down his ankle and soaking into the white, deep-pile rug. *God, no ... please, not again!*

Rushing along to Liam's room I knock on the door. 'Liam, what's happened ... are you OK?'

No answer, so I push the door open.

He's lying, motionless, in bed, dried blood over his head and face, with smears all over the pillow, too. A hollow emptiness consumes me.

'Liam,' I cry, rushing to his side and shaking his shoulder. 'Oh my God ... are you OK?'

His eyelids flutter and he stirs, emitting an undecipherable sound which could have been a word or just a groan. At least he's alive; the wave of relief which courses through me is overwhelming.

'Thank God,' I breathe, as he gradually comes to, eventually propping himself up on his elbow. His expression, as he registers the blood on the pillow is one of puzzlement. He raises his hand and tentatively probes his head, wincing as he finds the source of the blood.

'Christ Liam,' I breathe, 'you scared the shit out of me. What the hell happened?'

He looks genuinely confused. 'I ... I don't know. The last thing I remember was coming home last night, coming up the stairs and ... well, then you waking me up. I ... I don't know.'

'OK ... OK,' I soothe, 'we'll try and piece it together later. Let me take a look at that wound.'

It doesn't take long to find the gash in his head. It's not as bad as I expected, considering the amount of blood which has been spread around, but it does need stitches.

'Come on, let's get you down to A&E and get that wound closed up properly.'

'No … Mum, you know how I hate hospitals. Can't you sort it out? It's not that bad. You're a nurse … you do stitches.'

'Liam, I don't have any anaesthetic or any of the right equipment here … you need to go to hospital.'

'Come on Mum, you'll think of something … you always do.'

There it is … a glimmer of how my son used to be, the boy who could always wrap me around his little finger.

As I hesitate, he clearly knows I am about to fold. To clinch it, he gives me that smile which could always melt my heart.

'Weeell … there is an old-fashioned technique which can be used in emergencies …'

The method I use to treat Liam's wound is an old technique, intended for use in emergencies when no proper medical facilities are available. I first clean the wound itself and the surrounding area with antiseptic fluid and then tie strands of hair either side of the wound together, pulling them tight until the wound is closed. It isn't the neatest of closures, but it does the job.

When I clean up the hallway and landing, I discover the exact point which had inflicted the gash on Liam's head: there is a square wooden cap on the newel post at the top of the stairs; its corners are quite sharp. As I go to wipe some blood off from it, I encounter something which makes the bile rise in my throat: a small fragment of flesh with several hairs still rooted in it. In a flash, the whole scenario becomes as clear as a movie playing in my head: Liam had suffered a fit and fallen heavily, gashing his head on what, until now, had seemed an innocent household fitment.

My blood runs cold. What if it happens again … perhaps when he is crossing the road, or standing near a long drop of some sort? How much worse could the consequences be? A cold shiver runs through my body.

***

It's exactly a week now, since the incident, and thankfully there has been no sign of infection. It's time to see how well my makeshift treatment has worked.

First, I clean as much as possible of the dried blood which has reformed around the wound. Next, I snip away the knotted strands of hair – it would be impossible to untie them. Now I can see the wound more clearly – it has healed nicely, albeit it's a little lumpy. I shave off the last remaining remnants of hair around the wound and clean the area again. After a final few dabs of antiseptic fluid, I declare the procedure a success, handing Liam a mirror so that he can check for himself.

'Thanks, Mum,' he says. 'Really good job.'

'Well, I'm afraid you've got a bit of a bald patch now, but I think you can probably disguise it until it grows out with a bit of artful rearrangement of your hair.'

'No problem,' he says, and then, unexpectedly turns and gives me a hug.

This boy is just full of surprises: both good and bad.

Chapter 45

'The really bad one'

The fit responsible for his head injury is a wake-up call for Liam. He resolves to try again to cut down gradually on his drinking, but without the professional support of 'CLASP' he will have to manage the rate of reduction himself.

It doesn't work …

Every time he cuts down on his alcohol consumption, the fits recur. So, then he eases up a bit to try to control them and usually ends up drinking just as much as before. And so, what was supposed to be a carefully managed reduction programme becomes a desperate yo-yo between drinking too little and too much, with no sign that any sustained progress is being made.

Against the odds, Sienna is still standing by him, but she is clearly worried sick about him and, not for the first time, I fear that their relationship may founder on the rocks of his addiction.

And then comes the really bad one …

***

It's Saturday morning; I'm awake, but still in bed. As usual, Liam had been gaming and loudly talking through the small hours, but the house is quiet now; I assume he's finally gone to sleep. Amelia is staying over at her father's house and Grace always sleeps in late on a Saturday, so I have the house to myself for a while. I decide to go downstairs, make myself a cup of tea, and watch a bit of news on the TV before the others surface.

I fill the kettle and flip on the switch before starting to unload the dishwasher. Once that task is completed, I make my tea, switch on the small TV in the kitchen, and sit down at the kitchen table.

The news is just too depressing: war in the Middle East, a hurricane battering the Florida Keys, and raging inflation at home. After fifteen minutes, I switch off the TV and pour myself another cup of tea, sitting down again to think about my plans for the day ahead.

With the noise from the TV now absent, I become aware of some sounds from upstairs: first a couple or random bangs and thuds, but quickly morphing into a much more violent, intermittent series of loud bangs. It sounds as though the noise is coming from the bathroom, directly above me. A cold dread washes over me.

I jump to my feet and rush up the stairs, hammering on the bathroom door. 'Liam, is that you? What's going on?'

No answer, but the commotion inside the room continues.

I wrench at the door handle; the door isn't locked.

The scene which confronts me, as I burst into the room, thrusts a cold dagger of fear right through me. The shower is on, the bath full to the brim, with Liam thrashing about in it, seized by the mother of all fits, his head banging repeatedly against the side of the bath.

I rush over, straddle the bath and try to hold his head clear of the water; it's almost impossible with his body contorted by the seizure and thrashing uncontrollably. As I desperately struggle to keep his head above water, his mouth is emitting a bubbling mass of white froth and a terrifying, undecipherable sound.

'Grace!' I scream. 'Help me!'

No response.

'GRACE!' I scream again, at the top of my voice. 'Help me … NOW … IN THE BATHROOM.'

The next few seconds feel like an eternity as I struggle with this thrashing, wild thing in the water. I yell again, but finally she's here. Her eyes widen and her hand flies to her mouth as she takes in the scene.

'Help me,' I gasp. 'Turn off the shower … pull out the plug.'

She doesn't move; she seems frozen by shock.

'DO IT!' I yell.

My urgent scream shakes her from the trance which has gripped her. She rushes over and shuts off the shower.

'Now the plug!' I gasp.

She tries to do it, but Liam's wildly hammering feet pummel her probing fingers.

'I can't,' she wails, tears springing from her eyes and streaming down her cheeks.

'Yes, you can ... look, I'll try to lift him.' Finding strength I never knew I had, I heave him backwards, trying to pull his feet clear of the plug and chain. 'NOW ... do it NOW!'

She reaches in again and finally succeeds in pulling the plug clear.

'It's out,' she gasps, stepping back, panting heavily.

As the water level begins to drop, I ease him back down, cradling his head and trying to soothe him calmly with my voice.

'OK, well done,' I say, turning towards Grace and trying to sound a lot calmer than I actually feel. 'Now get the phone and call 999.'

She leaves the room and reappears a few moments later with the handset. 'What should I say? ... I don't know what to say.' She begins to cry again.

'Just call 999 and hold the phone to my ear.'

She does so.

By the time the ambulance crew arrives, the water has completely drained from the bath, and the seizure has eased considerably. My heartbeat has returned to something vaguely approaching normal. Liam is now responding coherently to my voice but, bizarrely, he has no idea what just happened. He seems more concerned at being naked in front of his mother, his sister, and strangers than anything else.

The paramedics get him out of the bath and into his dressing gown. They monitor all his vital signs and stay for a while until he is stable and safe to leave at home. They advise that he should consume a modest amount of alcohol to minimise the chance of another seizure. For Liam that equates to about half a bottle of vodka.

I stay home with him for the rest of the day. He is completely exhausted but, thankfully, no further dramas ensue.

That was a Saturday I won't forget in a hurry.

***

It's Sunday morning. Liam has gone to see Sienna and tell her what happened; Grace is having lunch with some friends. I'm on my own, lost in my thoughts.

Where do we go from here?

If these fits continue – and why wouldn't they? – I have to consider whether it is safe for Liam to be on his own at any time. There can be no showering or bathing unless I'm home … no going away overnight … definitely no holidays. The outlook seems bleak, to say the least. How do we break out of this vicious cycle?

My mind goes back to a discussion I'd had – without Liam's knowledge – with the people at CLASP after Liam had been removed from their self-managed addiction reduction programme.

'I'm sorry, Miss Fisher,' the clinician had said, 'but it's clear that, in Liam's case, a self-managed alcohol reduction programme just isn't going to work. The best approach, now, would be a supervised, full detox and rehabilitation programme.'

The trouble is, as I'd already been warned by the GP previously, such professional help is not available on the NHS and the cost of accessing it privately was – and still is – way beyond my means.

However many times I play it over in my head, the situation seems impossible.

Chapter 46

'A lifeline'

Over the ensuing weeks, Liam's seizures become more frequent, and his level of alcohol consumption becomes increasingly erratic as he struggles to deal with them. It's clear he needs professional help if he is to beat this crushing affliction.

With seemingly no other options available, I decide to go back to CLASP to see if they can help any further. As it turns out, I am able to speak to the same woman who had previously delivered the bad, but hardly unexpected news that Liam was to be taken off the self-managed alcohol reduction programme due to his lack of commitment to it. Her name is Felicity Hatfield.

'As I previously explained, Miss Fisher, I think what Liam needs now is a full detox followed by a rehabilitation programme.'

'But,' I respond, 'you know I don't have the means to pay for these services privately. Isn't there anything further that CLASP can do to help?'

She plants her elbows on the table, steepling her fingers and resting her chin on her thumbs, expelling a long, slow stream of breath. The silence which follows seems to last an age before she finally responds.

'Look,' she says, 'as you know, we have limited resources and can only afford to deploy them where there is a reasonable chance of success. On the basis of our previous experience, I'm not sure whether Liam would be able to—'

'Please …' I plead, 'I know he fouled up on the previous programme, but he's learned his lesson. These latest fits have been a real wake-up call. Give him another chance … he won't let you down this time.'

Her deep blue eyes bore into me for several seconds before her expression softens.

'Look, there is a possibility that an assisted home detox programme could provide the basis for a fresh start, but—'

'Oh yes,' I interject '…please … he's ready to try anything.'

She sighs. 'Look, it's not my decision alone. If we are to support Liam through a home detox programme, he will have to convince our assessment panel that he has the resolve to see it through.'

My heart surges … *another chance*.

'Thank you … thank you … you won't regret it, I promise.'

Her expression is hard to interpret. Sympathy? Compassion? Scepticism? It doesn't really matter, because she's going to give Liam another chance.

'Could he come here to go before the panel this Friday at 10a.m.?'

'Yes … yes, he'll be there. Thank you again.'

***

When the day of the panel interview arrives, I am, this time, allowed to accompany Liam. I make sure he has just a modest drink before the meeting: enough to ward off the possibility of a seizure in the middle of his interview, but not enough to cause him to turn up blind drunk. The panel consists of three people: Felicity Hatfield, who we had already met; and two strangers: Gareth Hooks and Linda Baker. I have the impression that Felicity is already on our side, so it's the other two who need convincing.

When he's sober, Liam can charm almost anyone, so after initial introductions, I stay very much in the background and let him do most of the talking. It works; it takes him just twenty minutes to convince the panel that he is a worthy case for further support.

In that moment, I am proud of my son.

As the home detox programme is explained to us, it becomes clear that it will impose a considerable burden on both of us. He will need to stop the alcohol dead on day one and replace it with a gradually reducing dose of a drug called chlordiazepoxide to control the seizures. For the first two weeks, I will need to be with him virtually 24/7. This is to to help control the administration of the medication and deal with any seizures or other emergencies which might arise as a result of the sudden withdrawal from a very high level of regular alcohol consumption. This will mean my taking unpaid time off work. How the hell can I afford to lose two weeks' pay? Will my employer even allow it, anyway? And how on earth will I manage the school run, shopping etc?

With no other options on the table, though, I bury those thoughts, cross my fingers, and assure them that we will be able to manage it.

And we have to ... somehow. I want my son back, not this zombie who is gradually descending into an ever-darkening spiral of self-destruction.

Chapter 47

'Home detox'

The day has arrived; the doorbell rings and I rush to the door.

'Miss Fisher? Good morning. I'm Katie Purcell … the nurse from CLASP.'

Katie Purcell is not quite what I was expecting. Aged probably only in her mid-to-late twenties; long, dark hair, tied back in a ponytail; restrained but immaculate makeup; and *very* attractive. Suddenly, I feel old and frumpy.

She smiles broadly, revealing a perfectly even set of dazzling white teeth, and extends her hand. It takes me a second or so to gather my wits and shake her hand.

'Come in … please go through,' I say, standing aside and ushering her through to the living room where Liam is waiting, expectantly. I follow her into the room.

'Ah, you must be Liam,' she says. 'I'm Katie.'

Liam's eyes widen and he jumps to his feet, displaying an alacrity which I haven't seen for some time. The nurse offers her hand, which Liam eagerly grasps. 'P-pleased to meet you.'

I smile, inwardly. This young woman has clearly made a pretty powerful initial impression on Liam. Perhaps he'll be so eager to please her that it will give him some additional incentive to stick with the challenging programme which lies ahead.

'Please, take a seat,' I say, indicating the chair facing Liam across the coffee table.

Her uniform is modestly cut but, inevitably, her dress rides up a little as she sits down. I can hardly miss Liam's self-conscious

174

glance at her slim, shapely legs. He swiftly swivels his gaze back to her face, clearly hoping she hasn't noticed.

'Can I get you a coffee ... or tea?' I venture.

'Thank you. Coffee, black, no sugar.'

I make my way through to the kitchen, leaving Liam to get acquainted with Katie Purcell.

When I return, five minutes later, the two of them are chatting as if already good friends. Liam has turned on that cheeky charm which always used to characterise the old Liam; Katie is smiling and nodding, animatedly.

I set down the drinks and biscuits and sit down beside Liam.

Once everyone is settled and has taken a sip of their drinks, I decide it's time to get down to business.

'So ... would you like to run through the programme with us, and explain what we have to do?'

'Of course,' says Katie, opening her bag and withdrawing a cardboard folder and some medication boxes.

Liam looks a little disappointed that we are moving on from the socialising but buckles down to pay attention.

Katie spends the next forty minutes or so explaining everything in detail. The first thing she emphasises is that every drop of alcohol in the house needs to be removed or locked away; the dosage of medication is calculated on the assumption of absolutely no alcohol in his system. She then introduces a drug chart which shows the gradually reducing dosage of chlordiazepoxide which is recommended. If the fits persist, however, we are to consult the nurse to discuss a variation to the schedule. The drug chart has space to record such variations and what dose has actually been administered. If all goes well, it should be possible to reduce the medication to zero in around one week – but I have to stay with Liam for at least another week in case the schedule has to be extended, or he suffers lingering withdrawal symptoms.

Sounds straightforward enough, doesn't it? I'm a nurse; I'm used to drug charts, comforting patients, and dealing with unexpected complications. But this is different; this is my son.

***

The first job, the following morning, is to get rid of all the alcohol in the house. Liam and I agree to do it together; we start in his room.

I haven't been into Liam's room for several days; the sight which greets my eyes is shocking, though I suppose I shouldn't be surprised. It's like a skittle alley: bottles all over the floor, some standing, some tipped on their side, most empty but some still part full. He turns his head and looks at me guiltily but says nothing.

I force a smile. 'First steps,' I say. 'I'll get something to put them in.'

I leave him gazing at the chaotic scene, returning a few minutes later with several stacking plastic storage crates and a large bucket.

'Right,' I say …' nudging his arm, 'come on … leftover liquids in the bucket and empties in the crates.'

Half an hour later, it's done: the bucket is half full, and three plastic crates are almost completely full of empty bottles. He's been oddly quiet as we've undertaken this task; I can't quite interpret his mood.

'OK, we're done,' I say. 'Come on, pick up the bucket … that's going down the loo.'

Finally, he speaks. 'Not quite done, Mum.'

He goes over to his chest of drawers and opens the bottom drawer, delving inside and turning back to face me, holding two brand-new, unopened bottles of vodka.

I smile; he's really serious about quitting this time.

'You know what to do,' I say, inclining my head in the direction of the bucket on the floor.

He gives a reluctant half-smile, sets one of the bottles down on the chest of drawers and cracking open the seal of the screw cap of the other. Stepping forward, he upends the bottle into the plastic bucket and places the empty bottle into one of the crates with the others. He does the same with the second bottle.

'Is that everything?' I ask.

He nods. 'Everything.'

'Then let's get rid of all this stuff.'

Ten minutes later it's done: the contents of the bucket have been flushed away and my recycling wheelie bin on the drive is half full of empty bottles.

By now Liam is showing signs of alcohol withdrawal: a noticeable tremor, a slight stammer, and a flushed complexion. I'm desperate to avoid his having another damaging seizure, so I quickly measure out his first dose of chlordiazepoxide, watching as he takes it, and recording it in his new drugs diary.

'Thanks, Mum,' he whispers. 'Think I'll lie down for a bit now.'

The fit never happens, and within fifteen minutes, he's asleep on the couch. I breathe a sigh of relief. Perhaps this really is the start of a new chapter in his life.

***

It's a full week now since every drop of alcohol in the house was removed. Liam has just taken what is scheduled to be his last dose of chlordiazepoxide. The gradually reducing doses of the drug must have done their job because – thank God - he hasn't had a single fit all week. His mood is strange though.

It's been a very long time since I've seen Liam completely sober, and he clearly doesn't quite know what to do with himself in this unfamiliar state. He seems tired, grumpy, and bored.

The people at CLASP had recommended someone should be with him 24/7 for at least another week, but I just can't afford to take any more time of work. Sienna, bless her, has said she'll come round as often as she is able, fitting around her work commitments as best she can. For the most part, though, Liam is going to have to fly solo. We need to talk ...

'Are you sure you'll be OK? You know I'd stay home longer if I could.'

He sounds rather disinterested. 'I'll be fine ... I've gone a week without a drink now, and there's none in the house anyway.'

'I didn't mean that ... I trust you to keep off the booze, but if you feel unwell, or there's any sign of the seizures recurring—'

'I'll be fine,' he repeats.

'Look, you can call me, or Katie, the nurse, anytime you need to ... and Sienna's not far away either.'

'OK, OK ... don't fuss.' Now there's a definite note of irritation in his voice.

I back off, trying to lighten the mood. 'I'm your mum ... I'm allowed to fuss.'

At last ... a smile ... a trace of the old Liam. 'I guess ...' He leans forward and gives me a hug.

There's so much more we need to talk about. Assuming he stays sober, what will he do with his life? Go back to college? Get a proper job? Settle down with Sienna? Who knows?

But this isn't the time; there's a very long way to go before he'll be ready to confront these issues seriously. I have to content myself with the knowledge that, for now at least, he's sober and healthy.

Baby steps …

Chapter 48

'Family'

Four weeks have now passed since Liam had his last alcoholic drink. Physically, he's doing well: he hasn't suffered a single seizure, and the only legacy of his former condition is a lingering tremor in his hands. His mental state is another story, though.

He seems unable to fill the void left by his drinking with other, more positive activities. At the weekends, when I am home, he has taken to lying in bed throughout the morning, finally dragging himself up well after midday. When he finally does emerge, his demeanour is sullen; he clearly feels low. I don't imagine things are any more positive on days when I'm at work and unable to observe what goes on.

Today, though, we're having a proper Sunday roast lunch with the whole family. Grace, Megan, and Amelia are all going to be here, and the occasion seems to have lifted Liam's mood. He was out of bed by 10a.m. and is now actually helping with preparations for lunch by peeling the potatoes. The vegetable knife with the aqua blue handle has long since been banished from the kitchen but, even so, I feel a cold shiver run down my spine as I see him wielding the new one with the black handle. But he's in good spirits today and doesn't seem to have noticed my momentary discomfort.

'It'll be really nice to see the girls,' he says. 'It's been quite a while since we've all been together … and I was probably acting like a complete dickhead when we were,' he adds, with a rueful smile.

'Well yes, you were, actually … but that was the old you. You're on the right track now.' *I hope to Christ I'm right.*

We are interrupted by the chiming of the doorbell.

'I'll get it,' pipes up Amelia, who is in the living room.

Moments later, both Grace and Megan come through the door into the kitchen.

'Wow!' exclaims Megan, smiling broadly as she eyes Liam up and down. 'Don't *you* look different!'

'Been dry for a whole month now,' replies Liam.

'Oh, well done bro.'

Liam puts down the knife and wipes his hands on a tea-towel before going over to the girls and enveloping them both in a group hug. How it warms my heart to see my family all together like this.

'Can we help with lunch?' says Megan, when they disengage from their long hug.

'It's mostly done now,' I reply. 'Why don't you guys go and sit down in the living room and catch up? I'll get everything into the oven and join you in a bit.'

'Come on,' says Megan, 'we have loads to talk about.'

They head for the door; seconds later, I am alone in the kitchen.

***

It's 2.30p.m. and we have just finished our main course. It's been a wonderful time … Liam, Megan, and Grace chatting away like a proper family should. Even Amelia refrained from making any cheeky remarks about her brother when his residual tremor sent the peas dancing from his fork.

'Anyone for seconds?' I ask.

'Uh uh …' said Megan, 'got to leave a bit of room for dessert.'

'Grace?'

She shakes her head, smoothing her hands down over her slim waist. 'Got to think about my figure.'

'Amelia?'

'I'm stuffed,' she says.

Liam doesn't hesitate; he's already reaching for the serving platter with the roast beef. 'All the more for me then!' he laughs.

As he recharges his plate with a second helping almost as generous as his first, I ponder on this unexpected side effect of his new-found sobriety.

Ever since he quit the booze, he has acquired a ravenous appetite. It's how he used to be, only more so.

We all chat away for ten minutes or so while Liam finishes his second helping, and then, as I move to start clearing the table, Liam unexpectedly stands up.

'Sit down Mum ... you've done enough ... I'll clear.'

'I'll get the dessert,' says Megan, pulling her chair back.

I can hardly believe it ... I have my family back!

***

It's just after 6.30p.m. Megan has gone home, Grace is out with friends, and Amelia is in her room, doing whatever eight-year-old girls do on social media. Liam has fallen asleep on the sofa in the living room. At least this time he's just sleeping off the effects of a very substantial lunch, not slumped comatose in an alcoholic stupor. I slip quietly into my armchair and put the TV on very low, taking care not to wake him up.

I'm not really paying any attention to the TV; it's just a subdued backdrop to the thoughts roaming through my mind. As I glance at Liam, whose breathing, slow and steady, can be heard over the sound of the TV, I reflect on how today's family lunch totally turned around his previously morose demeanour. All it took was something to occupy his otherwise structureless, pointless daily routine and awareness that there are still people who care about him.

I can't let him slip back now. His physical condition is vastly improved since the detox and, as far as I can tell, he hasn't touched a drop of alcohol since then. It's time to encourage him to get some purpose back into his life. It's time to talk to him about the future: going back to college or getting a job.

I'll need to choose my moment, though, if I'm not to turn him away, and I'll need to get Sienna to talk to him too. She has, thankfully, stuck with him through thick and thin. He listens to her.

For once, I think I can see the road ahead: not a smooth and easy road, but at least one that doesn't terminate in a dead end or a U-turn.

Chapter 49

'Relapse'

It's around three weeks since that agreeable family lunch. Liam's still dry, as far as I know, but his mood is unpredictable. I've been gently hinting that he should start giving some thought to what he's going to do for the future now that he seems to be finally defeating the destructive addiction which has been ruling his life. To my pleasure and relief, he says we can have a chat about it this evening when Amelia's gone to bed. Grace is out for the evening.

Liam's been in his room for most of the afternoon – nothing unusual about that, but it's after 7.00p.m. now, and dinner's ready. It's just the three of us for dinner: Amelia, Liam, and me. I've prepared Spaghetti Bolognese, which everyone likes.

'Liam,' I call out, 'dinner's ready.'

No reply, so I try again.

Still no reply.

'Amelia, can you go and fetch Liam, while I serve dinner, please?'

She scampers off, returning a couple of minutes later with an unexpected message. 'He says he's not hungry … he doesn't want any dinner.'

This is very unusual: since he's been sober, his appetite has generally been voracious.

'What? Is he feeling alright?'

She shrugs. 'Says he's not hungry.'

'Here,' I reply, setting her plate down on the table, 'You can start while I go and check on him.'

I knock on his door and push it open. Liam's lying on his bed, propped up on one elbow engrossed in his phone.

'Liam … are you OK? Amelia says you don't want dinner.'

'Er … yeah … not really hungry.'

'Are you sure? It's Spag Bol … your favourite.'

'Sorry Mum, I had a takeaway pizza this afternoon while you were at work … it was huge. Think I overdid it a bit.'

He breaks eye contact; something isn't quite right. I'm not going to push it though. 'Well, if you're sure. Look I'll save some for you in case you're hungry later … it won't take long to heat it up.'

'OK … thanks.'

He makes to turn his attention back to his phone, but I have something else on my mind. 'What about that chat we were going to have this evening?'

'Oh … er, yes still cool for that. I'll come down a bit later when Amelia's gone to bed.'

'OK … talk later then.'

***

It's 10.30p.m. Amelia's gone to bed; there's no sign of Liam.

I go and tap lightly on his door; no answer, so I push it open. Liam is fast asleep on the bed, still fully clothed. I guess our chat is going to have to wait a little longer.

I decide to watch a little TV before going to bed myself. It's no good though; I can't focus. Something is wrong, and I don't know what it is.

On a sudden impulse, I decide to check on something. I head to the kitchen and check the waste bin: no pizza carton. What about the recycling bin? Empty apart from a plastic milk bottle and a couple of paper leaflets. Finally, I grab my phone and switch on the torch, heading outside to check the big recycling wheelie bin: no sign of any pizza carton.

My son is lying to me. Why?

***

I should have realised what Liam's unexpected loss of appetite signified.

He covers it up well at first, but over the coming weeks the signs of a relapse become unmistakeable. Liam begins skipping meals more often and begins to spend even more time ensconced in his room. Soon, the noisy, nocturnal, online video battles start up again, waking both Amelia and me in the middle of the night.

My despair at his rapid decline is compounded when, one day, he emerges from his room so drunk that he can't even make his way down the stairs on his own two feet and resorts to shuffling down on his butt like a small child just learning to walk.

At my wit's end, and desperate for help, I decide to go back to CLASP once again – more in hope than expectation, as they had previously made it clear that they had reached the limit of what they were prepared to do unless Liam showed a clear dedication to getting himself well.

***

It is with a sense of *déjà vu* that I find myself sitting opposite Felicity Hatfield at CLASP once again. I have spent the last twenty minutes or so relating Liam's progress – and subsequent relapse – over the past few months. She has listened carefully, stopping me occasionally to ask questions, but now I'm spent.

'I know you said you had done everything you could to help Liam, but I'm desperate. You know I don't have the means to pay for private professional treatment … isn't there *anything* you can do to help?'

She exhales a slow, steady breath. 'In very difficult cases like your son …' *My son is not a 'case'*, I think, *he's a person* … *a young man who needs help.* I bite my lip. '… the only proven treatment is a supervised residential detox and rehab programme.'

'So what exactly does that—?'

She raises her hand, palm-outward, curtailing my question. 'The thing is, this treatment is very expensive. We don't normally have the resources to fund such a programme.'

'Then why are you telling me about it?' I ask, feeling a little annoyed.

'We have recently become a beneficiary of additional funds provided on a regular basis by a wealthy philanthropist. He has expressed a wish that our organisation should extend its reach to help in particularly difficult cases of drug and alcohol addiction.'

My heart surges. 'That's fantastic,' I enthuse. 'What do we have to do?'

'Please,' she says, her tone clearly intended to moderate my expectations, 'you have to understand that even with these additional funds we do not have enough resources to help every deserving case.'

'Of course ... but if you could help, what would we need to do?'

'Liam would need to go before a funding panel, just as he did previously. There are no guarantees.'

'I understand ... thank you, thank you so much. I don't know what I would have done if ...' My words dry up.

She smiles. 'Go home and talk it over with Liam. Call me back tomorrow and, if you're sure he's up for it, I'll arrange a date for a panel interview.'

I stand up and shake her hand, feeling as though a massive weight has been lifted. There's a long way to go from here, but it's a glimmer of light in a fog of darkness and despair.

Chapter 50

'A final chance'

When Liam and I sit down to discuss the unexpected possibility of a properly supported residential detox/rehab programme, during one of his increasingly rare sober interludes, he accepts that this is a final chance which must be grasped with both hands.

When the day of the panel interview arrives, Felicity Hatfield is, once again, on the panel and speaks convincingly in Liam's favour. The evolution of her attitude towards him over time has been remarkable; from reluctant sceptic, she has transitioned to persuasive advocate. Maybe she sees him as a challenge; maybe she just likes him – he's easy to like when he's sober – but whatever the reason, I owe her a debt of gratitude.

For his part, Liam behaves perfectly at the interview. He has consumed enough alcohol this morning to ward off the possibility of a seizure, but not so much as to turn him into a drunken fool. The combination of Felicity's backing and Liam's projection of a sincere commitment to the programme does the trick. He is accepted onto the programme, and we are invited to go and see the facility where he will be staying while undergoing his treatment.

***

Lockwood House looks more like a country house hotel than a medical detox/rehab facility. I bring the car to a halt outside the tall, wrought-iron, twin gates. I can see through them, at the end of a long, curving, gravel driveway, a large redbrick building, swathed in ivy. Liam, who is, uncharacteristically, reasonably sober today, turns towards me and gives a nervous smile.

'Looks pretty swish, eh?' I venture.

He nods but doesn't comment further.

I wind down the window and stretch to the limit of my reach to push a button on the intercom alongside the gate.

An electronically distorted voice answers, 'Can I help you?'

'Madeleine Fisher ... with my son, Liam.'

'Come on in, Miss Fisher ... we're expecting you.'

A click and a buzz ... and then the gates swing slowly open.

As we approach the house, the gravel crunches noisily beneath our tyres. When we get closer, it becomes clear that the glory days of this extensive house are long in the past. It's still impressive but clearly needs considerable time and money spent on it if it is ever to recover some of its former grandeur. The ivy has been allowed to run riot, playing havoc with the ancient brickwork; there are numerous broken and missing tiles on the roof, and the paint on the wooden sash windows is peeling away, revealing rotten timber beneath. The metal guttering is rusting badly, with some sections missing completely. Let's hope it's in better shape inside.

It is. We park the car and ring the doorbell; a smiling, middle-aged woman with a shock of curly, grey hair ushers us inside. Immediately, the impression is of a warm and welcoming environment. The entrance hall is in good decorative order, with peach-coloured walls and subdued lighting. The several chairs and sofas lining the walls are of simple, utilitarian design but look to have been recently re-upholstered in a nicely co-ordinated pale turquoise fabric.

Martha – for that is her name – is to be our guide. Over the next forty-five minutes she shows us around and answers our questions.

There are six bedrooms for patients, each housing two people sharing. The rooms are simply furnished but clean and comfortable, with all the essentials provided. The external doors are normally locked; only the three fire escape doors can be opened from inside without a key, and opening one of those sets off an alarm, so patients do not have the option to leave the house alone and undetected. They are, however, escorted outside regularly, accompanied by a member of staff, for walks and exercise. As Martha explains, although this may seem draconian, experience has shown that it is in the best interests of the patients, ensuring that there is no backsliding in the alcohol withdrawal regime.

There is a selection of non-alcoholic drinks and snacks available for purchase within the house, and patients are allowed to have a modest amount of pocket money provided by relatives or carers for this purpose. Sugary sweets are restricted as, apparently, the sugar increases the urge for alcohol. Meals and other essentials are all provided as part of the programme. Patients are, however, expected to take control of their own laundry and room cleaning, as well as helping with chores around the rest of the house and the cooking of main meals. There is also a full programme of activities each day. The idea is to keep patients fully occupied to help facilitate their recovery. There is, however, a certain amount of downtime, during which patients can watch TV, read, or play cards in the communal lounge. Lights out at 10.30p.m. and breakfast at 8.00a.m. ensure that everyone gets the right amount of sleep, essential for a successful recovery.

Liam has stayed largely silent throughout the tour of the house but for my part, I'm delighted that this programme will provide the structure in his life which has been so sorely missing. The only downside is that the earliest date which can be offered to Liam is still almost four months away, in the new year.

***

I never knew that four months could seem so long. Rather than try to ease down his alcohol consumption in preparation for the full detox he slides right back to his worst excesses. He is usually up most of the night, engaging in his noisy, online cyber-battles, and asleep for most of the daylight hours. When he is awake during the daytime, he is often abusive to both Amelia and me. When he's like this, there is no reasoning with him.

Christmas is a strange mixture of highs and lows. The whole family is together, and on occasion, the company of all three of his sisters seems to calm him; he becomes more sociable, and we even play some family board games. But then he will suddenly go right off the rails, shouting and arguing before stomping off to his room in a huff.

On New Year's Eve, he goes out for the evening – with whom I don't know – and rolls in, literally falling-over drunk, at 2a.m. He spends most of New Year's Day sleeping it off.

By now, I am counting down the hours to the day – just one week away – when his residential programme is due to start.

As a means of filling some of that time, and hopefully, getting Liam to start thinking positively to the weeks which lie ahead, I organise a shopping trip with him – to get him kitted out with enough toiletries and new clothes to see him through the programme. It turns into a disaster! He is drunk, noisy, and argumentative; other shoppers look on in disbelief, giving a wide birth to this crazy young man and the hapless, harassed woman trying to control him.

Still, there are only three days to go now – three days, hopefully, to a new start.

Chapter 51

'The day before'

We are due to set off tomorrow. Liam is preparing and packing – as well as he is able. He's drunk and confused, fumbling and forgetting what he's already packed. It's heartbreaking to see him like this. Unusually, he readily accepts my help, rather than shooing me away as I might have expected.

By 8p.m. we're done. 'Maybe you should turn in early,' I suggest. 'We have an early start and a three-hour drive tomorrow.'

He looks at me with puppy dog eyes, but his attention seems to be elsewhere. 'Yeah ... I just need to let my friends know what's happening ... why I won't be around for the next couple of months.'

'Oh, Liam, you've left it a bit late, haven't you? You need to get a decent sleep tonight.'

'It's OK Mum ... I'm not going to call everyone individually ... I'll just do a Facebook post.'

'OK ... well don't stay up too late. I'll wake you up early tomorrow.'

I leave him alone in his bedroom closing the door softly behind me. I suppose I should go to bed early too, but I know I won't sleep until I know he's settled down for the night. I decide to go downstairs and make myself a cup of tea.

I curl up on the sofa and start idly flipping through the pages of a magazine, although little or none of their contents really register with my distracted brain. After just a few minutes, I become aware of a muffled sound from above: it's Liam's voice. I can't make out any of his words, but it sounds like some sort of halting monologue. And then it dawns on me: he's recording a message to put on

Facebook. I lay down the magazine and try to focus on his words, but they merge to form a distant undecipherable stream of sound. As I let the sound wash over me, my eyelids begin to droop …

***

I snap awake. The sound has stopped. How long have I been asleep? I glance at the clock on the wall: 9.05p.m. It's only around forty minutes since I sat down. I listen again; all is silent. I decide to go and check on Liam.

I knock softly on his door; no response, so I gently push the door open. He is fast asleep, the covers pulled up around his neck. His laptop – lid closed down – is on his bedside table. I close the door quietly and head back downstairs. What to do now?

I know what I should do – go to bed myself – but my curiosity gets the better of me. I power up my laptop and navigate to Liam's Facebook page. Sure enough, there is a fresh entry, posted just twenty-five minutes ago. As I click to start the video, Liam's face appears – he looks melancholy, depleted, drained. My heart yearns to reach out, help him, hold him, but the image is just pixels on a screen.

He starts to speak, his voice slow and halting – and still slightly slurred.

'Hi everyone, I've got something important to tell you all. I know I've been a bit of a shit recently … well for quite a while I guess. I've let some of you down – some of my best friends – and you never deserved that. I'm sorry …'

He pauses for a few seconds, seemingly trying to compose himself. My heart is hammering.

'I want to explain … or at least try to. Some of you know already, of course, but everyone who's close to me deserves to know the truth. I have a drink problem.'

He pauses again to let those words sink in.

'You know I've always liked a drink … most of us do … but for me, it's gone way past that. I'm physically dependent on alcohol now … if I go for too long without any, I get violent seizures … fits. If I don't do something to break this addiction, it could eventually kill me.'

Those last words hit me in the solar plexus as surely as a physical hammer blow. I hear myself expel an audible gasp. And yet there is hope in those words: an acknowledgement of the imperative to beat the addiction and acceptance, in the use of the word 'I' that *he* must be the one to do it. I'm simultaneously terrified and proud.

His voice continues.

'Well, I *am* doing something about it. Tomorrow, I'm starting on a detox and rehabilitation programme … to get all the alcohol out of my system and then train my body to be able to do without it. I'll be away from home for … well, I don't know exactly … probably at least a couple of months or so. I won't be on social media or even have my mobile phone …'

He forces a small smile. '… guess I'll be sort of cut off from the outside world.

'So … you won't see or hear anything from me for a while now, but when you finally do, hopefully, I'll be a better person.'

He falls silent for several long seconds, as though considering whether to say anything more. Eventually, he does …

'I want to say my biggest sorry to my family … especially my mum. I know I've let you guys down more than anyone. So, if you see this, Mum – and I guess you will sometime – I'm going to make it up to you … and my sisters … I promise.

'I guess that's it … not much more to say.'

He gives a little wave. 'Bye then everyone … until I'm better.'

The tears have been welling up progressively as I've listened to his message but now, I can hold them back no longer. I descend into unconstrained sobbing, my breath coming in ragged, uncontrollable gasps.

We *have* to make it work this time.

Chapter 52

'Lockwood House'

Lockwood House is situated near to the seaside town of Freyton-on-Sea, normally at least a three-hour drive from home, and they want Liam there by 9.00a.m. We decide to set off at 5.00a.m. to beat the traffic and make sure we're there in good time.

When I go to wake Liam at 4.15a.m. I'm dismayed to find he's already pissed out of his head.

What the fuck? ... Has he been up all night, drinking?

I decide not to make a fuss; this is going to be a difficult and emotional enough day without provoking a row. Instead, I gently encourage him to get up and get dressed as soon as possible.

Breakfast is just a bowl of cereal, and then we're on our way.

Within minutes of setting off, Liam is fast asleep, his head lolling sideways against the window, so I just drive on in silence. We're making good time on the lightly trafficked roads at this early hour, and it soon becomes clear that we're going to arrive way too early. I'm not too sure whether we'll be able to check in if we're really early, so I decide to look for a roadside café to kill a little time and hopefully give Liam a chance to sober up a bit.

The best I can find is a rather down-at-heel transport café; it will have to do. When the car draws to a halt and I switch the engine off, Liam comes to, groggily.

'Uh ... what ... are we there?' he mumbles.

'Not yet ... we're a bit early. Want a coffee?'

'Uh, yeah ... I guess.'

As we walk up to the entrance, Liam is swaying unsteadily, occasionally grabbing my arm for support.

Just how much <u>did</u> he have to drink last night?

As we step inside, we attract curious glances from all directions. I suppose we must make an incongruous sight among the truckers mostly breakfasting alone. A forty-something, anxious-looking woman, and an obviously inebriated, much younger man. Maybe they think I've drugged and kidnapped him! However, they soon lose interest and return to their meals.

I order strong black coffee and a bacon sandwich for Liam, in the hope that the combination might help him sober up. I settle for a cup of tea, as usual.

Forty minutes later, we are on our way again; Liam seems barely any more sober.

***

We arrive at 8.45a.m. The unrelenting muggy gloom, which has persisted since early morning, shrouds the old house. We are greeted by Martha, the same woman we had met on our first visit, some months earlier. Liam still hasn't sobered up properly, and Martha can hardly have failed to notice this. However, she doesn't comment.

After a few pleasantries, she gets down to business. 'Liam, as you know, you'll be sharing a room, so the first thing today is for you to meet your roommate. If you'd like to take a seat, I'll go and get him.'

She disappears for a couple of minutes before returning with a tall, gangly young man, probably around the same age as Liam.

'This is Thomas … Thomas, Liam.'

'Hi,' says the young stranger extending his hand which Liam takes, rather disinterestedly.

Liam nods, 'Hi.'

That seems to be the extent of their initial conversation, so Martha encourages them. 'Liam … Thomas will show you to your room and help you settle in. Your mum can stay here and have a cup of tea or coffee while you unpack. I'm sure she needs a break before the long drive home.'

Liam looks rather bemused by it all, so his new roommate takes the initiative, picking up Liam's suitcase and gesturing for Liam to follow him. 'Come on … it's just down this corridor.'

Martha must have picked up on my anxious mood. 'Don't worry … he'll soon settle in. Thomas is a nice young man, and he's making good progress. He'll be a good influence on Liam.'

I smile, trying to look more positive than I feel.

'What can I get you … tea, coffee, a cold drink?'

'Thanks. Tea please … milk, no sugar.'

Once she has delivered my tea, and a plateful of biscuits, for which I have no appetite, Martha disappears to get on with whatever Martha does when not sitting at the reception desk. I am left alone with my thoughts.

After about fifteen minutes, Liam reappears. 'Hi Mum … I'm unpacked now.'

'Is everything OK? Do you need anything?'

'I'm OK.'

'How are you getting on with your roommate?'

'He seems OK.'

I guess 'OK' is about the most informative thing I'm going to get out of him just now.

'Well, I suppose I might as well be on my way then.'

He nods, looking at me with a forlorn expression; I feel the emotion welling up within me. I stand up and enfold him in a hug, which he weakly reciprocates.

After some seconds, we gently ease ourselves apart. 'Take care, Liam … and do everything they ask. We're lucky to have been given this chance. Whatever you do, don't waste it.'

'I won't, Mum.'

I ring the bell on the reception desk to summon Martha to let me out. Before stepping through the door, I turn to take one last look at my son. He looks pitiful, abandoned, lost.

I can't hold back the tears any longer. 'Bye,' is all I can manage before they start to flow.

***

I need to compose myself and get my head straight before setting off on the long drive home, so I decide to drive the short distance to the nearby town and have a walk around. It does little to lift my spirits. With many of the shops closed and boarded up, the entire town centre looks generally rather down-at-heel. This seaside town's best days are clearly behind it.

I make my way down to the beach, which is vast. I sit down on a seafront bench and gaze out to sea. As I sit there, the sky begins to change: it looks a little brighter as the murk begins to dissipate. My mood begins to lighten. I decide to linger a little longer.

Finally, the sun breaks through. The sea is calm today, but the low angle of the sun in the sky picks out myriad sparkling pinpoints of light on the dappled surface. Perhaps it's a metaphor for a light at the end of a very long tunnel.

Please God, Liam ... let this be the new start you need.

Chapter 53

'A setback'

Back home, everything feels so strange. When Grace and Amelia are at home, there is some semblance of normality – or what passes for normality in my decidedly abnormal life – but when they are out of the house, the silence and emptiness are crushing. My life was so busy when Liam was around – often, not in a good way, but it was what I did and how I lived. I didn't really know any different. Now, though, I feel lost and so sad.

Have I failed my son? I don't know what more I could have done, yet I am wracked with feelings of guilt. I long for him to be well, to be free of his addiction and to have a future, but for now, all I can do is wait. The rules of the rehab centre prohibit any direct contact with him for the whole of the first month, not even a phone call. It seems so harsh, when I desperately want to hear his voice, find out how he's coping, see how he's feeling. Right now, I can do none of these things; I just have to trust in the experience and judgement of the professionals.

The one concession I am allowed is to talk to the staff on the phone to enquire about his progress. Their initial feedback is encouraging; by the second day, he has settled well, made friends with his roommate and, so far, his body appears to be tolerating the detox.

Day three is a different matter though. My phone rings; when I go to answer it, I immediately recognise the area code as being the same as that of Lockwood House. I don't know anyone in that area outside of the detox/rehab centre itself. My blood runs cold; they wouldn't be phoning if all was well.

My worst fears are quickly realised. Liam's body has not been able to cope with the rate of detox; he has suffered a massive seizure and is in hospital, confused and slipping in and out of consciousness. My immediate reaction is to want to rush to his side, but the hospital assures me he is in the best place to receive the care he needs and there is nothing that I can do, particularly as I'm so far away. This happens sometimes, they tell me, and it just means that once his condition has been stabilised, the detox needs to be continued at a gentler pace.

It goes against all my instincts to stay away, but deep down, I know they're right. This is Liam's journey, and he must be given the time and space to see it through. Not only that, but I need to work, and who would look after Amelia if I were to rush over there? Reluctantly, I accept their advice.

When I hang up, the tears begin to flow.

***

It's two days since I learned of Liam's seizure. I've been calling the hospital regularly. They tell me that they have his physical reaction to the drug withdrawal under control but that his mental state is still erratic. They will keep him in long enough to complete the detox on the ward and only when they are satisfied that he is stable will they return him to Lockwood House.

It's barely an hour since my last update from the hospital when my phone rings; this time it's a mobile number – one that I don't recognise.

'Mum … it's me.'

'Liam? Is that you? Where are you?'

'In hospital … but I'm coming home.'

'You can't come home … you have to get better first. What phone are you using?'

'Ha! Borrowed it from Ryan … my mate in the next bed. The bastards won't let me have a phone here … and they've stolen my clothes … just got this poncy hospital gown … not even any pants or shoes.'

'Liam, you're not supposed to—'

'I need money for the train … can you send me some money?'

'Look, I can't do that … you don't even have a—'

'Doesn't matter, I'll just …'

His voice tails off, and then he starts rambling.

'They think they can just … but I know how to … I need that money, Mum. Oh shit! They're coming … get off me!'

I hear sounds of a scuffle, interspersed with an unfamiliar female voice.

After a few moments the new voice comes on the line. 'Hello … who am I speaking to?'

'I'm Liam's mother,' I yell. 'Who are you?'

'Amy Matthews – Staff Nurse.'

'What on earth is going on? Liam's talking about getting a train home.'

'It's OK … it's just that he's rather … oh, here's Doctor Singh … he'll explain.'

There's a brief, muffled conversation which I can't decipher and then a soft male voice with an Asian accent takes over. 'Hello … Doctor Singh here. I understand you are Liam's mother.'

'Yes … what's happening?'

'There's no need to worry. Liam is OK, but he's still a bit confused. This sort of thing isn't unusual while going through the detox process. We just need to slow down the process to a rate his body can tolerate. Please trust me on this.'

I'm not convinced, but what can I do?

'Should I come over?' I ask.

'That's not necessary or, to be honest, even desirable. This is a journey Liam needs to navigate on his own without reaching out to you when things get tough. He's in the best place here. We'll let you know if there is any cause for concern.'

Finally, I relent. 'Can I call every day to check on his progress?'

'Of course,' says the doctor, 'but it's best you don't talk to Liam directly at this stage.'

That's just so hard to take: to be told that if I see him or even talk to him, *I* become part of the problem. *Have I always been?* I do my best to banish that thought and just accept that I should do as the professionals advise.

***

Twelve days have passed, with no further drama. The hospital has kept me informed every step of the way, with Staff Nurse Amy having been especially helpful. The detox programme has been completed on the ward and Liam's mental state has settled back to some sort of normality. He is well enough to be returned to Lockwood House today. Would it have helped or hindered his progress had I rushed to his side? I guess I'll never know. The main thing is that he's on the mend now and able to commence his rehabilitation journey.

Chapter 54

One month later

'Rehab'

It seems to be going well. I haven't spoken to Liam once since that rambling call when he was in hospital, but the staff at Lockwood House have been wonderful, accepting my frequent calls with good grace and keeping me apprised of Liam's progress. Sienna, for her part, calls me regularly to check on how Liam is doing. He's so lucky to have such a wonderful girlfriend who is sticking with him through all these traumas.

The news is mostly good: the alcohol is completely out of his system and there have been no further seizures. His mental state is steadily improving, and he is embracing the rehab programme with something approaching enthusiasm.

He has been encouraged to write his life story, and with some assistance from the staff member assigned as his mentor, identify some of the triggers for his drinking. This will help him recognise the danger signs which could lead to a possible relapse in the future. His days are almost fully planned for him, full of meetings, group sessions, and chores. He has now been given various extra responsibilities, including cooking and house checks.

Finally, my son seems to be on the road to recovery.

One Saturday morning, the phone rings. For a few seconds, I don't recognise the calm, confident voice of the young man on the line … until he laughs that is. That laugh is unmistakeable.

'Liam? Is that really you?' I ask.

'Hi, Mum … yes, it's me.'

In just those five words, I can tell he's a changed person. Tears of joy spring from the corners of my eyes.

'Oh, Liam, so wonderful to hear your voice.'

'Yours too, Mum … it's been a while, hasn't it? Well, my first month is up now, and I'm allowed to talk to you now. I've only got ten minutes though, because everyone has to take turns on the phone.'

'OK,' I say, 'then let's not waste time. You have to tell me everything …'

That ten-minute call flies by, but it's enough for me to know my son has finally turned a corner. He now realises there can be life without booze; he's a changed person, both physically and mentally. He has forged friendships with others in the house; through a shared experience they have helped him, and now he's helping others too.

He still has a couple of months to go before his rehabilitation is complete, but right now – for this stage of the journey – I couldn't be happier.

***

Six weeks have now passed since that first phone call, and we have spoken regularly since then. Liam is now adept at the various jobs around the house and has even become a pretty competent cook – something which I would never in a million years have imagined! He has been appointed House Leader, responsible for helping the newbies settle in.

My heart feels full, relieved, and proud.

But now we need to start thinking about life beyond Lockwood House. It's only a few weeks until he is due to be discharged into a halfway house nearer to home. Regnum Court will be less regimented than Lockwood House, but still with absolutely no alcohol allowed on the premises. It is the final step in his rehabilitation programme before he faces the challenge of staying sober and maintaining a healthy lifestyle back in the outside world.

Meanwhile, I want to make his room back at home as welcoming as possible for when he can finally return home. It's in such an awful state: blood, urine, sweat, vomit, and booze have found their way almost everywhere over walls, furniture, and floor. I want to make sure there is no trace of what went before: nothing to remind him of his former life.

I set about taking the room back to a shell, removing furniture and carpet, and stripping off all the wallpaper, in readiness for redecorating and refurnishing his personal space.

Little do I know what lies just over the horizon, though …

Chapter 55

'Covid 19'

It starts with some news reports about a new, highly infectious disease which has broken out in China; hardly anything to occupy front and centre of my mind when I have things far closer to home to concern me. Even when the infection spreads to Europe, I still don't imagine it will radically impact upon my life.

But then come reports that hospitals in Italy are becoming literally overwhelmed; people are *dying* of this horrible disease. Before long, governments around the world are becoming so concerned that they begin imposing severe restrictions on international travel in an effort to limit the spread of the infection. Finally, the impact of Covid 19 – as the new disease had been named – becomes inescapable. On 23rd March 2020, the UK government imposes a complete lockdown, prohibiting people from even stepping out of their front doors except for essential purposes.

The image of the Prime Minister, on national TV, sternly admonishing, 'You *must* stay at home.' is still etched in my memory.

***

31st March: Liam was due for discharge today, but we've already been warned that it's not going to happen. Lockwood House has become *Lockdown* House – no-one being discharged, and no-one being admitted. Thankfully, there has been no outbreak of Covid 19 in the house, and they clearly intend to keep it that way.

Meanwhile, closer to home, the local centre which was to be Liam's stepping stone to life in the outside world is similarly paralysed … as are we. Our world has ground to a standstill, with no clue as to when Liam's journey can be resumed.

From an ever-increasing mood of optimism before this wretched disease struck, I am now plunged into the depths of despair.

***

Back home, our normal routine has been completely turned upside down by the Covid restrictions. Amelia's school is closed, with a combination of home schooling and online lessons being the only means of maintaining her education. But I can't be there with her; as infection rates rapidly escalate throughout the country, many private hospitals have been taken over by the NHS for adaptation as Covid treatment hubs. The hospital where I work is one of them, and all the nursing staff are to be given training on how to cope with the expected influx of patients, many of whom might be severely unwell. Any prospect of extended leave to look after Amelia is out of the question.

My saving grace, literally, is Grace. She's at university now, but the university has also been closed to students, with all lectures being delivered online. She has even been furloughed from her local part-time job so she's at home now, and able to look after Amelia, so we have been able to adapt, after a fashion, to this new, imposed routine. I just hope to Christ that I don't contract Covid 19 at work and bring it home to my family. There is never enough PPE – personal protective equipment – of the right type available when we need it. Fingers crossed!

Amelia seems to be adapting fairly well to remote learning but she's really missing her friends, whom she's not allowed to see in person.

Strangely, in spite of all the difficulties created by this enforced regime, there is, perversely, something positive coming out of it: we are pulling together and becoming closer as a family. Perhaps it's something to do with being united in the face of adversity, unfortunately, though, without Liam.

I've been so anxious during the last few weeks, worried that Liam's extended, enforced stay at Lockwood House might have set back his progress. The carefully planned programme of activities, talks, and meetings has been significantly disrupted during lockdown. All external speakers and services have been cancelled, and it seems that there are limits to what the staff can organise without such support. Consequently, Liam's continued confinement has become rather aimless and unfocused. I'm constantly on the phone to both Lockwood House and the local centre, Regnum Court, pushing, pushing, pushing for a date when Liam can finally make the move. So far, though, there is no sign that restrictions will be eased any time soon.

When will this nightmare end?

Chapter 56

'Regnum Court'

A month of constant pressure has borne fruit; they have finally relented. Although the national lockdown has not yet been lifted, the pressure to allow transfers to take place has now become irresistible. There are a growing number of patients at Regnum Court who have completed their programme and are waiting to be discharged to reclaim their places in society at large. Similarly, detox/rehab centres such as Lockwood House are overflowing with patients who, like Liam, are overdue for transfer to the next stage of their programmes. And, like a stack of dominoes poised to fall, there is a queue of sad cases desperately needing to begin their treatment. The pressure from carers and relatives like me must have finally become intolerable.

In the end, they have come up with a set of protocols to unclog the system without contravening government guidelines. Any patient who requires to enter either Lockwood House or Regnum Court will be required to test negative within forty-eight hours before the transfer. Any carer or relative accompanying them to either centre will also be required to show evidence of a negative test within forty-eight hours before attending and will not be allowed to physically enter the premises. Both Liam and I willingly accept the restrictions in order that he can move on with his programme.

***

The day has finally arrived; I can collect Liam and take him to his new temporary home to begin the next stage of his journey. This will be an important test for Liam, for as soon as restrictions are lifted, he will be trusted to leave the centre from time to time to visit the shops or meet friends while resisting the temptation to hit the booze. He will, however, need to sign in and out, and the staff will be watching out for any sign of a relapse. There will be strictly no alcohol allowed in the centre itself. It is, we are told, an important phase in his rehabilitation as he will, at last, be taking responsibility for his own wellbeing.

With all this in mind, I've been yearning for the day when Liam can make the move, yet now that day is here, I'm nervous as hell. The son I left was a dishevelled wreck, in need of constant and concentrated care and supervision. What version of my son is going to meet me today?

It's around three hours later that the large wrought-iron gates to Lockwood House swing slowly open in front of me. By now, my anxiety has intensified to fever pitch; my hands are shaking as I engage first gear and edge forward onto the gravel drive.

I know I will not be allowed on the premises; a quick handover at the door is all that can be permitted. I ring the bell and wait anxiously.

When the door swings open and Liam appears in the doorway, my fears evaporate in an instant. He is standing upright and tall, he is fuller in the face and has put on weight generally. His face breaks into the old, familiar smile that belonged to the son I used to have.

'Hello Mum … it's been a long time, hasn't it?'

I melt inside, unable to suppress the emotion welling up within me, as I enfold him in a massive hug. Not sure if hugging's allowed right now, but it's a moment when I *need* a hug – and so does he.

'Oh Liam,' I sob, when we finally ease apart, 'you look so *well*.'

'I am … this is the best I've been for … well, ages.'

Now I can see the tears forming in the corners of *his* eyes, too.

'We've so much to talk about,' I say.

'We have … but let's do it on the way home. They're probably desperate to shoo me out and shut the door.'

It seems a strange and unceremonious way to end such a significant phase of his life, but within minutes we are passing through those huge gates and on our way.

***

I have never known a three-hour car journey seem to pass so quickly. We have talked about everything: life in Lockwood House, what we expect during this next phase of his rehabilitation, and most of all, the *future*. Finally, my son is looking forward to life after alcohol.

I'm under no illusions, though. There have been so many false dawns that I can barely allow myself to believe we are finally on the road to a permanent recovery. I can't bear the thought of having my hopes dashed again. Right now, though, I have to banish such negative thoughts from my mind. Right now, I have my son back. Right now, he's sober. Right now, he's well.

I must have faith that he is on the threshold of a new and better life, a life where he can accomplish his goals, be a great son, brother, boyfriend and, who knows, perhaps in time, a great husband and father.

***

Regnum Court could hardly look more different from Lockwood House. A nondescript, blocky flat-roofed building, probably built sometime around the sixties. Apparently, it houses up to twenty guests, all of whom have completed their detox and rehab programmes and are ready for a less regimented environment as an interim step towards re-entering society.

As we draw to a halt, we exchange a sideways glance. For the first time since setting off, I spot the first signs of the mask slipping a little; the confident smile has been replaced by a nervous, almost pleading expression. It lasts but a second or so before the smile returns.

'Well, here goes then,' he says, unbuckling his seatbelt and pushing the door open.

His voice is firm, but I'm his mother: I know that underneath it all, he's a bundle of nerves. I resist the urge to let him know that I know, to smother him in hugs and tell him everything's going to be alright. Instead, I just step out of the car and help him retrieve his bags from the boot.

We step up to the front door and ring the bell on the intercom alongside, announcing ourselves to the disembodied male voice that answers.

'Please wait there,' says the voice. 'I'll let you in.'

But they don't let *me* in.

'I'm sorry, Miss Fisher,' says the young man who opens the door, but I'm afraid you can't come in ... Covid rules, you see.'

Liam looks at me helplessly.

'It's fine,' I say. knowing inside that it's anything but.

I give Liam a final hug and help him lift his bags across the threshold.

'I'll FaceTime you later,' I say.

He nods, forcing a smile, and moments later the door is closed.

Chapter 57

'The birthday from hell'

Two months have passed since Liam moved into the centre, and things are looking rather brighter now. Covid restrictions have been eased to some extent, and Liam is able to go out for an hour or so each day, as long as he wears a mask when entering shops or other public places. There is still not a proper programme of group meetings, external speakers, or other interventions in place at Regnum Court, but the relative freedom of being able to go out and about has lifted his spirts considerably. Opportunities to see him in the flesh, however, are few and far between as I can't just take time off work in the middle of the day to meet him, but we FaceTime regularly; he seems positive and easy to chat to.

Step by step, I am getting my son back.

***

It's just after 11.30p.m. Amelia is fast asleep and I'm alone in the living room. For some reason I'm just not ready for bed yet.

Tomorrow is Liam's twenty-first birthday. I've booked a day off work so that I can meet him for a coffee and give him his birthday gift: a lovely Tag Heuer watch. I can't really afford such an expensive gift, but he's been doing so well, and I want him to know how proud I am.

I decide to flick through Liam's social media pages; he's prolific on Facebook, Instagram, and Snapchat. I haven't looked at them for a while, and when I look at his most recent posts, I realise that something is wrong. Instead of the familiar backdrop of his room at

Regnum Court, he is framed by surroundings which I don't recognise. The room is basic and drab, with practically no soft furnishings visible. A creeping unease begins to infiltrate my mind.

I scroll to the next image, taken from a slightly different angle; there's something oddly familiar about this place, but I just can't put my finger on it. My anxiety begins to morph into a feeling of dread, gradually tightening around my stomach like a tourniquet. *What is this place?*

And then it hits me: it's a local homeless shelter. I visited the place some time ago during my nurse training. *What the hell is my son doing in a homeless shelter?*

I scroll forward again. This time the image which confronts me hits me in the guts like a physical piledriver. Liam is sitting on the bed, looking sad, lost, and broken, but the thing which has evoked such a visceral reaction is the cord looped around his neck. The date and time stamp indicate this post is just seven minutes old.

In a blind panic, I struggle to recall the name of the shelter. *'Turning ... something'? ... 'Turning Point'? ... 'Turning Tables'? ... no ... 'Turning Fortunes' ... yes, that's it!* Frantically, I Google the name and find the website. With trembling fingers, I grab my phone and call them.

'Hello, Turning Fortunes refuge. How can I help?'

Struggling to control my breathing as the words spill incoherently from my mouth, I blurt, 'My son, Liam ... is he there?'

'I'm sorry ... who is this?'

'Madeleine Fisher ... where is he? Is he there?' I gasp.

'Sorry, Ms Fisher ... what's this about?'

'My son, Liam,' I yell. 'Look, I think he's there, with you. I've just seen an Instagram post, and he's got a bloody rope around his neck! For fuck's sake can you check on him ... NOW!'

Now she's got the message. 'Oh ... yes, Liam ... he's been here for two days, but—'

'Then PLEASE go and check on him ... or do you want a bloody suicide on your hands?'

Now I can detect the rising panic in *her* voice, too. 'OK, OK ... I'm going right now. I'll call you back'

She hangs up.

The minutes tick by; no news. *How long is it since I spoke to her? I don't know; I've lost track of time. It seems like an age.*

Then it occurs to me: *maybe she doesn't even have my number.*

I call the shelter again: only an answering machine. *Fuck! I'm going to call the police.* But just as I am about to hang up, a breathless voice cuts in.

'Yes ... I'm here ... who's that? Is it about Liam?'

'Yes ... is he alright?'

'Yes, he's OK ... physically at least ... but he's in quite a state emotionally.'

'Where is he ... can I speak to him?'

'The paramedics have just taken him away. The ambulance is just setting off.'

My stomach is performing somersaults now. 'Paramedics? Ambulance? You said he was OK.'

'He is – physically – but his head was in such a state when I got to him that I decided to call an ambulance. They got here really quickly and have given him something to settle him down. But they decided it was best to get him to hospital for the night ... for his own safety. That way someone can keep an eye on him right through the night.'

'So he'll be safe tonight?'

'Yes, but I'm so glad you called. I had no idea ... I mean nothing much normally ever happens during the night shift ... I'm here on my own ... I can't possibly know exactly what ...' She stifles a sob. 'I'm so sorry ... Madeleine, was it?'

'Yes, Madeleine ... and you are?'

'Oh sorry, yes ... it's Rochelle.'

'Well, thanks Rochelle, for what you have done. The main thing is that he's safe now.'

'I only wish I'd ...' Her voice tails off.

'Look,' I say, 'what was he even doing there in the first place? The last thing I knew was he was in Regnum Court recovery centre and doing well. Next moment, I find he's in your homeless centre and apparently in the depths of despair. What on earth happened?'

'Well, I don't know all the details, but I understand Liam has a drink problem.'

'Yes, but he's been through detox and rehab, and he was well on the road to recovery.'

'Well, like I said, I don't know the full details but, apparently, he was smuggling alcohol into the centre and has started drinking again. It seems that, in spite of several warnings, he kept on doing it. Eventually, they evicted him and put him in touch with us.'

I can hardly believe what I am hearing. 'And they did all this without even informing me … his mother?'

'It seems that way,' says Rochelle, her tone helpless.

The sense of befuddled confusion which had beset me now begins to transform itself into a simmering anger. *How dare they throw my son out without a word to me?* I vow, there and then, that they'll be held accountable for such gross negligence. But that's a battle for another day; right now, Liam's wellbeing is my only thought.

I must have fallen silent, for the next thing I know, Rochelle is gently prompting me. 'Is there anything else I can help with?' she says. 'I don't really know what more I can tell you.'

'No … thank you for everything. I'll take it from here.'

I hang up and glance at the clock on the wall: just after 1.00a.m. I probably can't do much more tonight. Liam is at least in a safe place for the night. I don't know if he still has his phone or if he's in a fit state to use it, but I send him a message anyway.

Liam, I heard what happened last night. I'll be with you in the morning, and we'll work something out. I love you and I'm thinking of you – Mum x

Chapter 58

'Square one'

It's 5.15a.m. and I just can't sleep. The hours drag by interminably, as my restless mind searches for answers which just will not come.

Why, when he seemed to have been doing so well, has he relapsed yet again? What happens now? Where will he live? What does the future hold? How can I help him claw his way out of this living nightmare?

The futility of lying there, wrestling with this cloying mire of unanswerable questions gradually sinks in, so I decide to get up and face the day ahead. He needs me now, more than ever.

With a weary sigh, I haul myself out of bed and shuffle through to the bathroom, taking a pee before daring to confront the sight staring back at me from the mirror. *Jesus Madeleine, you really do look like shit.*

A shower and a hair wash help a bit, but it takes rather more makeup than usual to restore some semblance of normality to my haggard features. Even after my best efforts, fear and anxiety are clearly written across my face. I try effecting a relaxed smile, but it looks as unconvincing as it feels. Nevertheless, false smiles will just have to do today.

My first task of the day is to drop Amelia at school. She doesn't seem to notice any difference in either my appearance or demeanour. That, at least, means I don't have to field a torrent of questions to which I have no satisfactory answers. Listening to her usual early-morning chatter helps to distract me from thinking about what might lie ahead today.

The traffic on the way to the hospital is awful, but finally I find myself turning into the car park, which is already almost full. I find a space and park up, but I need a minute or two to compose myself before going in. The minute or two turns out to be more like five as I watch people stepping out of their cars and heading for the hospital entrance. I study their faces, trying to interpret their expressions, wondering what story lies behind each one: joy for a friend getting better; tragedy of a loved one near the end of their life; or like mine, fear of the unknown. Behind every smile or every blank expression lies a secret, hidden from the casual onlooker by the mask on display.

Finally, I pull myself together and open the door, stepping out into the chill morning air.

I understand that Liam is still in the Accident and Emergency department. I'm not sure if that's good or bad really: does it mean he's in a bad way, or that they are not expecting him to stay long enough to warrant admitting him to a ward?

The nurse shows me to a small bay behind the main assessment area. 'He's just having some breakfast,' she says, indicating the curtained-off space. 'He only wanted orange juice and dry toast ... says he doesn't like butter.'

Well, that's true – he never did.

'Take as long as you like,' says the nurse, with a smile. 'Doctor North will be along shortly. He'll be able to answer any questions you or Liam may have.'

As she steps away, I put my false smile on and pull back the curtain. Liam has obviously heard us talking, as he is already looking expectantly in my direction.

'Happy Birthday, Liam. Not quite how we hoped it would be, huh?'

He puts his arms out for a hug. 'Sorry Mum.' He murmurs, as he pulls me towards him. 'I've let you down, I've let everyone down, I've even let myself down.'

I feel the burning sensation of the tears welling up. 'No, you haven't,' I say, easing myself gently away from the hug. 'You are trying your best ... we knew it was never going to be easy.' I look him directly in the eyes; he looks so fragile, so vulnerable. 'The important thing is that you're OK. We need to look forward, not back ... work out where we go from here.'

He nods, wordlessly.

'The doctor is coming back soon; we can discuss it with him then.'

'OK,' says Liam, forcing a small smile.

As though that has somehow deferred the substantive discussion for the moment, our chat turns to more everyday things: what Amelia's been up to, how the older girls are doing, how I've redecorated his room, and so on.

It's around 10.20a.m. when the doctor appears, but he's not alone, he's followed by a gaggle of around half a dozen white-coated young medics whom I take to be trainees. *How on earth are we going to have a private conversation about Liam's situation with this bunch all around us?*

'Hello Miss Fisher,' says the doctor, 'I'm Doctor North ... Liam has been under my care since he was admitted last night. These people are F2 doctors ... do you mind if they listen in as part of their training?'

As a nurse, I'm well aware of what an F2 is: a doctor in the second year of their foundation training. Well, they all have to learn their trade, of course, but I'm certainly not too happy about having them here while we discuss Liam's future. However, I'm too disorientated to respond before Liam interjects, 'Yeah, that's fine.'

I guess we're stuck with them then.

The doctor then proceeds to tell me what I already know: Liam has been through detox and rehab and appeared to be well on the way to resuming a normal life but has relapsed and found himself in the homeless shelter. *No shit, Sherlock.* I feel as though this summary is more for the benefit of his trainees than either Liam or me. I sense a simmering anger begin to grow within me.

The doctor then delivers the news that there is really nothing the NHS can offer Liam, as there is no state-funded service for helping people in this situation. He could, of course, go into private rehab, the cost of which he would know, if he had bothered to ask, is well beyond my means. The other option is to go back to the charity which had funded his previous failed bids to get sober, but given his history, he would be at the bottom of a very long list.

Now my anger is threatening to erupt. I'm looking for help here, not confirmation that the situation is hopeless. Somehow, I manage to contain my emotions and respond in a calm and civil manner.

'Doctor North, I still have a number of questions, but could I suggest that we perhaps continue the discussion in private?'

I don't know quite how to interpret the frown which wrinkles his brow, and the tone of his reply gives nothing away. 'Of course; I should be free in around an hour if you are able to stay that long.'

'Yes, that's fine … see you back here?'

He nods, delivering his best professional smile before setting off with his entourage in tow.

Liam is looking tired, and I can feel the beginnings of a headache coming on, so I suggest he tries to get a little sleep while I step outside for some fresh air.

***

Outside the front entrance, there are quite a few people gathered: some in pyjamas and dressing gowns; some in regular outdoor clothing. Most are dragging furiously on cigarettes, despite the notices directing them to a designated smoking area.

I make my way through the cloud of smoke and move away to find some solitude around the side of the building. I find a quiet corner alongside a crumbling wooden perimeter fence, on which I prop my elbows and peer at the tangle of brambles beyond.

I had hoped for some helpful advice from the doctor, but instead all I get is confirmation of my worst fears. There is nothing the NHS can do, I have already exhausted all the possibilities for charities to help, and private treatment is way beyond my means. As the reality of the situation hits home, I begin to cry, at first just a few ragged sobs, but then the dam bursts and releases a full-blown torrent of tears.

I don't know how long I have been crying when I finally begin to compose myself, but I do know that admitting defeat is not an option. Liam and I are going to have to tackle this together, without further professional help. The first question is where will he live? With all other options closed off, the only possibility is for him to move back home to his old room. I am acutely conscious of the advice I had received that it was inadvisable for him to return to a place which he associated with previously drinking alone, but what else can I do?

All his old furniture and carpets have been thrown out so, right now, the room is nothing more than a shell, but at least it's clean and freshly decorated. I'll have to sort out carpets and furniture in the coming days.

The very process of beginning to formulate a plan has helped to lift me out of the depths of despair to which I had sunk just minutes earlier. I look at my watch; almost forty minutes have elapsed since I left Liam. I need to get back before the doctor returns, though I'm not optimistic that he's going to offer any further help.

Liam isn't asleep when I get back; he's already chatting to Doctor North who had returned a little earlier than expected. However, my pessimism about further help being offered, turns out to be well-founded.

The doctor basically spends the next twenty minutes reiterating our complete lack of options, closing with, 'Sorry I can't be of more help.'

Finally, he says that as Liam's condition is now stable, he can be discharged.

We're on our own, then.

Once the doctor has gone, I tell Liam about my plan, formulated while leaning on that crumbling fence and gazing at the brambles.

He reaches out for a hug. 'Thanks, Mum.'

'Let's go home,' I say, putting my arms around him.

***

The first thing we need to do is collect Liam's things from Turning Fortunes homeless shelter, as he won't be going back there.

When we arrive, and step out of the car, there is a small group of people sitting on garden chairs outside the front entrance, some smoking, some drinking, some both. They are a motley bunch – poor unfortunates who have hit rock bottom yet finding some solace in the company of others in a similar situation. I shudder at the thought that this was the point Liam's life had reached. At that moment I know that, however difficult it may prove to be, bringing Liam home is the right decision.

A scruffy-looking man in a tattered parka jacket raises a beer bottle in our direction. 'Hi Liam ... what's occurring?'

'Hiya Jim ... this is my Mum. She's taking me home.'

He shifts his gaze to me, his weather-worn and leathered features creasing in a lopsided smile. 'Bless you ma'am. Liam's a good lad ... he doesn't belong here.'

Suddenly, I'm filling up. This man, who has literally nothing, can still find space in his heart to care about his fellow man.

Whatever words I'm trying to form choke in my mouth; the best I can do is offer him the same forced smile which has already been heavily over-used this morning.

We hurry towards the entrance and step inside. The young woman at the desk inside looks drawn and pale, but she manages a smile when she sees us. 'Liam, thank goodness ... are you OK?'

'I'm OK, thanks. Er this is my Mum. Mum ... Rochelle ... I guess you spoke to her last night.'

'Yes,' I say. 'I can't thank you enough for what you have done for Liam.'

She manages a weary smile. 'I'm just glad he's OK.'

'How come you're still here?' I ask, looking at my watch.

'Fourteen-hour shift,' she sighs. 'But I'm nearly done ... Brenda will be here in around an hour.'

I nod – I know all about long shifts from my work as a nurse.

'Mum's taking me home,' says Liam.

'That's great,' replies Rochelle. 'You make sure you don't let her down.'

'I won't,' he says.

I wish it were that easy, I think.

'Anyway, we've come to collect his things.'

'Oh, sure ... go ahead.'

Fifteen minutes later, we have said our goodbyes to Rochelle and are making our way through the smokers and drinkers.

Jim, the guy in the tattered parka, acknowledges us with that lopsided smile and the beer-bottle salute. 'You make sure you do it right, son. Don't let this lovely lady down.'

Oh, God ... now I'm almost on the brink of inviting this poor man to come home with us as well. Madness, of course ... I can't save every unfortunate soul who's in dire straits. I don't know if I can even save my son.

We sit in silence for the first five minutes of the journey home. As I glance across at Liam, I notice his hands are clenched tightly on top of his knees.

'Are you OK Liam?'

He meets my sidelong glance with a fearful gaze. As he lifts his hand, the tremor is obvious. 'I'm getting the shakes, Mum. I need some alcohol.'

Of course: he's become physically dependent on alcohol once more. They'll have stabilised his condition at the hospital, but the meds will be wearing off now. Why on earth didn't they give us more supplies before we left to give us a chance to wean him off gradually?

'OK … look, I'll stop at a supermarket and get some vodka. That should ward off the fits for now, but you are going to have to be strong, Liam, and gradually reduce your intake until we can get you sober again.'

'Yes, yes, I will. Look … there's a supermarket … ahead on the left.'

At this moment, he'll say anything to get his hands on that bottle.

I pull up on a double yellow line and pass him some money, which he gratefully grabs before running into the store. As I wait for him, a wave of fatigue sweeps over me. I feel tired, numb, and totally disheartened.

This wasn't the birthday I'd planned or hoped for.

Chapter 59

'The contract'

We're home now. Liam is exhausted after his ordeal and is already a little drunk, having consumed over a third of the bottle of vodka we bought on the way home; he just wants to sleep. Trouble is, right now his room is nothing more than a shell: no carpet, bed, or furniture.

The best I can do for now is blow up one of the old inflatable airbeds I still have from those happier days when he was just a normal, boisterous kid who loved putting up a tent in the garden and sleeping out overnight. The room looks utterly forlorn: a single airbed, a pillow and a couple of blankets in splendid isolation on the bare floorboards. But he just wants somewhere to crash, and doesn't complain as he disappears into his room, clutching the vodka bottle and a glass of water which I ask him to take, more in hope than expectation that he'll drink some of that rather than just the vodka.

I check on him half an hour later; he's fast asleep, the bottle – now less than half full – and the glass of water – untouched – standing on the floor alongside where he lies.

I glance at my watch; it's time to collect Amelia from school. Liam looks as though he'll probably be asleep for hours, so I won't wake him. That can wait until I get back with Amelia.

***

Amelia comes skipping out from the school entrance, clutching her coat, bag, and lunchbox. She dumps all this paraphernalia in my waiting arms before waving to her best friend, Alexis, who has also just been collected by her mum.

'Good day?' I enquire.

'It was alright,' came her typically brief reply.

'What did you do today?'

'Oh, usual stuff: sums, reading … bit boring really.'

It seems as though that's about all I'm going to get out of her, so I prepare to give her the news of which she has absolutely no idea at the moment.

'OK, well here's a question for you: can you remember what today is?'

Her forehead crinkles in puzzlement. 'Well, it's Wednesday of course … that's a silly question.'

'Ah, but what *date* is it?'

'Oh, I don't know … does it matter?'

I smile; life is so simple at that age. 'Well, it's the eighteenth of May. Can you remember why that date is special?'

'Oh Muuum … what's this all about?'

'It's Liam's birthday; he's twenty-one today.'

Understanding dawns. 'Oh, I get it … what's he doing then?'

'He's home.'

'Home where?'

'Our home.'

Her eyes widen and her mouth makes an 'O' shape. 'What, you mean he's back home with us?'

'Yes … we're all together again.'

She squeals with delight. 'Are we having birthday cake?'

I smile; birthday cake is the last thing on my mind, but seeing the joy on Amelia's face melts my heart. 'Well, I didn't have time to make one so let's stop at the supermarket on the way home and buy cake and candles, shall we?'

She nods vigorously, grabbing my hand, almost making me drop all the stuff she has loaded me up with. 'Come on,' she says, dragging me in the direction of where the car is parked.

When we arrive home, Amelia bounds up the stairs to greet her brother but minutes later comes back down, looking despondent.

'He's asleep.'

'Well, he's been really tired. Let me go and check on him.'

I can hear the snores even before I reach the top of the stairs. I knock gently before pushing the door open. He's out for the count; the vodka bottle is empty now. He must have woken up and finished it off while I was collecting Amelia. *Good thing I had the foresight to buy another bottle when I stopped to buy cake.* I call his name: no response. I try touching his shoulder gently: still no reaction.

I decide to leave him a while longer.

When I go back down, Amelia looks at me expectantly. 'Is he alright?'

'He's fine ... just really tired. Let's leave him for a while ... I'm sure he'll be awake soon.'

'OKaaay ... can I go on my iPad for a while before tea?'

'Homework first ... then you can have half an hour on the iPad.'

'Ha,' she cries, 'Miss Evans was off sick today, so we had Mrs Pocock. She didn't set us any homework.' Her expression was nothing short of triumphant.

'OK, well, in that case you can have an hour on your iPad.'

'Yes!' she exclaims, punching the sky – all thoughts of her brother's birthday apparently forgotten for the moment.

***

It's 8p.m. and Liam still hasn't surfaced; Amelia is watching TV. She has school in the morning, and she needs her sleep, so it's time to break the news that birthday celebrations are on hold until tomorrow.

'OK ... TV off in five minutes ... time to get ready for bed.'

'Oh, Muuum, you promised we would have cake with Liam.'

'I know sweetie, but Liam's still—'

A loud thump from upstairs announces the fact that Liam has finally woken.

'He's up!' she cries.

I don't have the heart to bundle her off to bed now. 'OK, you can stay up a bit longer.'

'Yay! I'm going to see him.' She scampers off and scoots up the stairs.

Ten minutes later, the two of them come down.

'We're doing cake now,' declares Amelia.

The cake is football themed, steeped in E numbers and food colouring: not what I would have ideally chosen when Amelia needs to sleep, but it was the best I could find in the supermarket. Anyway, they both attack it with gusto after we sing together, and Liam makes a theatrical show of blowing out the candles. I join in with a small slice even though it's way too sweet for me, really.

Liam is in a jokey, happy mood, with absolutely no sign that he has just drunk a whole bottle of vodka. Amelia is obviously loving catching up with her brother and I don't have the heart to break up the reunion.

It's 10.30p.m. by the time I finally manage to get Amelia ready for bed. By now she's dead on her feet and tumbles into bed without any of her usual delaying tactics. *Let's hope I can get her up on time in the morning!*

Liam has already discovered the extra bottle of vodka which I bought and insists it's essential that he drinks a glass or two before bed to make sure he doesn't have severe withdrawal symptoms or a full-blown fit during the night. I reluctantly agree but draw the line at letting him take the rest of the bottle up to his room.

After he's gone to bed, I end up having a little myself, heavily diluted with fresh orange juice: it's been a shitty day, and I figure I deserve it. As I sit there sipping my drink, the TV playing softly but barely registering in my consciousness, I wonder where the hell we go from here and how we are going to succeed with getting Liam sober when all the professionals have failed.

Time for bed; maybe things will seem clearer in the morning.

***

They do – up to a point, but I have to take Amelia to school and go to work today so I can't have a serious chat with Liam until late in the evening, after Amelia's gone to bed.

I have already noticed that the second bottle of vodka is empty and there's a third in the kitchen, already started. We sit down to talk.

'Liam, we can't go on like this. Unless we make some big changes, you are not going to get better, and your sisters are going to suffer.'

He nods but doesn't comment.

'If you are to settle back at home with Grace, Amelia, and me, we need to agree some ground rules.'

225

'Like what?' he says, inclining his head, wrinkling his brow, and narrowing his eyes.

I reach for my handbag, which is lying on the sofa alongside me, withdrawing a sheet of paper with hand-written notes I'd made during my lunch break.

'We are going to have to make a contract with each other.'

'A contract? Oh, Mum, you have to be joking.'

'I'm not joking, Liam. We've tried everything else. You can only stay here if you agree to this.'

Whether it's my tone of voice or the expression on my face which has hit home, I'm unsure, but one way or another he gets the message. His smile evaporates, and his face falls. He seems lost for a response, so I press on, reading from my notes.

'OK, as long as you agree to your side of the contract – which we'll discuss in a moment – this is what I propose for my part of the contract …

'I will re-carpet and re-furnish your room at my own expense. It won't all be new stuff, but it will be liveable.

'I know you can't work in your present condition, so I will cover all the costs of your board and lodging until you can.'

I look up at him. 'OK?'

He appears to be dumbstruck. 'Well, I sort of assumed you'd have to …'

His words tail off.

'Don't assume anything,' I admonish him. 'Right, now your part … you have to commit to the following …

'You actively follow a written plan to gradually reduce your alcohol consumption, until you are no longer physically dependent. You will not bring any alcohol into the house; the only alcohol allowed will be brought in by me.'

'But Mum, I—'

'I haven't finished.'

His open mouth closes.

'You will keep your room clean and tidy.

'You will sleep during the night and get up in the day; no online gaming after midnight.

'You will agree to share housework, doing cleaning and hoovering while I'm at work.

'You will re-engage with CLASP and—'

'But Mum … they'll never have me back after everything that's happened.'

'Well, it's true that you've blown your chances of their offering a detox and rehab programme, but you can start attending regular meetings again. I want you to tell them about our contract and share details of progress every time you go.'

I pause to wait for a response; there is none, so I continue.

'Finally, as soon as you are able to go for at least ten hours continuously without alcohol, you will actively seek a job and contribute to the cost of your board and lodging.'

I pause and look up. 'Understood?'

He looks stunned and takes several seconds to respond. 'Mum … isn't this all a bit … formal?'

As I regard his bewildered expression, I'm on the brink of folding. I just want to give him a hug, but I'm convinced this is a time for tough love. With some difficulty, I maintain my stony expression.

'Sorry Liam, but if it's going to work, this is how it has to be. Now … do you agree?'

He hangs his head. 'Yes,' he mumbles, 'I'll do all that. I know you're only doing it for the best.'

The release of tension feels almost physical. *I got through it without crumbling.*

As I fight back the tears which are threatening to erupt, I enact the final part of my plan.

'Well, in that case, here's your birthday present.'

I withdraw a small package from the shelf below the coffee table and pass it to him. As he unwraps it and registers the familiar red and green logo on the box within, his jaw drops in disbelief. He opens the box to reveal the beautiful Tag Heuer watch I have been keeping for him. He stares at it for several long seconds before looking up at me, tears welling up in his eyes. He comes over and hugs me tightly.

Now we are both sobbing, uncontrollably.

Is this the start of a new, and better, chapter? I hope, with all my heart, that it is.

Chapter 60

'Will it hold?'

Almost two months have passed since we agreed on the contract, and summer is here.

I've re-furnished his room with a combination of items we had around the house and some things purchased from the local charity shop. He's doing a reasonable job of keeping it clean and tidy, but the part of the contract which requires him to help with other housework seems to have gone by the board. At least he's sticking to his promise to keep reasonably sociable hours. He's usually up before I take Amelia to school and the noisy nocturnal online battles seem to have largely stopped.

He has no income other than benefits, so I'm having to cover most of his expenses, which puts a hell of a strain on the household finances. Thank God for Grace's contribution; she's such a treasure.

I've been strictly controlling Liam's alcohol consumption which we have managed to get down from two or more bottles of vodka per day to just over half a bottle per day. Even so, the cost of the booze is yet another financial burden, so we've recently switched to strong cider, which is cheaper, but still seems to do the job. He's had a couple of seizures when we've tried to reduce his intake too quickly but, overall, we're making progress.

He's been accepted back into regular meetings at CLASP. He complains that most of the others there are much older than him and difficult to engage with, but apart from missing a few meetings he's hanging in there. He has also started going to a 'Narcotics Anonymous' support group in a local church every Friday evening.

Apparently, it's for addicts of any sort – drugs, alcohol, medicines – and the others there are closer to his own age.

Against all the odds, Liam's girlfriend, Sienna, has stuck by him through everything. With the advent of the long summer evenings, they often go to the nearby park to play ball or have a picnic.

She's such a good influence on him; I'm not sure we'd have got this far without her.

Will she stay the course? Will he? Who knows? Right now, though, the contract is holding and so is their relationship. I guess it's as much as I could have hoped for right now.

Chapter 61

Two months later

'Slipping back'

I'm getting concerned.

As summer begins to fade into autumn, progress on the alcohol reduction seems to have slowed virtually to a standstill. Liam hasn't had any more seizures recently, but every time we try to cut down his consumption a little, he says he's getting the shakes and feels as though a fit is coming on. I'm not sure whether he's being entirely truthful, but I'm terrified that if we overdo it, he'll suffer a really bad seizure, with who knows what consequences.

He's started missing some of his CLASP meetings and I'm not even sure if he's still attending the Friday evening meetings with Narcotics Anonymous.

His adherence to household rules seems to be slipping. The midnight cut-off for online gaming has been gradually stretched, night by night, to the point where it's often more like 1a.m. or even later. When I mention it, he brushes it off, saying he doesn't do it intentionally but sometimes just loses track of time.

He's doing nothing to help with household chores, and I don't really know how well he's even looking after his own room, as he locks it when he goes out and doesn't like me going in there, even when he's at home.

Each of these things, individually, is worrying enough, but taken together, they paint a foreboding picture of an impending relapse. I resolve to have another heart-to-heart with Liam before things get worse. Before I even get a chance to sit down with Liam and thrash it all out, though, events overtake me.

***

It's Sunday night. I've been asleep for a while when I feel something shaking my shoulder.

As the fog of sleep disperses, a small voice penetrates my befuddled brain. 'Mummy, I can't sleep.'

In the dim light cast through the open door by the plug-in night light in the hall outside, I discern Amelia's anxious face.

'What is it, sweetie ... a bad dream?'

'No, it's—'

She doesn't need to finish her sentence. 'YES!' comes the triumphant shout from Liam's room, accompanied by a loud thump.

I glance at the bedside clock: 2.37a.m. The surge of anger which erupts within me feels like some physical thing which could explode at any moment. With some difficulty, I control it sufficiently to avoid frightening Amelia. Now fully awake, I step out of bed and place a comforting arm around her shoulders.

'OK, Liam is behaving very badly ... I'll make him stop at once. Now you go back to bed and try to get to sleep.'

I guide her gently out of the door and towards her own room, where she stops in the doorway, turning to give me an enquiring look. I smile and nod my encouragement for her to go inside. As she pushes the door to, leaving a gap of just an inch or two – she never likes to have it completely closed – I turn and stomp determinedly towards Liam's room.

I don't even knock, such is the anger which I need to vent. As I barge into the room, my nostrils are assaulted by the sickening stench of alcohol, vomit, and urine. The floor is strewn with empty bottles, cardboard fast-food cartons, and clothes cast carelessly aside. Liam is fully dressed, sitting in front of his games console. His head spins around at my sudden and unexpected entrance, his eyes wide and his jaw hanging open; at that moment, though, he is apparently lost for any words to respond. Well, I'm not about to give him time to find some.

I slam the door shut behind me and rip into him. 'What the FUCK do you think you're doing? It's almost three in the morning, and you're up, yelling and screaming, waking Amelia and surrounded by … THIS!' I cast my hand in a wide arc across the squalid, chaotic scene.

He gawps at me, wordlessly, like some stranded goldfish, evidently overwhelmed by the ferocity of my outburst.

'WELL?' I demand.

Finally, he finds his voice; his words are slurred. 'You shouldn't juss come in here like that … iss not allowed … iss my personal shpace and you—'

I cut him off. 'Now listen to me, you impudent, ungrateful prick. *You* do not get to tell *me* what to do in my own house. I've bent over backwards to try to help you sort your life out, I'm paying for everything, I'm giving you the roof over your head, and THIS' – I sweep my hand once again across the shit-heap his room has become – 'is how you repay me.'

Now that he has recovered from the shock of my initial onslaught, he's in combative mood – no doubt fuelled by the copious amount of alcohol he's obviously consumed. *Where the hell did he even get it from?* He tries to stand up and face me but is so unsteady on his feet that he slumps back into his chair. He's still ready to do battle, though.

'Thassnot fair … issmy room and you've no right to dissreshpect me like that … in any case you're my mother … issyour job to give me shomewhere to live.'

That's it – my patience snaps; I step forward and slap his cheek … hard. The expression on his face is one of astonishment rather than pain, as he raises his hand to touch his cheek.

'I can't talk to you when you're like this. Now shut this fucking thing down,' – I yank the power cord from his games console – 'get yourself sobered up, and we'll thrash this out tomorrow.'

I stomp out of the room without giving him time to reply.

'Bitch!' I hear him hiss, as I close the door behind me.

***

It's 6a.m. the following morning. The house is silent now, but I haven't slept a wink since my flaming row with Liam. I could spend another forty minutes or so in bed before getting up and making breakfast but what would be the point? I'm hardly likely to get to sleep now, and I imagine Liam will be completely out of it for hours yet. I haul myself wearily out of bed and make my way to the bathroom to have a pee and splash my face with some cold water, before going to check on Liam. My anger has subsided now, and I am already regretting some of the things I said last night, so this time I knock softly on the door and call his name. No response, so I push the door open. The smell is no less revolting than before, but at least I'm prepared for it this time. Liam is sprawled on the bed, breathing heavily, still fully clothed. As I expected, he'll be asleep for some while yet. In any case, I can't get involved, just now, in what will surely be a very difficult heart-to-heart; I have to get Amelia to school and go to work. I cannot afford to take any more unplanned time off work. I leave him to sober up while I go to make myself a cup of tea and watch twenty minutes of news on the TV before rousing Amelia.

***

It's around 4.30p.m. by the time I get home. Amelia is usually allowed half an hour on her iPad when she gets home, after she has first done her homework, but today I tell her she can have an hour as I need to have a serious talk with Liam. She scampers off to her room to get her homework done as quickly as possible.

But where is Liam? He's not in the living room or the kitchen, so he must have either gone out or be in his room.

I go and knock on his door and call his name.

'Come in, Mum,' comes the softly spoken reply.

As I push the door open, bracing myself for the sickening stench which I know is coming, I receive a huge surprise: an overwhelming smell of cleaning fluid and disinfectant. Liam is on his hands and knees, scrubbing away at his bedside rug. He looks up and smiles – the kind of smile I haven't seen for quite some while.

'Hi, Mum … thought my room needed a bit of a clean.'

I look all around. No bottles or discarded clothes on the floor, but a plastic crate full of empties by the side of the bed and an overflowing laundry basket. The bed has been stripped of sheets and covers and a damp patch on the mattress is evidence of some of his earlier cleaning efforts.

'Looks a bit better, huh?' he says, dropping the scrubbing brush into the bucket alongside him and standing up.

'I … I don't know what to say.' And I really don't.

233

He sits down on the dry part of the mattress and gestures for me to pull up the chair from his computer desk.

As I sit down opposite him, he rescues me from my dumbstruck state. 'I'm really sorry, Mum. I said some awful things last night … and I really didn't mean them. I was completely off my head and when you came in suddenly like that, I just reacted … I've never seen you so furious, and it really caught me off balance. I was so drunk that I just lashed out back at you. I'm sorry.'

My heart melts as I look into those big, blue eyes, full of contrition. 'Well, I said a few bad things myself … not because I really meant them … it was more because I was so devastated to see how you had slipped right back after all our efforts to make progress.'

'So can we wipe the slate clean and make a fresh start?' he says.

In spite of the wave of love and affection I am now feeling for my son, I know I must be firm with him.

'I'd like to do that Liam, but it's going to be down to you. We can't just have another reset today and then slide back again tomorrow.'

'I know,' he says casting his gaze downward.

'You need to be honest with yourself – and me – about why you relapsed and what you need to do to stop it happening again.'

He is silent for several long seconds. 'It's Sienna.'

'Sienna?' I exclaim. 'What has she done? She's been amazing, sticking with you through thick and thin.'

'That's just it … she has … but I'm so afraid of losing her. I can't bear to think of that, and I get so anxious about it that I start drinking again to dull the pain.'

'Oh Liam … can't you see what a vicious circle you're creating? The more you drink the more likely it is that her patience will run out. If you want to keep her, you have to get sober.'

'I know … but it's not so easy,' he says, hanging his head.

I must be firm and resolute now. 'And while we are on the subject of the booze, where the hell have you been getting it from? We were gradually reducing the amount you were drinking, and I know you don't have the money to be buying more.'

He doesn't't immediately reply, instead continuing to stare at the floor.

'Liam,' I say, raising my voice a little for emphasis, 'look at me.'

He does so, but still doesn't reply.

'Well?'

Finally, he answers me. 'My mates have been bringing it round while you're at work and Amelia's at school.'

'Your "mates" … what sort of "mates" are they to encourage you into a complete relapse?'

He shrugs, helplessly.

'Right,' I say, 'which of your mates have been doing this?'

'I don't want to get them into trouble, Mum.'

'Trouble?' I say, now aware that the tone and volume of my voice are involuntarily getting away from me. 'Well fuck that … I'm more concerned about the trouble *they* are getting *you* into. Now who are they?'

He recoils slightly. 'OK … OK … it's mainly Mickey and Wayne.'

'Right … like I said, fixing this is going to be mainly down to you … but I'll help you as much as I can. This is what we're going to do.

'First, you have to tell Mickey and Wayne that you're making a fresh start, and they must NOT bring any more booze round, whatever you might ask in a weak moment.

'Second, I'm going to talk to their parents, explain the situation, and ask for their help to make sure it doesn't happen again.'

'But, Muuum—'

'No "buts".'

He thinks better of further protest.

'Third, we're going back to the routine where we agree a gradual alcohol reduction programme, and *I* control how much is available to you until you can kick the dependency completely.

'Finally, you and I are going to have a chat with Sienna together to tell her what we're doing and try to convince her that you're really serious this time.'

'Oh, Mum … that's going to be a bit …' he pauses.

'A bit what? Embarrassing? Awkward? Look, Sienna is a lovely girl, and she loves you. And she's *my* friend too. But you've stretched her loyalty almost to the limit. If you want to keep her, you need to fully involve her.'

Liam casts his eyes downward. 'I guess you're right.'

I extend my hand towards him. 'Deal?'

'Deal,' he agrees, looking up at me and taking my outstretched hand.

Have we really laid the foundations for a fresh start? I'd love to think so, but with so many false dawns behind us, how can I be confident? I guess only time will tell.

Chapter 62

One year later

'Fear'

Fast forward one year; it has not gone well: the reset was short lived. Within weeks of our agreement, Liam began returning to his old ways. Now, after a full year, he is even worse than before. He is, once again, up for much of the night, shouting at his computer or games console, disrupting Amelia's sleep … and mine. By the time I set off for work each morning he is almost always flat drunk, fast asleep, and impossible to wake. He has often only just got out of bed when I get home from work; I'm usually exhausted and in no mood to argue. But frequently, he *is* in the mood: he has become disrespectful and argumentative, pursuing issues that make no sense whatsoever, picking a fight before I have even taken my coat off. It is pointless to try and reason with him when he is drunk, irrational, and angry. Even Amelia has felt the sharp end of his tongue on occasion, and when I intervene to protect her, it incenses him even more. My home has become a battlefield, and I now dread coming back to it each day.

Everything that has been tried in an effort to help Liam has failed. The professionals have failed, detox and rehab have failed, and my own attempts have also failed. I am at my wits' end as to what to do next.

***

It's a Monday afternoon, and I've had a particularly stressful day at work. Liam launches into me the moment I get home. He's very drunk and very angry – about what, exactly, I cannot say, as he's totally irrational. He's cussing and swearing and using the most obscene language.

I've had enough. 'Liam!' I yell … 'not in front of Amelia.'

'Not in front of Amelia,' he repeats, mimicking my voice. 'You only care about that little runt … you don't give a shit about me. Issnot fair.'

Now I'm furious, but with a superhuman effort of willpower I contain the urge to slap his face.

Amelia is whimpering now, tears beginning to flow.

'Amelia,' I say. 'Liam doesn't mean it … he's just very drunk. Now, why don't you go to your room and get your homework done before tea? I need to have a talk with Liam.'

She glances uncertainly at me and then at Liam, whose florid face is a mask of anger.

I place a hand on her shoulder and smile. 'Off you go then.' She heads off to her room, still sobbing.

Once I hear her door close, I turn back to Liam. 'Don't you EVER speak to me like that again in front of Amelia.'

'Why the fuck sh-shouldn't I? Why's she sho fucking shhpecial?'

That's it, I finally snap: I slap his face, hard enough to make him recoil and take a step backwards. 'Get out of my sight.' I hiss.

He takes but a second to regroup before drawing back his fist and stepping forward, his eyes wild with rage.

'LIAM – NO!' comes a shout from behind me.

He stops, suddenly raising his gaze and looking past me to where Grace has just come in, unnoticed by either of us, preoccupied as we were by our flaming row.

I turn back to Liam, locking eyes, challenging him. He thinks better of what he was undoubtedly about to do.

'Shtupid bitch!' he mutters, before turning round and stomping off towards his room.

'Are you alright, Mum?' says Grace.

'Not really,' I reply, trembling now.

'What was that all about?'

'All about nothing really – just one of Liam's crazy tantrums.'

'He's getting worse, isn't he?'

I nod, miserably. 'Yes, he is.'

'I think he was really going to punch you in the face, you know. He could have broken your nose ... or even worse.'

'I know.'

'This can't go on, Mum. We have to do something.'

She's right of course, but WHAT?

***

Several hours have passed. Amelia is in bed, asleep, while Grace and I are watching some banal quiz show on TV, although to be honest, I think both our minds are elsewhere. There has been no further sign of Liam. Hopefully he's passed out or gone to bed. No such luck ...

Just as I'm thinking of turning in early myself, he comes staggering into the living room. He's unsteady on his feet, and his voice is heavily slurred.

'You're shooo fucking high and mighty ... issnot fair. Issmyy housh too ... you shouldn't dishrespect me like that.'

Grace tries to intervene. 'Oh, Liam ... leave her alone. She's had a tough day at work and doesn't need all this grief.'

He whirls on her. 'Wassit got to do with you, you ... shlutt?'

I jump to my feet shooting him a furious glare. 'Don't you DARE speak to your sister like that.'

He loses his balance and just manages to fall into the armchair alongside him rather than collapse on the floor. 'I'll shpeak whatever fucking way I like ... 'cosh I ... I got ...' His voice peters out as he loses whatever thread was in his addled brain.

And so it goes on, for about another twenty minutes. He is just spouting utter gibberish, all the time winding himself up to even higher levels of anger. I've had enough ...

'Grace, I'm going to bed ... I can't take any more of this shit. Can you turn everything off before you come up?'

I push past Liam – he's on his feet again now ... just about, anyway. As I do so he turns to follow me, mimicking my voice as best he can in his inebriated condition. '*III'm* going to bed, blah blah blah. Well, go to bed, shtupid bitch ... you're pathetic.'

He follows me all the way to my room, muttering incoherently. Even when I reach the sanctuary of my bedroom he won't give up; he follows me in, getting right in my face as I try to back away, laughing at my obvious distress as my resolve to stay strong crumbles.

'Look at you … crying now. Ha! Like I shaid, you're pathetic … weak and pathetic.'

'GET OUT!' I scream, summoning all my strength to push him away.

He's so unsteady on his feet that my shove is enough to put him flat on his backside on the floor.

'GET OUT!' I yell again.

With some difficulty, he levers himself off the floor and onto his feet.

He points an accusing finger at me. 'Fuck you … isssnot worth even talking to you.'

I summon the most threatening tone I can manage. 'Get out now or I'm calling the police.'

'Pah! Fuck you, and fuck the poleesh. I'm going.'

Finally, he staggers out of the room; I rush to slam the door behind him and grab the chair from my dressing table, wedging it firmly under the door handle. I slump down on the bed, my breath coming in ragged sobs. I can hear loud bangs and shouts coming from his room.

After about ten minutes, the commotion subsides. He must surely have passed out now. I wait another five minutes before there is a soft knock on the door.

'Mum, are you OK?' It's Grace.

I remove the chair and open the door to reveal her anxious face.

'Are you OK … did he hurt you?'

I manage a small smile. 'I'm fine … he's gone to his room … probably passed out for hours now.'

'Want me to stay here with you tonight?'

'No, I'll be fine … you go and get some sleep now.'

'Well, if you're sure …'

I smile, patting her on the shoulder. 'I am.'

I'm nowhere near as confident as I try to sound, so as soon as I'm sure Grace has settled down for the night, I set about providing some early warning should Liam try to come back during the night while I'm asleep.

I put various obstacles between his room and mine: a chair. A stack of books, an empty waste bin, and a few aerosol cans. In the darkness of the hall and considering how drunk he will still be, he'll be bound to fall over something and wake me up.

Finally, I retrieve from the dressing table the tall, heavy, glass perfume bottle which I have saved for years as an ornament. I test its satisfying heft with a trial swing; yes, that will do as a weapon if I need it.

I climb into bed, keeping the weighty bottle in my hand, under the pillow.

So, it has come to this: I am now seriously concerned about the likelihood of physical assault by my own son, either against me, or worse still, against Amelia or Grace.

What am I going to do?

Chapter 63

'Jekyll, Hyde, and the final straw'

There is no nocturnal collision with any of the obstacles I set up, and Liam is completely comatose when I set off for work. All day long at work, I am dreading the confrontation which will await me when I get home after collecting Amelia from school. Now, that moment has arrived. I stop by the front door and talk quietly to Amelia.

'Now sweetie, I need to have a serious talk with Liam, so can you go straight to your room and do your homework while I do that?'

A fearful shadow flits across her eyes; she's still too young to fully understand what is going on but she knows it's something bad. Nevertheless, she doesn't comment but just nods.

I open the door and we both step inside, closing the door quietly behind us. There is no obvious sign of Liam.

'Off you go then … you can have a bit of extra time on your iPad when you've finished your homework.'

She trots off to her room.

No sooner have I put my bag down and hung up my coat, than I hear sounds from upstairs and Liam appears at the top of the stairs. He looks awful: pale and gaunt, clothes crumpled, and hair a tangled mess.

He comes down the stairs slowly, picking his steps carefully. An awkward silence fills the air. *Who is going to speak first?*

He does. 'I'm so sorry, Mum.'

He steps forward and puts his arms around me, hugging me tightly. I'm completely thrown by this unexpected show of remorse and just don't know how to react. For now, I just hug him back. We cling together for several long seconds; when he eventually pulls away, his red-rimmed eyes are brimming with tears.

'I was an absolute arsehole last night.'

My instinct is to just hug him again and tell him all is forgiven, but whatever part of my brain remains rational tells me that's the last thing he needs. 'Yes, you were,' I reply.

'I'm so sorry,' he repeats. 'I was completely wasted ... I didn't mean to behave like that.'

'I don't suppose you intended to, but the fact remains that you *did.* Come and sit down ... we need a serious talk about this.'

We go through to the living room and sit opposite one another, either side of the coffee table. He looks at me expectantly, his big blue eyes sad and regretful. I'm on the brink of folding – but I don't.

'You crossed several red lines yesterday. You used obscene, disgusting language against me and, more importantly, your sisters. You threatened us with actual physical violence.'

'Oh, Mum I wouldn't have actually—'

I raise a finger to interrupt him. 'Oh yes you would ... I'm sure you would have punched me in the face if Grace hadn't walked in at that exact moment. She's sure of it, too.'

He hung his head. 'It's the booze ... that's not the real me ... you know that.'

'Oh, Liam ... I know it's the booze, but that's the whole point. It's not how you are when you're sober – like now – but how often is that?'

He doesn't respond.

'When you're drunk – which is a great deal of the time – it *is* you.'

'I guess ...'

'The thing is ... you're like two different people ... and I never know which one to expect next. Unless you sort yourself out – and urgently – I can't trust you with Amelia ... or, come to that, even Grace or me.'

'Oh, Mum ... I wouldn't do anything to hurt my little sister ... or any of you.'

'How do I know that?' I demand. 'You just said it yourself: when you're drunk, you're not yourself.'

He doesn't respond.

'So here's the deal: you get back on track ... right away ... or I can't have you living here anymore.'

His big blue eyes widen as my words sink in. He is silent for several seconds before replying. 'OK … I get it. I'm really going to try this time. We'll do it like the contract we made before, but this time I'm really going to stick to it. You can take charge of the alcohol, so you know how much I'm taking.'

'Don't blow it this time, Liam.'

'I won't.'

'OK … now go and apologise to Amelia for the things you said to her yesterday.'

He slinks off to do so.

Will it work? It's hard to be optimistic. But this time I'm resolute. I love my son, in spite of everything, but I love my daughters too, and I will not put them at risk. Liam's on notice now.

***

Almost two weeks have passed since our heart-to-heart, and so far, things are going OK. Liam seems to have been keeping to his gradual alcohol reduction programme and has been far less objectionable as a result.

It's Saturday evening. Sienna has come over and spent most of the day with Liam. This morning, they went for a walk and a pub lunch. I don't know whether Liam used the opportunity to have extra alcohol which wasn't on the schedule, but he seemed reasonably sober when they got home; if anything, it was Sienna who was a bit giggly. Anyway, they've gone to his room now, where they are watching a movie on the small TV he has there. Grace has already gone to bed, and I've no idea when, or if, Sienna's likely to go home tonight. I'm really tired after a tough week at work, so I decide to turn in too.

The volume of the TV emanating from Liam's room is much too high, and the soundtrack is occasionally interrupted by loud peals of laughter. I can't be bothered to go and intervene, though; God knows what I might be interrupting! At least they're having a good time together, and Liam is behaving himself. As far as I know, both Grace and Amelia are managing to sleep, so I just pull a pillow over my ears and try to ignore the noise.

I'm not quite sure whether the noise finally stopped or whether I managed to doze off in spite of it, but I must have been in a deep sleep when the next onslaught of noise shocks me awake. There is a loud shriek, then a flurry of banging and crashing, punctuated by angry shouting.

What the hell is going on? I leap out of bed, wide awake now, and shrug into my dressing gown, hurriedly tying the cord around my waist as I rush towards the door. As I step out into the hallway, I see Liam pushing Sienna roughly towards the top of the stairs. He's fully dressed but she's wearing nothing but her knickers and a loose-fitting sweater.

She's screaming at him to stop, but he bundles her to onto the staircase; it's all she can do to grab the banister and stop herself tumbling down, out of control.

'Go on, bitch ... get OUT!'

She manages to get her balance and rushes down the stairs to escape his onslaught. At the bottom she turns to face him as he follows her down.

'Liam ... PLEASE!'

By now, I'm yelling at him, too, but he ignores both her pleas and mine, charging down the stairs after her and pushing her roughly towards the front door. He grabs the key hanging on the hook alongside the door and tries to insert it into the lock, but he's so drunk that it takes him several seconds to fumble it into place, by which time I'm down there with the two of them.

'LIAM!' I yell, grabbing his shoulder, 'what the hell are you doing?'

He grabs my wrist and casts me aside. 'None of your fucking businesssh!'

Finally, he succeeds in unlocking the door and wrenching it open. He grabs Sienna and pushes her out of the door. 'Go on ... FUCK OFF, BITCH!'

She backs away, wailing, half-naked and barefoot, pleading with him to let her back in. He slams the door in her face.

I lunge forward, summoning all my strength to push Liam aside, and pull the door open. 'SIENNA ... WAIT!' I yell, but she's already through the gate and out into the street.

She casts me a desperate glance, her eyes wide with fear. She shakes her head. 'It's too late,' I hear her cry, 'he's gone completely crazy.'

Suddenly Liam wrenches the door from my hand and slams it shut again. The last thing I notice before the door slams is that she is clutching her phone. *Funny,* I think, *how, for this generation, the instinct is to protect that most precious possession, your phone, no matter how dire the situation.*

I turn to face Liam. 'What the fuck was all that about?' I demand.

'She's a fucking BITCH ... dessherves everything she gets. Leave her to pissh off.'

He's drunk, angry and irrational; there's no point trying to talk to him while he's like this. But right now, my concern is Sienna: she's out there in the street, alone, half-naked at 1a.m.

I grab my phone from the small table near the door and hurriedly tap out a text to Sienna.

Stay in this street – I'm coming for you

Liam is mumbling incoherently as he hangs onto the post at the bottom of the stairs for support.

'You absolute bloody DICKHEAD!' I hiss, as I push past him and bound up the stairs to my room to get dressed.

This is one occasion when my bedtime habit of just flinging my clothes on the chair when I undress has paid off; I don't have to rummage in the drawers or wardrobe for something to wear. I pull on my knickers, jeans and sweater; no time to mess about with my bra. I slip on my shoes and rush back downstairs, grabbing my phone again. There's a new text.

Still here – have called a taxi

I glance through into the living room, where Liam is slumped on the sofa, still muttering gibberish.

I rush out into the street. Sienna has not gone far; she is sitting on the low wall of a neighbour's front garden, sobbing softly.

'Oh, Sienna, I'm so sorry ... what on earth happened?'

She tries to compose herself enough to answer but before she has a chance, I see Liam stumbling unsteadily after us. She jumps to her feet, backing away, holding her hands up in a defensive posture.

'Leave me alone,' she cries.

'Go back Liam ... leave her.'

He is undeterred – still staggering towards her.

'Leave me alone,' she repeats, '... or I'll call the police.'

He takes no notice – still pushing forward as I try to restrain him. She hurriedly taps out 999.

As I jostle with Liam, simultaneously trying to reason with him and hold him back, the taxi shows up. The driver lowers the window, his expression a mixture of puzzlement and unease about the scene he is witnessing.

'Who called for a taxi?

'I did,' says Sienna, stepping towards the car.

Liam shakes himself free from my efforts to restrain him.

'You fuck off mate … 'sno fucking businessh of yourssh. This bitch is my businessh.'

The driver doesn't need telling twice. 'I'm not getting involved in this … sorry.' The window goes up, and the car speeds away, leaving the three of us alone once more.

'LIAM,' I say placing both hands on his chest, trying to hold him back, 'go back inside … you're not helping here.'

He brushes me aside, his angry gaze fixed on Sienna. 'Get out of the fucking way,' he growls, taking an unsteady step towards her.

At that moment, the insistent wail of a police siren interrupts him. 'Wassat?' he mumbles, confusion written all over his face.

'It's the police … now back off.'

The police car slews around the corner and, seconds later, pulls up sharply, with a squeal of tyres. Two officers step out: a man and a woman.

'Alright, what's going on here?' enquires the male officer.

Liam piles right in. 'It's all her fucking fault,' he mutters, raising an accusing finger towards Sienna and taking a step forward.

'Whoah there,' says the officer placing a restraining hand on Liam's chest. 'Now who made the emergency call … was it you, Miss?' He's looking at Sienna, quickly taking in her state of undress and obvious distress.

She nods.

'OK what's your name, Miss?'

'Sienna … Sienna Parvis.'

'OK, Miss Parvis … why don't you get into the car with PC Baker and tell her what has happened.'

The female officer puts a comforting arm around Sienna's shoulders and guides her towards the car.

'Yeah … fuck off, bitch,' adds Liam, unhelpfully, jabbing the air with his finger.

'Liam,' I cry, 'for God's sake shut up … you're making things ten times worse.'

'And you are?' says the officer, turning his attention towards me.

'Madeleine Fisher … I'm his mother.'

'And a fucking ushelesss one at that,' hisses Liam, swaying precariously on his feet and placing a hand on the police car to stop himself falling over.'

His words cut me like a knife, even though I know it's the booze talking.

'OK, Ms Fisher, your son is obviously in no fit state to give us any sort of statement at the moment, so I think we need to get him down to the station to sober up overnight.'

I glance at Liam who is, by now, sitting on the pavement with his back leaning against the car. 'Yes … that's probably best,' I agree.

'I'm going to radio for an ambulance to take him to the station,' says the officer. 'I don't think he should be in the same car with the young lady in his current mood, and in any case, it would be good for the paramedics to check him over.'

'No … you're right, of course. Look, he's not really a bad boy at heart. He isn't normally like this … it's just …' My words tail off; *what can I say?*

'Don't worry, Ms Fisher we'll take care of both of them and call you in the morning. Now where is your house?'

'Just there,' I say, pointing it out.

'OK, well I suggest you go back inside and try to get some sleep. We'll let you know tomorrow if we need you to make a statement.'

Liam appears to have passed out, his head slumped forward on his chest. The officer picks up on my obvious concern.

'Don't worry, we'll take good care of him. Now, go home … get some sleep.'

***

When I get back inside, Grace is anxiously waiting in the living room. 'Mum, are you OK? I saw most of what was going on through the window, but I couldn't leave Amelia on her own.'

Amelia – with all the drama, I'd completely forgotten about her. 'Oh God, is she alright?'

'She's fine … incredibly, she's slept right though it all.'

I shake my head in disbelief.

'What on earth happened to spark such a flaming row between them?' asks Grace.

I sigh. 'I have absolutely no idea. Liam's completely wasted, and Sienna can hardly get a word in edgeways. All I know is he's behaving like an absolute bastard, and she's desperately upset.'

'So what's happening now?'

'I don't really know. They've both been taken to the police station, so I guess we'll find out more tomorrow.'

'Is there anything I can do?' she says, her caring nature shining through.

I smile. *How can I have produced two children who are so, so different?* 'No, there's nothing either of us can do right now. Go back to bed and get some sleep. We'll talk about it tomorrow.'

***

Sleep completely eludes me for the remainder of the night, such is the maelstrom of thoughts whirling round in my head. I have some big decisions to make.

The following morning I'm on my own, sitting in the kitchen, drinking tea, warming my hands around the cup, listening to the silence, waiting for the phone to ring. Amelia has gone on a pre-arranged playdate with her best friend; Grace dropped her off before going to meet a friend herself. I'm still wrestling with what to do next.

The trilling from my phone pierces my consciousness like an ice-cold dagger, jerking me back to the here and now in an instant. It is the call I've been simultaneously waiting for yet dreading.

The lady from the custody centre explains the situation …

Apparently, Sienna was taken to the police station, provided with some temporary clothes, and asked to give a statement, before being driven home to her anxious parents. She does not wish to press any charges against Liam but insists she never wants to see him again for the rest of her life.

So sad, when she has been such a rock for Liam, but I can hardly blame her.

Liam is still in the custody centre. He's sobered up and apologised for his behaviour last night. He can come home now and has named me as the person who will pick him up. They'd like to know when to expect me.

I have steeled myself for what I have to say, but it still doesn't come easily. 'I'm afraid I won't be coming to pick him up.'

'Oh, who will be doing that then?'

'No, you don't understand … I can't have him living with me any longer.'

'Oh, but … well, where is he to go? Who will collect him?'

'I don't know. He's become abusive and potentially violent. I can't cope with him any longer.'

She sounds completely nonplussed. 'But he can't stay here … can't you take him back for a while until you can sort something out? Maybe Social Services could—'

I cut her off. 'Look, I have a young child – my daughter – living at home. I can't risk her safety, even for a short while. I'm sorry, but that's it … you'll have to find somewhere for him to go.'

I hang up, and immediately the tears I have been holding back start to flow. Liam's younger years flash before me: his big blue eyes, his tousled blonde hair, his innocence and unfaltering love. But that child is gone, to be replaced by a young man I don't know or trust living in my house and dictating the rules.

I feel like shit, but what else can I do?

I sit there crying – for how long I have no idea. My world is shattered, and I have no idea what will happen next.

Chapter 64

'Where is he?'

Three hours have passed since that pivotal phone call, and I have heard nothing further. I can't stand it; I have to know what has happened, so I call the custody centre. The voice on the line sounds like the same lady I spoke to earlier.

'So can you tell me where you have sent him?' I ask, after identifying myself.

'Well,' she replies, sounding rather nonplussed by my question, 'we haven't actually *sent* him anywhere.'

'What do you mean … is he still there?'

'No, he's sobered up now, and as the young lady does not wish to press charges, we've released him.'

'Oh … but where has he gone then?'

'I don't know. We had no reason to keep him any longer, so he's gone.'

My stomach performs a flip. 'But don't you have a responsibility to ensure that those you release have a safe place to go?'

For the first time, I detect a hint of irritation in her voice. 'Look, we're the police, not social services. We are here to fight crime, not look after …' – she hesitates, as though choosing her words carefully – 'everyone who gets themselves into difficulties. And we're desperately under-resourced to even do that. I'm afraid you'll have to talk to Liam yourself. He still had his phone with him when he was discharged.'

I'm too numb to argue; I hang up.

I take a few minutes to settle down and compose myself, before messaging Liam.

Are you alright … where are you? Call me.

The next three minutes, which I spend staring at my resolutely silent phone, seem more like thirty. Finally, it chimes.

As if you give a shit. You've made it pretty damn clear that I'm on my own now so, why should you care where I am? Fuck off and leave me alone.

My heart sinks. This is not how it's meant to be. Somehow, I need to help him understand that I still love him. I'm not disowning him, and I'll still look out for him. I just can't have him living with me and the girls any longer, though. We need to talk.

I dial his number, but the ring tone is cut off after a few seconds. I try again, but he won't pick up.

I'm worried sick now. It's February, and the nights are cold. He doesn't even have a change of clothes. Where is he? Does he have any shelter? What about food and money?

I'm wracked with guilt for allowing this situation to come about. I should have talked it through with him, explained why he had to move out, helped him find somewhere to live. Instead, we've parted on the worst possible terms.

I try, again and again that day, to get in touch, but he blocks me every time. I spend another largely sleepless night, turning over in my mind a myriad of what-ifs and regrets. What the hell should I do now?

***

Monday morning, and I can't face going into work; I call in sick. Maybe that wasn't such a good idea, for without the distraction of work, the hours drag by interminably, and there is still no word from Liam. On Tuesday, though, there is finally some news. Megan, my eldest daughter, calls me that afternoon; she has seen Liam and spoken with him.

Apparently, she had gone for a pub lunch with two work colleagues and, by chance, spotted Liam drinking alone in a quiet corner. When her friends were ready to return to work, she had made her excuses and stayed behind to talk to Liam. He wouldn't tell her where he had been staying for the past couple of days, but it turns out that he does have some money, which he has managed to put aside from his meagre state benefits. He has been in touch with the council to see if they can find him some emergency accommodation and has to report to their offices this afternoon for, hopefully, a placement.

The wave of relief which washes over me is palpable. At least he will have some food and shelter, and a little money. Maybe he'll be ready to talk now. I decide to leave it until tomorrow to try contacting him, by which time, hopefully he'll have been settled somewhere.

That night, the cumulative effect of several sleepless nights finally kicks in. The combination of exhaustion and relief results in my first reasonably solid sleep since Liam was arrested.

***

Feeling somewhat refreshed after several hours sleep, I return to work the next day, but my relief is to be short-lived. During my lunch break, I try calling Liam, but he blanks me again. Minutes later, though, I get a call from Megan; she has spoken to Liam again. It turns out that he spent the entire afternoon in the pub yesterday and failed to make it to the council offices before they closed at 5.30p.m. He slept in a shop doorway overnight.

The reality of the situation hits me like a sledgehammer. *Oh Christ! How has it come to this?*

Now I absolutely *have* to speak to him. I'm going to tell him he can come home, sleep in his own warm bed until we can find him some accommodation. I try calling him again: no answer. In desperation I call Megan back; maybe Liam will be more willing to talk to her.

My lunch break is over. I need to get back to work; I've already stretched the patience of my employer to the limit in recent weeks.

***

I don't get a chance to speak with Megan again until the evening, after I have got Amelia settled down for the night. Liam is now refusing to take her calls as well as mine.

Grace has gone out for the evening, so I find myself alone in the living room, the TV playing softly in the background. I'm not registering a word of what is being said, though; I'm sick with worry.

Where will he stay? Will he be safe? Will he have enough to eat? How will he cope?

As I wrestle with these, and hundreds more questions, I keep coming back to the one which really matters most: what can I do? Irrespective of all my regrets for everything which has led up to this situation, I must confront the reality of Liam's situation – and mine. What can I do when he no longer respects me or is even willing to talk to me?

It begins to dawn on me that the only one who can truly help him turn a corner is Liam himself. I've read about others battling addiction and despair, who have to hit rock bottom before they will make the decision to turn their own lives around. Do I need to step back and hope it will be so for Liam? That's a hell of a tough call. I'm his mother and, in spite of everything, I love him. And if he doesn't turn that corner, what then? I can only see one other outcome to the downward spiral which has sucked him in, and it's not one that I can dare to contemplate.

Chapter 65

'Homeless'

Three days later, and I have still heard nothing from Liam. Neither has Megan. The anxiety has become unbearable; I can't concentrate on my work, I can't be bothered to eat properly, and I'm starting to drink too much myself.

Amelia asks me, for the hundredth time, where Liam is. I try to explain that he's not well and needs some time on his own to get better, but she's just too young to understand. She misses her big brother – and I miss him too. I'm clinging to the belief that inside the shell of drunk, vengeful Liam, the other Liam, sober and kind, is still in there somewhere. But, in my darker moments, I am also starting to face the possibility that the worst may have happened.

***

Household chores have become some sort of weird therapy, providing a welcome distraction from the persistent, nagging fear gnawing away at my brain. And so it is today. It's quite late – 11.00p.m. – but rather than go to bed and face the whirlpool of dark thoughts that I know will consume me, I am busy hanging up the laundry.

My phone rings – unusual so late in the evening. I dump the damp sweater I was holding back into the laundry basket and take the call.

'Mum … it's me.'

It takes me a second or two to recognise the breathless, ragged voice on the line. 'Megan … is that you? What's the matter? You sound … odd.'

'Sorry … been running … need a moment.'

'What is it … what's happened.'

'It's Liam … I don't know exactly, but … oh, Mum … I think he's in trouble.'

My stomach lurches. *What the hell this time?* 'Slow down, take a moment, and tell me what you know.'

After a few stuttering sobs, she manages to compose herself sufficiently to tell me. 'My friend, Emily, just called me. She's just bumped into Liam, running towards the train station.'

'The train station … why … where was he going?'

'Well, it was all a bit garbled but, apparently, he was at a party; a bunch of guys there were pretty drunk and harassing some girl, who was really terrified. Seems it all got out of hand, so Liam took it on himself to call the police.'

Well, I thought, *that's a first – someone else is the drunken idiot and Liam's the sensible one.*

'So, what happened?' I urge.

'Well, it seems that the police came, broke up the party and arrested one of the guys, but his friends figured out Liam was the one who shopped them, and they snatched his phone.'

Oh God … his phone … the one hope I have of contacting him.

'So, what's all this got to do with his running towards the station?'

'He slipped away from the party, but he's scared that they're coming after him. Says he needs to get away from the area … something about a friend who will put him up for a while.'

'But who? Where?'

'I don't know … that's why I came running to the station … to try to find him.'

'But no luck?' I ask, rhetorically.

'No. If he was going to catch a train, I guess he's already gone.'

She sounds so desperate, so anxious. I try to reassure and calm her, even though I'm barely any less apprehensive myself.

'OK, don't worry … he'll probably show up shortly, but in any case, I'll take it from here.'

'Sorry, Mum … I tried my best to find him.'

'Don't be sorry, you did everything you could. He'll turn up eventually … he always does. Now, go home and get some sleep. We can talk again tomorrow.'

'OK … bye.'

After I hang up, I sit in silence for several minutes wondering what to do. I have no idea where he's gone, and I have no way of contacting him. I eventually decide to phone the police and report him as a missing person. They listen sympathetically enough but, given all the circumstances, they suggest we leave it for a few days before assuming anything sinister has happened.

It seems all I can do, for now, is sit and wait.

***

Two days later, the police call me back. Liam has been in contact with them to report his phone stolen. He is OK and staying with a friend. However, he doesn't want the address revealed to me, and as he's over twenty-one, they have to respect his wishes.

The sense of relief is overwhelming but is soon overtaken by the anxiety and frustration of being unable to contact him, to tell him I'm sorry, to say he can come home.

Days slip by with no change but, eventually, there is some news.

He's finally relented and broken his silence, though not to me. It is Megan whom he has decided to contact.

Apparently, the police have recovered his stolen phone and returned it to him. So far, so good, but the rest of his news is unrelentingly bad …

It seems that relations with the 'friend' with whom he was staying have broken down. How and why, he didn't exactly say, but the result is that he's been thrown out and is now sleeping rough on the streets. He's been mugged at knife point and had his wallet stolen, so the only things he has left are some cash, which he'd hidden inside his shoe, and his phone, which his assailant somehow missed. In spite of all this, he's still too angry with me to swallow his pride and make contact.

Oh Liam … my boy. How has it come to this? It's all gone way too far.

Megan has urged him to come home, to bury the hatchet and work things out – but to no avail. He just says he'll manage.

When Megan ends the call, I just sit there in a trance – for how long I cannot say – I'm numb, hollow, grief-stricken.

I eventually gather my wits and start to think about what can be done.

At least he still has his phone, so the first thing I do is try calling and messaging him, but he blanks me every time. I call Megan back and ask her to call him and tell him I need talk to him. No luck – he won't even answer her call.

I can only think of one more way to try to reach him, and it will be hit and miss at best …

***

It's Saturday morning. I'm not at work again until Monday and I've arranged for Amelia to have a sleepover at her best friend's house. That gives me most of the weekend to enact my latest, desperate effort to track Liam down without stretching the already-fragile patience of my employer any further.

I'm counting on Liam still being somewhere close to home so I'm starting with the local town centre. I've parked my car in the multi-storey car park and now I begin my quest. It's 7.00a.m – around two hours before the shops will open.

It doesn't take long before I encounter the first little encampment in a shop doorway. At first it just looks like a bundle of rags, but then I can see there's a supermarket basket containing some scraps of food and an open beer can. There's a small dish with a few coins in it and, alongside it, a pair of well-worn sneakers. No sign of any occupant though – until I hear a subdued groan, and the bundle of rags moves slightly. He – or she – is in there somewhere.

My heart is hammering in my chest as I moisten my lips and prepare to speak. 'Hello … are you OK?'

No response, so I try again, a little louder this time. 'Hello … are you OK?'

Still no response, so I risk reaching gently for where I judge the shoulder of this poor soul to be. This time the reaction is instant; a deeply lined face, framed by a shaggy, dark mop of hair and an unkempt beard emerges as its owner props himself up on one elbow. It's not Liam, of course; what would be the chances that the first rough sleeper I found would be him?

He's groggy, disoriented. 'Whassup … whadya want? I ain't done nothing wrong.' His eyes look fearful.

'It's OK, sir … I just wondered if you might have seen this young man anywhere around here.' I show him the photo of Liam which I have brought with me.

He blinks as he tries to focus on the image. 'Nah … looks like a posh boy ta me.'

Posh? If only he knew. I guess it's all relative, though.

He's about to settle back down into his ragged sleeping bag, but I reach into my bag and produce a five-pound-note, holding it towards him. 'Are you sure … can you take another look?'

The man's eyes light up, and he squints as he studies the photo more closely. He shakes his head. 'Sorry Ma'am – I ain't seen him. Maybe worth looking round the back of the big supermarket up there …' – he gestures with a nod of his head – 'a lot of us guys set up round there.'

I manage a small smile as I hand him the banknote. 'Well thank you anyway, sir … good luck.' *Seems a pretty crass thing to say, really. His luck is anything but good.*

He eagerly snatches the banknote and stuffs it into his pocket. 'God bless you Ma'am.'

He reaches out to touch my hand and gently squeezes it. I'm ashamed to say that my first thought is to find some hand sanitiser in case he has transferred something unpleasant to me.

Is this what Liam's life has become also?

With a sigh, I move on, heading for the location he has pointed me towards. Maybe I'll have better luck there …

Chapter 66

'The hostel'

My weekend is unproductive. In spite of the hours spent trawling the streets, doorways, and alleys in the local area, speaking to around a dozen poor homeless men and one desperately sad woman, no information about Liam comes to light. Five more days have passed now, and I am no nearer to finding him. I've been repeatedly calling and messaging him, but still, he won't – or can't – pick up. I'm at my wits' end, sick with worry and fresh out of ideas. But then, out of the blue, comes the following message.

> I know you've been trying to reach me … I don't know why, as you've obviously given up on me, but anyway I thought you should know the council have finally found somewhere for me to stay. So you can forget about me now.

My heart leaps – *he's safe!* But my joy is tempered by the cold, hard-edged tone of his words. *Oh Liam, you are so, so wrong.*

My clumsy fingers fumble with the keypad on my phone as I rush to send a reply – using the first words that come into my head.

> Liam, that's not how I feel at all. I'm sorry for the way things have worked out … we need to talk about it. Where are you staying? Tomorrow's Saturday - can I come and see you?

There is an agonisingly long wait before the phone pings again.

You can come if you like. It's Heathfield's Hostel, Victoria Road
– it's nothing special.

Still so cold and distant, but at least we're talking. I send a brief
reply.

About 10a.m. OK?

The reply is curt.

I guess.

I sit back, relieved but also apprehensive – nervous about seeing my
own son!

***

Heathfield's Hostel is an unremarkable, flat-roofed, utilitarian-
looking building, probably built in the fifties. The metal window
frames are badly rusted, and what passes for a garden outside is
unkempt and overgrown. Still, it's a roof over my son's head.

I message Liam to let him know that I've arrived and head for
the front door. The door is wedged open and there appears to be no
reception or security, so I walk straight in. The first thing that hits
me is the distinctive and overwhelming smell of cannabis hanging in
the air.

Liam appears from the corridor off to the left. He is barely
recognisable: thin, bearded, and scruffy. I try not to display my
shock and instead step forward to offer him a hug. He shrugs me off.

'My room's this way,' he says, indicating the corridor from
which he's just emerged.

I dutifully follow. As we move down the corridor I note, with
some dismay, numerous empty spirit bottles and beer cans stacked
alongside the skirting board. But there's something else, potentially
even more disturbing: the smell of pot is fading, but being replaced
by a strange chemical aroma, overlaid with what smells almost like
burnt rubber or plastic. I have no idea what it is, but the spectre of
more serious drug abuse hangs heavy on my mind.

We stop at the last door in the corridor: number seven.

'Seven,' I say, trying to lighten the mood. 'Always used to be your lucky number.'

He gives a wry smile. 'Not so lucky now.'

He pushes the door open and ushers me inside. The room is small and sparsely furnished. There is a metal-framed single bed, a tall metal locker like those you see in sports changing rooms, a basic folding table and two chairs. Disturbingly, there is a large, two-litre bottle of strong cider on the table. I don't comment.

I take a seat on one of the chairs while Liam perches on the edge of the bed.

'So ... what do you want?' he says.

I have thought long and hard about what I will say to him. I hope it comes out right.

'Liam, I'm your mother, and whatever you might think, I love you. I want you to be well, to be safe.'

He stifles a cynical chuckle. 'Is that why you threw me out?'

Oh shit – this is already unravelling. 'I didn't "throw you out", I just ... oh, look, I'm sorry about ... well, what happened. It's just that ...' *Oh hell, I'm struggling here.*

'Go on,' he goads, 'I'm listening.'

Is he actually _enjoying_ my discomfort here? It's all the encouragement I need to pull myself together and tell it like it is.

'OK ... look I *do* love you, and I *do* care what happens to you. I'd like you to be well, to kick your addiction and get your life back on track, but when you're drunk, you're a different person: you're rude, abusive, and violent. I'm worried for Amelia's safety, and frankly mine and Grace's too.'

'Wow!' he says, expelling a long, slow stream of breath, 'don't hold back then, will you?'

'I'm sorry, but that's the way it is. When you're sober, like right now, you're my son ... the Liam I know ... but when you're drunk, you're a danger to yourself and everyone around you.'

There's a tense silence for several seconds as he digests what I have said.

'So is that what you came here to say? Because if it is—'

I cut him off. 'No, it isn't ... I came to see that you're OK but also to explain that I can't have you living with us long term until you succeed in beating your alcohol addiction.'

'Well, you've already made that clear enough, so I don't know why—'

I interrupt him. 'I know … but I never expected things to get this bad. Look, if you want somewhere to stay while we find you somewhere more suitable than this place, your room is still there for you … as a temporary measure. Longer term, if you can kick your habit, I'd be more than happy to have you back for as long as you like.'

He pauses for several long seconds – then takes a deep breath before replying. 'Thanks, but no thanks. If I'm so bloody dangerous, you don't really want me there, do you?' He doesn't give me time to respond to his question, which is clearly rhetorical anyway. 'And I don't want to be there either … I'm ok here, where the people around me don't judge me.'

His words hit me like a sledgehammer. 'Oh, Liam, I'm not—'

He cut me off, sharply. 'So I guess you should go now … you've said what you came to say.'

'Can't I just—?'

'Bye then.'

He steps over to the door and holds it open, gesturing with a nod of his head that I should leave. I feel drained, empty, lost.

My final words are, 'I'm there for you if you want to talk some more … you know how to reach me.'

***

It's Sunday morning. I barely slept at all last night as I wracked my addled brain trying to find a way to reach him, to repair our shattered relationship. In the end, though, I have concluded that it's too soon; I have to give him some time before trying again. At least, for now, he has a roof over his head and somewhere to sleep, though I'm worried sick that the environment may exacerbate his addiction rather than help him escape it. I can, at least, try to make his stay a little more comfortable.

I spend the next couple of hours packing a suitcase with several changes of his clothes and various toiletries, then another bag with his laptop, his PlayStation, and some cash – which I hope to Christ doesn't get spent on booze.

I try calling him, but he doesn't answer. *Fuck it! I'm going over there anyway.*

I debate whether to take Amelia, but decide against it – I don't know what sort of mood he will be in. My neighbour, Jenny, is happy to look after her, though I don't share with either of them the full story of why I need go out for a couple of hours.

When I arrive at the hostel, I try calling Liam again but, once more, he blanks me. I drag the suitcase and bag from the car and make my way up to the front door which, as the day, before is wedged open. The smell of drugs in the air is even stronger than it was the day before. Undeterred, I move down the corridor to room seven and knock on the door.

'Whoissit?' comes the heavily slurred voice from within.

'It's me … Mum.'

After a few seconds the door opens. Liam is wearing nothing but a pair of shorts; his long, shaggy hair is wild and unruly; he is swaying unsteadily on his feet. He blinks at me erratically, as though trying to focus.

'What the fuck? Waddya want? I told you issa waste of time. I'm sshtaying right here.'

The smell of alcohol on his breath as he utters the words manages to cut though even the drug-fuelled haze in the corridor. It's clear he's in no fit state for any lucid conversation so I keep it short and to the point.

'I've brought some of your things,' I say, depositing the suitcase and bag in the doorway.

He looks down at the case on the floor, blinking stupidly as he dimly registers what it is. 'I didn't ask for any sshtuff.'

'Well, I brought it anyway. Goodbye, Liam … call me if you want to talk.'

Realising that any further discussion is pointless, I turn and leave.

***

Several hours have passed and I've heard nothing from Liam. Amelia has two of her friends over this afternoon, so I have my hands full keeping an eye on them and maintaining the inevitable supply of drinks and snacks. Keeping busy and listening to their laughter as they play is a welcome distraction from the gloomy thoughts which, these days, occupy most of my waking hours – and a lot of my sleeping hours, too.

Grace is out this evening, so once I have got Amelia settled down for the night I am on my own. As I switch on the TV and slump down on the sofa, my phone pings.

Thanks for the stuff, Mum.

A wave of relief courses through me. It's a small step but after we have been on such acrimonious terms recently, it's a very welcome one. Could it be the first tentative step towards repairing our relationship?

I hope so.

Chapter 67

'A narrow escape'

My hopes turn out, once again, to be unfounded.

Months have passed, during which time things have, if anything, become even worse. Liam is barely communicating with me at all, and when he does, his messages are usually angry and hateful. It is clear that the environment in which he is living is desperately unhelpful; alcohol and drug abuse is rife, and I suspect that he is now experimenting with cocaine.

He has started hanging around with down-and-outs, both within the hostel and out in the streets, and is regularly getting arrested for being drunk and disorderly in public.

His health is rapidly deteriorating, too; he's been in and out of hospital and has been told he has acute pancreatitis and the beginnings of liver failure. Despite all this, he won't let me advise him; he still bears a deep grudge against me for excluding him from the family home.

At last, though, something *does* get through to him. Following his discharge from his latest stay in hospital he calls me – something he hasn't done in weeks. The doctors have told him that if he carries on as he is, he will be lucky to make it to thirty. Finally, the reality of his situation has dawned on him and the shield he has built around himself falters; he's ready to listen. For once he appears sober and lucid.

'I don't want to die,' he sobs.

My heart is breaking as the vulnerable soul within the harsh, angry, belligerent young man is revealed. My son is still in there, somewhere.

'We have to get you out of that place, Liam; it's not good for you.'

'I know, but ...' he mumbles.

'Let's try and get you on the waiting list for a housing association flat ... away from all the bad influence around you right now.'

'Do you think I stand a chance of getting one?'

'Well, we'll only know if we try, won't we?'

'I guess ...'

'Come on ... let's do it.'

'Will you help me, Mum?'

My heart melts. 'Of course I will ... and meanwhile, why don't you come home until we can find you somewhere?'

'I don't know about that ... you said yourself that wouldn't be OK.'

Don't push it, Madeleine. 'Well, think about it. Meanwhile I'll look into what we need to do and get any forms and stuff we might need.'

'Thanks, Mum.'

I sit in silence for a while, after hanging up. This is nothing more than a tiny, tentative step towards resolving Liam's situation, and yet, in the context of mending our relationship, it feels like a breakthrough.

***

Four weeks have passed since our phone conversation. Liam's application has been accepted, and he's on the waiting list for a flat. He's decided against coming home while we wait, though. Nevertheless, our relationship has thawed considerably, and we're communicating regularly.

Today is Wednesday, and I've just finished my shift at work. I'm sitting in my car, just about to set off to collect Amelia from school when my phone rings. It's the police custody centre; I recognise the voice of the woman I spoke to last time Liam was in there.

My stomach clenches. *What the hell this time?*

'Miss Fisher? I'm calling about Liam.'

Well, who else would it be about? 'Yes,' I answer, weakly, 'What's happened?'

'I'm afraid Liam has been arrested.'

I feel my shoulders slump as I sigh deeply and try to prepare myself for whatever bad news is about to be delivered.

'What's he done this time?'

'Well, it started with a 999 call from Heathfield's Hostel, where I believe your son is currently staying.'

'Yes, he is ... go on.'

'It seems Liam was very drunk,' – *big surprise there* – 'and someone there feared he was suffering some sort of medical emergency, so they called an ambulance. When they arrived, Liam was incoherent and abusive; he even went as far as threatening the paramedics with a rifle.'

'A rifle! What the ...? He hasn't even got a rifle. Well ... as far as I know, anyway.'

'Well, I don't know where he got it from, but as there was a potential danger to life, we had to despatch firearms officers to the scene.'

I feel the prickle of cold sweat breaking out on my face and neck. *This just can't be.*

'Oh, no ... is he hurt ... is anyone else hurt?'

'No, no ... he's OK ... after a brief standoff, he gave himself up to the officers and handed over the gun. Turns out it wasn't a firearm at all, but a BB gun that just fires pellets. It was realistic enough for the officers to believe it was a genuine firearm, though ... and even a BB gun can cause significant injury to the face and eyes.'

Relief washes over me. *He's stupid ... but unharmed.*

'Oh God! I can't believe he would be so reckless ... I'm so sorry.'

'Well, hardly your fault, Miss Fisher.'

'So what happens to him now?'

'Well, the paramedics seem to know something about Liam's medical history. Taking into account his alcohol addiction and his mental health issues, they don't want to press charges. Now that he's starting to sober up, he seems genuinely remorseful, so he's been let off with just a caution for wasting police time. Under the circumstances, I think he has gotten off very lightly. I think the outcome will be very different if he does something like that again.'

I'll bet ... 'Thank you ... thank you so much.'

'Anyway, he's ready to be discharged ... are you willing to come and collect him this time?'

Oh – 'this time' – she clearly remembers the previous incidents when I was unwilling to collect him. 'Yes,' I reply. 'I have to collect my daughter from school first, but I can be there in about an hour and a half.'

I hang up. *Where on earth do we go from here?*

Chapter 68

'A squandered opportunity'

As is often the case, once he is sober, Liam is full of remorse for the stupidity of his actions. The trouble is, I know full well that it won't last. When he's blind drunk again, or high, or both, what will his next crazy stunt be?

I've tried, once more, to persuade him to come home while we wait for a flat to become available, but he refuses to do so. He argues, quite reasonably, I suppose, that we have no idea how long it will take, and he doesn't want me to take on an open-ended commitment. I think the reasons run deeper than that, though: I think that, deep down, he knows how dangerous he can become; I think he's genuinely concerned for his little sister's safety – and perhaps mine and Grace's too. Underneath it all, my selfless boy is still in there. Meanwhile, though, he's still in that awful place – that den of druggies and boozers. In spite of all evidence to the contrary, I still can't bring myself to accept that my son is one of them.

***

Thursday evening, and we've just finished dinner. Grace is helping me with the clearing up; Amelia's surfing the web, as usual. *I must try and restrict her time online a bit more; heaven knows what she's viewing.*

My phone rings; it's Liam. He sounds excited – and sober. 'Mum, it's come through.'

I don't initially register what he means. 'What has … what do you mean?'

270

'The flat ... they've found me one ... only a few miles from here.'

My heart jumps – a lifeline. 'That's fantastic! When will it be available?'

'Right now – I can go and see it tomorrow.'

'Oh wow! That's great ... look, I'm not working tomorrow ... can I come with you?'

Grace has obviously picked up on my animated tone. She mouths a silent 'What?'.

I cup my hand over the phone and hold it away from my mouth. 'It's Liam ... I'll explain in a moment.'

I return to Liam. 'So, can we go together?'

'Sure ... what time?'

'Er ... let's think ... I'll need to drop Amelia at school first. So can I pick you up around nine-thirty?'

'Yeah, that's fine ... the housing association rep says she can meet us with the keys any time tomorrow. I'll let her know we'll be there about ten.'

'Great ... see you tomorrow.'

I hang up and give Grace the good news; she seems almost as excited as I am. She knows full well the stress I am under with Liam's current situation, and she worries about me. Such a lovely, considerate daughter.

***

The flat is not what I had hoped for. It is a one-bedroomed apartment in a large block of flats. Right now, it's an empty shell; quite small, with living, dining area, and kitchen, all in one room. Only the bedroom and a tiny bathroom are separate. Furthermore, it's cold and damp, with only one small window, admitting very little natural light. It's also badly in need of decoration. I try not to show my disappointment, but Liam has obviously seen it written all over my face.

'Come on Mum, it's not so bad. We can easily do it up, and once it's had some heat on for a while to get rid of the damp, and we've got some furniture in, it could be quite cosy.'

What's with the 'we' bit, I think, with some trepidation. But it soon becomes clear that he's not referring to me: he's hoping to lure Sienna back with the prospect of a shared project and somewhere they can both live together. I'm doubtful about this – I think he's well and truly burned his boats with Sienna – but who knows? In any event, I'm not about to say anything to dampen this rare show of optimism and enthusiasm. At least it gives him something to focus on other than his drinking, and moving here will get him away from all those malign influences evident in Heathfield's Hostel. Maybe this is the opportunity for him to sort out his life.

Let's hope she's willing to give it a try, I think. If *she dashes his hopes this time, I dread to think where he'll end up.*

It's just two days later that Liam gives me the news that I'd barely dared hope for. Against the odds, Sienna has agreed to help him with the renovation of the flat. However, she's making no definite commitment to resume their relationship, let alone move in with him, until she can see that he's seriously cutting down on his drinking, and they have a realistic prospect of building a life together. He's confident he can win her over. I'm hoping against hope that he's right.

Don't screw this up Liam.

***

But he does – it's clear from the outset that things are not going well, and it's less than three weeks before it all falls apart completely.

I'm at work when I get the call; it's around 10.15a.m. The woman introduces herself as Maria, but she really doesn't need to, because I immediately recognise the voice: it's the woman at the custody centre. Although I have never met her, I'm beginning to feel I know her. My whole body slumps in resignation.

'It's about your son, Liam.'

No shit. I think, as I grab the nearest chair and sit down, ready to absorb whatever is coming next. 'What's he done this time?' I sigh.

'I'm afraid he was arrested yesterday evening following reports of a disturbance in his flat. It seems he had a flaming row with his girlfriend and threw her out on the street.'

A dead weight descends in the pit of my stomach. *Oh, Liam ... won't you ever learn?*

Maria continues. 'A neighbour called the police; when they arrived, Liam and his girlfriend were still arguing in the street. Your son was very drunk indeed and abusive towards our officers. The young lady was extremely distressed.'

'Oh ...' is all I can think of to say. I'm too numb to come up with anything else.

'We've kept him in overnight ... he has sobered up now.'

'I'm sorry ... I thought he was getting ...' *Oh, what's the point of trying to explain?* 'I really don't know what to say ...'

'We took the young lady back to her parents' home last night and called her this morning. She does not wish to press charges, but she doesn't want your son anywhere near her ever again.'

My worst fears for the fate of a reconciliation with Sienna have been realised.

'So what's the situation now?' I ask.

'Well, although the young lady was extremely distressed by Liam's behaviour and abusive language, she doesn't wish to report any actual physical violence. She's content to let the matter lie. As far as our officers are concerned, they are well used to dealing with drunk and disorderly behaviour, and abusive language is, to them, like water off a duck's back. Since he didn't cause any actual harm or damage to persons or property, it's been decided to release him without charge.'

'Oh ... thank you,' is my emotionless response.

'He's been very lucky,' she continues, her tone hectoring now, 'to get away with just a caution, but you have to understand that if he carries on like this, he *will* end up being charged with a criminal offence. He's taking up a great deal of police time and public money.'

I know, I know, you self-righteous bitch ... can't you understand he's ill?

I'm too drained to pick a fight so I roll over. 'I know ... I understand.'

'Anyway,' she says, 'he's ready to be released now. Can you come and collect him?'

'Well, it's difficult ... I'm at work.'

'Well, he has no money on him, and we're not going to waste yet more police time and money by taking him home.'

My God, I could happily strangle her. I have no energy to protest, though. 'I'll try to get an extended lunch break – will it be OK to collect him about 1p.m?'

Her exasperated sigh is clearly audible. 'Very well ... no later though.'

'I'll be there.'

I hang up, depleted and exhausted. *When will it ever end?*

Chapter 69

One year later

'Mark'

The final break-up with Sienna marked the start of Liam's descent into an even more hellish state than ever. His drinking has now accelerated to unprecedented levels, and his health has rapidly deteriorated. The nerves in his hands and feet have been affected, and he can no longer walk unaided. Consequently, he never leaves his flat, except on those increasingly frequent occasions when he has to be carted off in an ambulance. His 'normal' day – if you can call it that – is to sit in bed most of the day drinking vodka, which he orders online. He is not eating anything like a proper diet: mostly, he just rips open a loaf of bread – also ordered online – and eats the middle without butter or any accompaniment. The rest is cast aside and adorns the floor of the flat as it goes gradually stale and mouldy. His weight is plummeting, and he looks absolutely skeletal. The flat has frequently become almost uninhabitable: filthy dirty and reeking of urine, vomit, and decay.

I'm doing what I can – of course I am – in spite of everything, he's still my son. I clean the place once a week, but it always descends back into squalor within days. I cook him a proper meal when I can, but he invariably brings it up, adding to the filth in the flat. I do his washing once a week, but it's barely enough, given the rate at which he soils his things.

His memory is completely shot, so even when I've spent hours with him, he often forgets that I've been; then he calls me the very same day to complain that I've neglected my visits. I've resorted to taking selfies of the two of us together and sending them to him after each visit to jog his memory.

When I can't get there in person, I call him practically every day, but he often forgets those calls too and calls me back to scold me.

It's so, so difficult. I have to work, look after Amelia, do the school run, and maintain my own household. I'm just about at breaking point.

But then, Mark walks into my life.

***

It happens, bizarrely enough, during my weekly supermarket shop. Not sure if I've mentioned it previously, but I'm not particularly tall – five feet two inches to be precise. Consequently, I sometimes have difficulty reaching items on the highest shelves. On this occasion, I'm stretching for a bottle of household floor cleaning liquid – I use a lot of that these days!

'Can I help you with that?' comes the soft, warm, male voice from behind me.

I turn to see the smiling face of a tall man, probably in his mid-fifties. He's good looking, in a rugged sort of way, with sparkling blue eyes and neatly trimmed grey hair. I feel an involuntary flush.

'Oh, thank you,' I say, standing aside to allow him to reach the bottle. 'Perils of being vertically challenged.'

As soon as I hear the words coming out of my mouth, I realise how crass they sound; all of a sudden, I'm a tongue-tied teenager.

He laughs. 'Don't know why they stack stuff up so high … there are plenty of women who are a lot shorter than you.'

'I guess …' I reply, feeling stupidly self-conscious. 'Well, thanks for your help.'

'You're welcome,' he says, flashing a warm smile as he places the bottle in my trolley. 'Nice to meet you.'

And then he is gone.

Ten minutes later, I'm pushing my trolley through the car park. As I approach my car, I can't help noticing it's even more filthy than usual; with everything else on my mind, keeping the car clean isn't exactly high on my list of priorities. Even so, it really is just *too* disgusting to leave. I decide to invest seven pounds with one of the hand car wash guys who operate in the car park, although how much of that sum he will actually keep is debateable, given the sinister, lurking presence of the 'supervisor' in the background. I hand over the money and head back to the coffee shop in the supermarket for a well-earned break, while the hapless guy with the bucket and sponge battles the baked-on bird crap and mud adorning my car.

Just a few minutes after I set down my pot of tea and generously sized slice of carrot cake, I hear a vaguely familiar voice. 'Mind if I join you? There don't seem to be any empty tables just now.'

I look up to see my tall, top-shelf helper holding a tray and eying the chair opposite me.

'No ... I mean yes ... please do.'

He takes his seat with a weary sigh. 'I'm Mark,' he says, extending his hand.

'Madeleine,' I reply, as I accept his handshake.

'I always like to have a sit-down and a coffee when I've finished shopping,' he says.

Does he? I think. *Did he really just happen to arrive at the exact moment just after I did and when all the other tables were occupied? Is it possible that he has engineered this situation as an excuse to talk to me?*

Suddenly, I'm acutely conscious of my appearance: my hair's a mess, and I paid only scant attention to my makeup before stepping out this morning. And my clothes: jogging pants, trainers, and sweatshirt are hardly the height of elegance. Nevertheless, it looks as though this rather attractive man has made the effort to make my acquaintance. Well, I'm not about to pass up the opportunity for some pleasant male company as a welcome interlude in the unremitting stream of crap which my life has become.

And so we talk ... and talk ... and talk. He's just so *easy* to talk to. Turns out he's a retired Detective Inspector in the police, recently divorced, and finding new things with which to fill his life. He's now devoting much of his time to charitable work, helping unfortunate souls who have lost their way in life. He works with the homeless, the destitute and, significantly, those addicted to drugs or alcohol.

When I tell him about Liam's predicament, he's only too eager to offer his help.

By the time we finally part company, having exchanged contact details, over an hour has passed. I've no way of knowing whether

Mark's involvement – if indeed he even goes through with it – will make a significant difference to Liam's situation. God knows, I've had too many let-downs in the rollercoaster ride named Liam to harbour unfounded optimism. And yet … there is a certain something about this man.

When I climb back into my car, I'm feeling so much better than when I stepped out of it a couple of hours earlier. At the least, maybe I've found someone with whom to share my problems, and you know what they say about a problem shared …

Chapter 70

'A helping hand'

Mark is as good as his word; he wants to meet my son. When I call Liam to say there's someone I'd like him to meet, he sounds fairly coherent – which is unusual these days. He is, however, rather guarded about the idea, clearly suspicious of my motives. When I explain that Mark is a friend who genuinely wants to help, he eventually agrees to meet him. Whether he'll remember that when the time comes is another matter …

***

The following day, as we approach the door to Liam's flat, my heart is hammering furiously. *What will we find inside? What state will Liam be in? Will he be openly hostile to the intervention of this stranger? Will Mark turn and run, realising he has bitten off more than he can chew?*

I knock on the door, calling Liam's name. No answer. I try again. Still no answer.

I have a key to the flat, so I unlock the door and gingerly push it open. The stench is overpowering. Liam is sprawled on the bed, motionless, mouth lolling open. An empty vodka bottle lies on its side alongside him.

'Liam!' I cry, rushing forward, fearing the worst.

No response, so I grab his shoulder and shake it hard. To my relief he utters a guttural groan and his eyes flicker.

'Whassup? Whassamatter?' He heaves himself up onto one elbow, blinking in confusion.

'Liam, are you alright?

'Yeah … why'd you wake me up?'

I ignore the question, instead going over to the one small window in the flat and opening it wide. 'It smells disgusting in here.'

'Issnot that bad … wassup, anyway?'

'I've brought Mark to come and meet you. Remember? We talked about it yesterday.'

I turn around, half expecting to find an empty space with Mark having run a mile, but he's still there. He steps forward extending his hand towards Liam, who eyes him suspiciously but eventually offers a rather weak-looking handshake.

'Pleased to meet you, Liam. Your mum's told me all about you.'

Liam utters an ironic chuckle. 'Bloody train crash, huh?'

If Mark is shocked by what he has seen, he doesn't show it. 'I know you're battling some difficult issues, but your mum's here to help you and I'd like to think I can help too.'

And so the discussion begins. Against the odds, Liam shows little hostility to this stranger who has been thrust upon him, so I leave the two of them to chat, while I try to restore some semblance of order and cleanliness to the flat. It is more than two hours later that we finally leave. The flat looks and smells rather better, and Liam has managed to eat a cheese and ham sandwich and a bowl of soup without throwing up. More importantly, he seems to have cautiously accepted the offer for Mark to help me to help him try to find a road to recovery.

All in all, it's about the best I could have hoped for in a first meeting.

***

Mark offers to buy me lunch while we discuss the outcome of his first meeting with Liam. We find a table in a quiet corner of a local pub.

Once we have got some drinks and placed our food order, I ask the question. 'So what do you think?' As soon as I say it, I realise that's a very big, and open-ended question. I'm apprehensive about how he may respond.

Mark purses his lips and expels a long, steady stream of breath. 'Well, from everything you've told me, and what Liam himself has said, it's clear that you've both been navigating one hell of a difficult journey. To be honest, I just don't know how you've coped while working, looking after Amelia and all the other pressures you're juggling.'

I stifle a sigh. 'Well, I don't really have an option, do I?'

He smiles. 'I guess not. Look, I'm not sure I would have done anything differently, but maybe if we work together, we can make some headway.'

'You think so?'

'Maybe. Look, you've done everything you possibly can in the time you have available after going to work, providing for your daughters, and running your home. You've had no-one with whom to share the burden; no single mum could have done more. But there are two of us now, and *I* don't have to go to work. If we join forces, we surely stand a better chance of success.'

Hope surges within me. He hasn't actually suggested any concrete steps, but his positivity is infectious.

'I do hope so. I'm just so exhausted … the prospect of some help to share the burden is just …' I feel the tears welling up; I hardly really know this man, yet he fills me with an optimism I had long forgotten. 'I can't thank you enough.'

He smiles. 'So let's make a plan.'

I look at him, expectantly.

He's clearly already given the matter quite a bit of thought. He continues, 'From what you have both told me, the closest you have come to success has been when working with CLASP, the addiction charity, right?'

'Well … yes, I suppose so, but when Liam relapsed after rehab, they made it pretty clear that they weren't prepared to sink more money and resources into his case. I think they consider him a lost cause.'

He places his hand on top of mine on the table, shaking his head. 'I don't believe anyone is a "lost cause". It so happens that I know a couple of the people in CLASP through working with a young girl I was trying to help a year or so back. Do you know Felicity Hatfield?'

'Well, yes, I do. She was on the panel which approved Liam's admittance to the detox and rehab programme last time.'

'OK, well why not let me go and talk with Felicity, explain that we're now working together on Liam's case and determined to get him sober. Maybe she'll relent and offer some further help.'

'You think so?' I feel like a person drowning who has just been thrown a lifebelt

'I don't know,' he says, 'but it can't hurt to try.'

'No, it can't,' I smile.

'OK, I'll do that. Now, meanwhile, it's clear that Liam isn't really coping with living on his own.'

'You can say that again.' I say, stifling a wry chuckle. 'You saw the state that things get to when he's on his own.'

'Yes, I did. Look, I know you're going round there as often as you can, but how often is that, typically?'

I think for a moment. 'Probably about twice a week on average, I suppose.'

'OK, well here's what I was thinking. I had the impression that, after a bit of initial wariness, Liam took to me reasonably well.'

'Oh, he did … he likes you.'

'Well, why don't I drop in on him on the days you can't make it?'

'What … every day?'

'If he's OK with that … on the days you can't go. Maybe I can encourage him to adopt some sort of daily routine to keep things more in order. I've found that simple things like that can help give a bit of purpose to people whose life has gone off the rails.'

'You'd do that for him?'

'As long as he doesn't find it too intrusive.'

The wave of emotion which engulfs me is overwhelming. Without even thinking about what I am doing, I stand up, move around the table, and kiss him.

At which point, the barmaid turns up with our meals. 'Er … should I wait a moment? I can …'

I feel my cheeks flush. 'No, it's fine … thank you.'

Chapter 71

'A lifeline'

Felicity Hatfield comes good. The first thing she does is to send a nurse – Kayleigh – to assess Liam's physical condition. She is clearly shocked by what she finds.

His weight has dropped to a skeletal forty-eight kilograms; he can't walk more than a few steps unaided; and at times, he suffers from uncontrollable tremors and severe nosebleeds.

Kayleigh's response to what she has seen is brilliant! She recognises the urgency of Liam's situation and promises to push for Liam to be given another chance at residential detox and rehab. Meanwhile, she arranges for him to receive meal replacement drinks which will be less likely to be rejected by his ravaged digestive system, until he can be gradually weaned back onto regular meals. She also undertakes to visit Liam at least once per week to administer vitamin injections and check on his condition.

I am just *so* grateful for the help that this young woman is giving to my son.

***

Just over two months have passed since Kayleigh's first visit. During that time there has barely been a single day in which Liam has not been visited by Kayleigh, Mark, or me. His physical condition has improved a little, and the flat is at least habitable. But he's barely cut down on his drinking at all; every time he tries, he suffers more debilitating seizures. He is desperately in need of professional help, a point which Kayleigh, Mark, and I keep determinedly emphasising to Felicity Hatfield.

Eventually, our combined entreaties bear fruit. I can barely contain my joy and relief when we get the message that Liam is to be given another chance at residential detox and rehab!

The detox, lasting one to two weeks depending on his tolerance of the alcohol reduction regime, will be at a nearby hospital. We may be allowed to visit him during this period, subject to his being well enough to receive visitors. The subsequent rehab programme will last at least eight weeks, and may have to be even longer, given Liam's history of relapse. *No-one* wants to see him fail yet again. The nearest rehab unit capable of handling such a challenging case, and with available capacity, is over a hundred miles away. But as visiting will be strictly limited anyway, the distance is not really an issue.

Detox is due to start in just two weeks. I'm simultaneously excited and apprehensive. With help and support from me, Kayleigh and Mark, and the expertise of the medical professionals who will supervise his recovery programme, surely Liam has a fighting chance this time. And yet … so many times in the past, my hopes have been dashed. I can hardly dare to believe.

*　*　*

If things are looking more hopeful for Liam now, then he's not the only one. For months and years, I have felt that I'm battling alone to try to help my son beat his addiction, but now I have allies.

Kayleigh has been like a breath of a fresh air. Her unalloyed joy at learning Liam is to be given another chance at detox and rehab seems almost as boundless as mine. She's promised to follow his progress every step of the way. We've become good friends now; although she's some twenty years younger than me, we're bound together in common purpose.

And Mark … he's admitted now that he engineered our meeting in the supermarket coffee shop because he found me attractive and hoped to win at least a dinner date, although when I think back to my dishevelled state that day, I can't help but wonder why! But there is no doubt whatsoever that his interest in helping Liam is completely sincere; he's such a caring and compassionate person. Could I have got this far without his help? I don't know, but I would never have given up trying.

Anyway, it probably won't surprise you to learn that Mark and I are lovers now. Where our relationship goes in the future, and how it might be affected by the outcome of Liam's recovery programme is something I just can't predict. For now, though, Mark and I are happy with each other's company and united in our desire to see Liam beat his addiction and return to full health.

Chapter 72

'So near yet so far'

I have never known two weeks to pass so slowly. Liam's health continues to deteriorate. He is dazed and confused, seemingly unable to distinguish hallucination from reality. Most of the time he doesn't even remember that he's about to embark on another cycle of detox and rehab. He is suffering repeated nosebleeds, and sometimes complete blackouts. It's almost as though, even as help is just around the corner, he's given up completely. The flat is impossible to keep clean, the rancid combination of blood, vomit, and urine rendering all our best efforts next to hopeless.

It's clear that he can't be left alone for even a single day at a time, so Mark and I have stepped up our visits as much as we can. Given my work commitments, and the patience of my employer already stretched almost to breaking point, Mark is shouldering much of the burden. Every day, he takes round meals which I have prepared and heats them in the microwave oven which I bought. Sadly though, Liam often brings what he has eaten straight back up, adding to the squalor. By the time Mark has attended to Liam's needs, collected up the empty bottles strewn across the floor, cleaned up, and restored some vestige of habitability to the flat, he is spending several hours every day there. And yet he sticks with it …

Two weeks become three … three weeks become four … four weeks become five. We are all just about at breaking point. I'm now calling Felicity Hatfield almost every day. She is very apologetic as she tries to explain the various competing pressures the charity is juggling but I'm no longer listening, and I can sense she is becoming exasperated with my increasingly fractious tone. Mark is trying his best to keep things on an even keel, calming me down when I'm fit to explode and calling Felicity to keep her onside. Meanwhile, Liam is descending deeper and deeper into the suffocating pit which is enveloping him.

The whole thing just feels like it's unravelling.

***

It's Wednesday morning, I've just arrived at work, trying my best to focus on the day ahead and, once again, putting my trust in Mark to deal with the daily grind of caring for Liam. *How long will his patience endure?* I wonder.

My thoughts are interrupted by the ping of a text message arriving on my phone. Wearily, I open the message; I need to read it twice before it registers properly with my addled brain. Liam is booked into the hospital to start detox this coming Monday!

Five days! We just need to hang in there for five more days. I call Mark, who is just about to go round to Liam's; the relief in his voice is palpable as he digests the news. We decide that Mark won't say anything to Liam during his visit this morning, reasoning that it will be best if we are both there together when we deliver the good news and try to explain what will happen. We agree to go together this evening.

I try to focus on my work for the rest of the working day, but my mind is elsewhere. My joy and relief at the prospect of another round of detox and rehab are tempered by waves of trepidation and doubt. *Will it really work this time?* I have to believe; if not, how can I give my son the help and support he needs to tackle the forthcoming battle?

The day seems interminable, but finally, I am able to collect Amelia and go home. Mark is already there, waiting for me. We haven't yet taken the significant step of moving in together but we both have keys to each other's homes.

Amelia is about to scamper off to her room for her customary routine of homework followed by a screen-time fix before dinner, but first I want to give her the news about Liam.

She listens carefully before delivering her judgement. 'But isn't that just the same as what happened before? Why should it work any better this time?'

The last thing I need right now is a twelve-year-old reinforcing all my doubts and threatening my resolve.

Mark rescues me. 'Well, it is similar to what was done before, Amelia, but we're all *determined* to make it work this time. Liam won't come home until everyone is completely sure that he's well again. And this time your mum has Kayleigh and me to help her support him.'

A puzzled frown creases her face as she takes a few seconds to digest this assessment. 'I guess ...'

'And ...' adds Mark, '*you're* so much more grown-up now, so I'm sure you'll be helping, too.'

She still doesn't look entirely convinced but has evidently decided to decline any further analysis of the situation. 'OK – I will. Can I go on my iPad now?'

'What about homework?' I enquire.'

'Done it!' she declares, triumphantly. 'Miss Parkins was off sick, so we had a free period this afternoon; I did it then.'

'OK then,' I smile. 'I'll call you when dinner's ready.'

***

Grace offers to clear up the dinner things so that Mark and I can get over to Liam's as soon as possible. We gratefully accept her offer and make our way over there straight after dinner.

Despite Mark's best efforts this morning, the flat is an absolute tip again, and Liam is completely off his head. He's clearly been drinking heavily and is barely coherent. We do our best to explain what is about to happen, but he just doesn't grasp what we are saying. In the end, we decide to just help him into bed and give the flat yet another clean up as he sleeps it off.

It's another three hours before we finally get home. Grace and Amelia have both gone to bed. I suggest Mark stays over as it's so late, but he says he has things to do in the morning and decides to go home. I'm too tired to enquire what 'things to do' means. It's not often he declines an invitation to share my bed, but it's not exactly been an ordinary day. I'm shattered, and I'm sure he is, too.

Five more days ... no, more like four now, I guess. It doesn't sound like much, does it? Yet with Liam's condition worsening with every passing hour and day, I am wracked with anxiety about whether he will even make it. We're so very close now, but those four days seem to stretch out ahead of me like an eternity.

Chapter 73

'The wait is over'

In the event, the four days pass quickly, even though my thoughts are constantly dominated by anxiety about Liam. There is, of course, the usual constant round of tidying and cleaning the flat, as well as caring for Liam, who is in no fit state to care for himself. On top of that, we have to prepare and pack for him what could be a very long stay away from home – if his squalid quarters can even be called 'home'. As I try to sort out what I should pack for him, it becomes evident that many of his clothes are ruined, either by dampness or various unidentified and unsavoury-looking stains. I spend most of Saturday shopping for new things for him. By Sunday evening I finally have everything packed and ready – or at least, everything I can think of.

***

The first glimmers of dawn announce that Monday has finally arrived. I don't really need to get up just yet; Mark is not due to get here for another hour and a half. However, I hardly slept at all last night, and I can't see myself suddenly being able to do so now, so I drag myself out of bed and pull back the curtains. The bruised sky is an amazing mix of colours: deep purple-black clouds, suffused, in places, by an orange glow, interspersed with the first patches of watery blue. Kind of reflects my muddled mix of emotions. I take a few seconds to absorb the view before setting about preparations for the day ahead.

Mark and I arrive at Liam's around 8.15a.m. He is due to be admitted at 9.30a.m. The hospital is nearby, so we should have plenty of time.

A gentle knock on the door evokes no response so we let ourselves in; Liam is fast asleep. We wake him gently and remind him about his hospital appointment; he smiles but has absolutely no recollection of what is to happen today.

By 9.00a.m. we are ready to go, but Liam is so unsteady on his feet that we have to support him, propping him up either side, which isn't easy, given that Mark is a full twelve inches taller than me. It must make an amusing spectacle for anyone who may be watching this lopsided, six-legged ensemble shuffling towards the car! At least we'll have access to a wheelchair when we get to the hospital.

On arrival, they show us to a side room, where, Kayleigh, the nurse from CLASP, is waiting. Liam still doesn't seem to grasp what is going on, but when he sees Kayleigh's smiling face he seems immediately to relax. Those two really seem to have established a bond. What a lovely young woman.

There are two other nurses present, who introduce themselves as Sandra and Holly. They explain that they will be Liam's primary carers during his detox, with Kayleigh visiting daily and acting as the link between the hospital and CLASP. They run through the detox process with us – superfluously in my case, but perhaps useful for Mark.

I explain that I am a nurse myself and tell them about our experience of previous detoxes and Liam's propensity for severe seizures if the process is rushed. Sandra, the older of the two hospital nurses, assures me that they have plenty of experience of managing such detoxes and will take utmost care not to withdraw the drugs too quickly.

I feel bad, talking with strangers about Liam like this as though he's not even in the room, but the presence of Kayleigh, who is gently holding his hand and soothing him, is so comforting for Liam that he remains calm and unperturbed. To be honest, he's so completely out of it that I don't think he's even registered that he's the subject of the discussion.

The doctor who will be supervising Liam's detox turns up. It turns out that I already know him: his name is Matthew; he's the father of one of Amelia's school friends and a really nice man. He speaks to Liam in calm, reassuring tones, explaining what will be happening over the coming days. I don't think Liam really grasps any of it, but he seems to accept the doctor readily enough.

Having established an initial relationship with Liam, Matthew turns his attention to me and Mark to answer any questions we may have, but I've been through it all before and have discussed it endlessly with Mark, so we have very few.

He writes up Liam's medication plan and hands it to Nurse Holly before leaving. She administers the first dose of chlordiazepoxide there and then, followed by infusions of vitamins and sedatives. Before long, Liam has drifted off to sleep.

Nurse Sandra turns to me to me. 'OK … I think you can leave Liam with us now; we'll take good care of him.'

I'm so reluctant to go, to leave my boy to face what I know will be an incredibly tough withdrawal process, but I know it's time to let go and place my trust in the professionals.

'Can we come and see him tomorrow?' I ask.

She seems initially reluctant but, perhaps cognisant of my anxiety, eventually agrees. 'Call first though, so that we can judge whether he's in the right condition to accept visitors.'

'Thank you. Look, when he's settled on the ward, can you leave this with him, please?'

I hand her a small card; on it is printed the Alcoholics Anonymous version of the well-known Serenity Prayer.

God, grant me the serenity to accept the things I cannot change, the courage to change the things I can, and the wisdom to know the difference.

It's something which Liam was introduced to during his previous rehab; it seems to resonate with him and give him some comfort. He often recites it, even though it's often jumbled when he's in one of his incoherent states.

The nurse smiles as she slips it into her uniform pocket, without reading it. 'I will.'

And so it begins. Mark and I say our goodbyes and turn to leave.

Be strong and stay safe my boy. Get through this and get well. I'll be back tomorrow and with you every step of the way.

Chapter 74

'Detox'

I have booked a week's holiday to coincide with Liam's first week of detox. It is stretching the already-threadbare forbearance of my employer even further, but I know that, if I were at work, I would not be able to concentrate on my duties properly. When I suggest this could potentially put my patients' welfare at risk, they agree to grant my request. I resolve to visit Liam every day ... assuming the hospital will let me.

Day one Now I understand why they were reluctant for me to visit during the early stages of detox. Liam looks and sounds awful. His thin, bony face, covered in straggly facial hair, looks years older than the young man to whom it belongs. His eyes are tinged with yellow: something I hadn't noticed before. He is drifting in and out of consciousness, and when he *is* conscious, he is rambling and incoherent. The nurse assures me that in cases of severe addiction these things are not unusual in the early stages of withdrawal. I stay for around two hours, feeling more and more despondent with every minute that passes.

I hardly sleep at all that night.

Day two Mark comes with me today; it helps to have someone with whom to share the burden. It's just as well, because Liam is no better: a mere shell of the person he should be. As I become increasingly discouraged about his condition, Mark is there to remind me what we had been told: that things would get worse before getting better. Nevertheless, I'm wracked with fear and anxiety.

Once again sleep eludes me for most of the night. It is only sheer exhaustion which eventually drags me into the welcome oblivion of sleep, though not until almost dawn, and then only for an hour or two.

Day three I detect the first tentative signs that we may be approaching some sort of turning point. He is conscious for longer periods, though still talking gibberish much of the time. Nevertheless, there are moments of lucidity, and a little of his memory seems to be returning.

I am further buoyed up when Kayleigh shows up, and Liam immediately greets her with a smile.

Suddenly, he utters his most coherent sentence since arriving at the hospital. 'Hi Kayleigh. Want to come with Mum and me down to the Costa shop?'

I am astonished and delighted in equal measure. I didn't think he even knew of the existence of a Costa Coffee shop in the hospital. Kayleigh and I exchange a hope-filled glance.

'Yeah … let's do that,' she says.

Unfortunately, his physical body has not kept up with the meagre progress of his mind: when we try to help him out of bed, his legs will not support him. We help him into the hospital wheelchair alongside his bed and set off for the Costa shop.

His brief period of lucidity, however, seems to desert him as swiftly as it had arrived; by the time we get down to the coffee shop his conversation is, once again, sporadic and muddled. Nevertheless, he consumes half a cup of coffee without vomiting and seems to enjoy our company.

It's progress!

Day four After yesterday's hopeful signs, today turns out to be so difficult. Apparently, he fell out of bed last night, dazed and confused. He dragged himself to the door to get help, not even knowing where he was. Even now, he is restless and bewildered, and his conversation just doesn't make sense. I immediately recognise the signs from the experience of his previous detox programme: they are reducing his dosage of chlordiazepoxide too quickly. I stay with

Liam until he drops off to sleep but then ask for a meeting with the doctor, Matthew.

To his credit, Matthew interrupts what he was doing and, just thirty minutes later, I am sitting with him; the two nurses, Sandra and Holly; and the ever-caring Kayleigh.

When I relate my observations of the last few days and explain how I had seen the same pattern during his previous detox, Matthew endorses my suspicion that the rate of reduction of Liam's medication is perhaps more than his body can cope with.

'OK,' said the doctor. 'Look I know it's tough, but to be honest, it always is. I'm reluctant to increase his dose at the moment, as his body may then crave more, leading to a backsliding in his progress. I suggest we hold the current dose for two or three days and see if his body will learn to tolerate the current level of medication before resuming further reduction in dosage.'

I am so relieved that he has taken on board my concerns, but now I have another. 'Thank you, Doctor' – I didn't want to address him by his first name in front of his colleagues – 'but that gives us another problem. He won't be fully detoxed by the date he's due to go into rehab, and they won't take him until he is.' I'm starting to panic now, as I can see it all unravelling.

Kayleigh jumps in, 'I'll talk to them and see if they can hold his start date open for a few days longer until he's ready.'

'Thank you,' I say, 'but won't that cost more?'

'I'll talk to Felicity and see what we can do.'

A wave of relief courses through me. 'Thank you so much,' I say. *I really owe this girl.*

Day five Liam seems rather better today. Perhaps the slowing down of his detox is already having an effect. He is much more lucid and wants to go walking again. I decide to try for the hospital restaurant; it's a bit further than Costa, but there is a handrail along the corridor which he holds onto while I support him from the other side. It's slow progress, but we make it without mishap – only to find the restaurant is closed! There is nowhere to sit and take a rest, so I suggest we go to Costa again. However, this is downstairs and back along the long corridor. I'm really tired, but Liam is up for it.

It turns out to be a stretch too far. When we get to the staircase Liam grabs the handrail and takes some of his weight with his arm across my shoulders. It's too much though: about halfway down, his legs buckle, and we both end up half-sitting, half-standing on the stairs as he hangs on desperately to the handrail. *What the heck do we do now?* I think.

As I glance around, looking for help, a nurse appears at the top of the stairs. She swiftly comes to our aid.

'Wait there, I'll get you a chair,' she says, easing Liam down so as to sit on the stairs.

She disappears for a minute or two, before arriving with a wheelchair at the bottom of the stairs. She helps me to get Liam down the remaining stairs and into the chair. He is panting furiously, his energy completely spent.

'Where do you need to get to?' she asks.

'Oh, we'll be fine now,' I reply. 'It's not far ... thank you so much for your help.'

'Well, don't try to do too much.'

'We won't. Thank you again.'

Day six Liam seems much better today. He is lucid and coherent in his speech, and, physically, he seems to have recovered from yesterday's exertions. We go walking again; I'm pleased to see that he can manage by just holding onto handrails without the need for me to prop him up. Nevertheless, we steer clear of stairs this time!

Day seven The detox programme was supposed to have finished by now, but due to the need to slow it down, we're going to need at least a couple more days. The good news, though, is that he is now back on the reducing dose of chlordiazepoxide, so far without further ill effect.

Day eight Kayleigh and I visit Liam together. He is now totally lucid, and we are able to hold a proper conversation. Kayleigh delivers the good news that his start date at the rehab unit is being held open for him and CLASP have agreed to fund the extra cost.

Day nine Liam is now walking short distances completely unaided. He had what we hope may be his final dose of chlordiazepoxide this morning. The next twenty-four hours will determine whether his detox can be considered complete. Fingers crossed!

Day ten I've had to go back to work today, but Mark and Kayleigh are at the hospital this morning. I've been desperately anticipating a call or message to let me know Liam's situation. Finally, at around 11a.m. I get the call: his detox is more or less complete, though, as a precaution they are going to keep him on a very low dose of chlordiazepoxide for a few more days.

My heart sinks as I realise this will take us beyond the already-postponed admission date at the rehab unit.

But then comes the good news: as his detox is essentially complete, he *can* be discharged tomorrow, and they will administer the final doses of medication at the rehab unit. Tomorrow, as it happens, is my birthday; what a birthday present!

When I announce to my employer that I want to book yet *another* day's holiday for tomorrow, after having been back at work for just one day, they aren't exactly over the moon, but they understand my situation and agree without too much fuss.

And so … the next phase begins!

Chapter 75

'The Helen Hope Unit'

I wake up on my birthday feeling every one of my fifty-one years, and more, consumed by the strangest mix of contradictory emotions. I'm elated that we've finally reached this crucial milestone in Liam's journey, yet, at the same time, anxious, uncertain, and wary. *Will it really work this time?*

I glance at the clock: 5.28a.m. Mark will be here in about an hour and a half, and we're due to collect Liam from the hospital at 8.30a.m. Time to get up.

The rehab centre, named the Helen Hope Unit, is just over a hundred miles away; it should take about two and a half hours if the traffic's not too bad. Amelia is off school, recovering from a cold, so she will need to come with us.

Amelia has only a sketchy understanding of what is going on, and as I prepare breakfast, she is constantly firing questions at me, most of which I have no answers for.

'Is Liam going to be alright? Can he walk properly now? Can he play Fortnite soon? When can he come home?'

I try to deal with her questions as patiently as possible, but I wish she would stop and give me time to process my own thoughts and doubts.

I try to bring the questions to a close with the most honest answer I can give. 'I don't really know, sweetie, but what I do know is that, today, we are taking him somewhere that provides hope … hope that, in time, he can do all these things. It will take time, though.'

It isn't the definitive answer which will satisfy a thirteen-year-old's need for certainty, but she seems to sense that it's the best answer she is going to get. She stops asking questions and turns her attention to her corn flakes.

After breakfast, I gather together the things we will need to take with us and place them by the front door: Liam's suitcase, containing new clothes and toiletries, and some snacks and drinks for the journey.

It's 6.45 a.m. now, and we're all ready to go, but it's still fifteen minutes before Mark is due to arrive, so I sit down with a glass of chilled water to wait. My thoughts turn to what my research has revealed about the rehab centre where Liam will spend the coming weeks.

The centre is run by a man named Jonathan who has battled, and overcome, just about every setback life could throw at him. He was addicted himself once: to alcohol, gambling, and cocaine; and as if that were not enough, he lost his daughter to a brain tumour. At his lowest point, he even ended up in prison for a while. Well, they say you have to hit rock bottom before you can rise back up, and this man certainly has. He has turned his life around and dedicated himself to helping others who, like my son, are at their lowest ebb.

My thoughts are interrupted by the chiming of the doorbell; Mark is here.

***

We arrive at the hospital and park near the entrance. Mark goes in to retrieve Liam while I stay outside with Amelia.

A nurse I trained with years ago walks by; she's a sister in Accident and Emergency now. Tess has known Liam since he was a child, and due to his frequent visits to A&E in recent years, she has witnessed his heartbreaking descent into the depths of addiction. I explain why we are here and where we are going; she hugs me, exuding genuine delight that there is now hope for Liam.

Suddenly, she looks past me, over my shoulder; I turn to see Liam emerge from the entrance, with Mark just behind. Liam looks somewhat bewildered, as though he has been dragged from a deep sleep.

Tess rushes over and gives Liam a hug, offering words of encouragement. 'You've got this, Liam … I believe in you. Be strong … I know you can do it.'

Liam smiles and reciprocates the hug, but he still looks a little perplexed by it all. We say our goodbyes and turn towards the car.

***

Mark is driving, so that I can sit in the back with Amelia. Liam sits up front, with a sick bowl, just in case. He's tired and confused and still on a low dose of medication, so conversation is sporadic at best.

I glance at my watch: 9.15a.m. – around fifteen minutes behind schedule. As long as the traffic's not too bad, though, we should still have plenty of time to get there by midday, which is Liam's scheduled admission time, The traffic is heavy to start with but, thankfully, once we hit the motorway, the traffic thins out and speeds up. We should be fine for time.

No sooner do we get into a decent flow, when Amelia announces that she needs the toilet. We pull into the next service station, and as we now seem to have a little time in hand, stop for tea and coffee – and for Amelia, a caramel frappé. Liam just wants water. He's quiet, looking lost and distant; we reassure him everything's going to be OK, but I'm not sure he's really in the moment.

When we get moving again, progress is good for a while … until we hit the inevitable roadworks. We eventually arrive about thirty minutes late.

The unit is housed in a plain, blocky building, probably built around the 1970s. We stop at the tall iron gates and press the buzzer on the intercom, and after Mark exchanges a few words with the person who answers, the gates swing open. We park up and enter the reception area, which is clean, freshly decorated, and un-fussily furnished. The receptionist invites us to sit down while she calls Jonathan, the manager of the centre.

Jonathan arrives a few minutes later. He's probably around fifty years old, bald, apart from dense patches of dark hair at the sides, framing a round, friendly-looking face. Hardly the stereotypical hardened druggy ex-con! He is softly spoken, and his soothing manner quickly puts us at ease. It turns out his family used to live very close to me; I even went to school with his cousin! Small world, eh?

After we have exchanged pleasantries for a short while, he asks to take Liam's bags for the nurses to check. I know there's no booze in them as I packed them myself, but as Jonathan explained, they have strict procedures in place, and everyone has to follow them. Somehow, he says it so nicely that I take no offence whatsoever.

It's time to say our goodbyes and entrust Liam to these people who, I hope and pray, will make Liam well. Liam levers himself to his feet but has to rely on Mark for support until he establishes his balance. I start to explain to Jonathan that Liam's mobility is still not good, and he is not fully off his medication yet. Jonathan doesn't seem fazed at all as he assures me they have all the notes from the hospital and will smoothly manage the final phases of his withdrawal from medication.

Suddenly, the emotion is too much; I can feel the tears welling up. I quickly excuse myself and head for the ladies' toilet, taking a few minutes to compose myself before rejoining the others.

It's time… Mark shakes Liam's hand, and Amelia gives him a tentative hug, averting her eyes to avoid showing the upset which I'm sure she's feeling. Finally, I hug him tightly; my composure fails completely now, and I'm in floods of tears.

Jonathan judges the moment. 'I'll show Liam to his room now. Don't worry, Miss Fisher … he's in good hands.'

***

The atmosphere on the drive home is quiet, empty … a bit like that blank, doleful feeling you get when returning home after a wonderful holiday. Amelia has moved into the front seat vacated by Liam and popped her earbuds in to listen to who knows what. I sit in the backseat.

And so, the next phase of Liam's journey begins …

Chapter 76

'Rehab Mk 2'

It's been two days since we dropped Liam off at the Helen Hope Unit, and I'm going out of my mind with worry. *Is he off the medication yet? If so, how is his body coping? Are they watching his condition closely enough? Is he able to walk unaided?*

I just feel this overwhelming urge to protect him, watch over him, but I've been told that there is to be no contact with him for at least the first seventy-two hours, while he settles in. I just can't stand this tension though; I call the unit and ask to speak to Jonathan. His calm tone of voice is immediately reassuring.

'Don't worry, Madeleine,' – funny how his use of my first name seems entirely appropriate even though I've only met him once – 'Liam is settling in well. Physically, he's in a pretty fragile condition … but you know that, anyway … however, he's adjusting well to his new situation.'

I have so many questions, but somehow, I just can't frame them coherently. 'But is he *OK* ... I mean … oh, I don't know *what* I mean.'

Jonathan is patient – giving me time to try to articulate what I'm clearly incapable of articulating. After a few seconds he rescues me.

'I understand your concern, Madeleine … I really do … but he's in good hands here. Helping people like Liam is what we do. As I said, his physical condition is poor, and that will take time to improve, but we'll help him every step of the way. For now, he's doing as well as can be expected.'

Jonathan's manner is so reassuring, and yet still I have doubts. 'Can I talk to him?'

I detect a faint sigh through the phone. 'You need to understand, Madeleine, that one of the important elements of Liam's rehabilitation is to live within a structured environment ... where rules are adhered to and routine is the norm. He has been told no phones for the first three days, and he has accepted that. We should not undermine that contract.'

'I guess ...' I murmur, 'but ...'

Jonathan seems to sense my uncertainty. 'Look, tomorrow is day three. Assuming all continues to go well, he will be given his phone back after dinner. You can call him then up until 10p.m. The phone will then be confiscated again ... rules and routine, you see?'

I reluctantly accept the situation, remembering that, during his previous rehab, phone access was even more restricted than this. These people are professionals; I have to believe that they know best what to do. I say my goodbyes and hang up, a little less anxious than before, but still full of doubts.

***

Day three, and time seems to have slowed to a crawl until I can finally call Liam.

'Hi Mum, how are you?' His voice sounds steady, calm, if a little subdued.

'How am *I*?' I laugh. 'More to the point how are *you*?'

'I'm OK, I guess. It's nice here; everything's so calm and peaceful, and the staff are really kind. I've already made two new friends.'

I can hardly believe this is my son talking; he's lucid, calm, and engaged. His speech is a bit slow, but for now he's still on a low dose of chlordiazepoxide which could explain that. Overall, though, the transformation from where he was is barely credible in just three days.

And so, we have our first sensible and coherent chat in ages. That night, I have my first decent sleep in weeks

***

Over the next few weeks, I call him every evening. Before long he's off the medication completely, and each day I can sense his condition gradually improving. The subjects we discuss are mostly pretty pedestrian, revolving largely around his daily routine and what he has been eating, but I don't care; it's comfort enough to hear his voice, sense his progress, and know he's getting better.

Chapter 77

'The first visit'

It's been four weeks since we dropped Liam off at the Helen Hope Unit, and now, finally, we're allowed to visit. It's a school day, so Amelia isn't coming with us today. My neighbour, Jenny has offered to collect her from school and look after her until we get home.

I'm a bundle of nerves. Which version of Liam am I about to meet today? Will it be the lovely, intelligent boy I once knew? Will it be some version of the sick, resentful addict that I've come to know? Will it be some new Liam that I've never met before and have to learn from scratch? And how should I approach him, depending on which Liam it is? My emotions are an unfathomable miasma.

A familiar voice penetrates my thoughts. 'Penny for them?'

As I turn to face Mark, who has been doing the driving, I realise we are stationary. The M25 is doing what it does best: grinding traffic to a standstill.

'Not sure I could put my thoughts into words even if I tried.'

He smiles across at me. 'Big moment, huh?'

I nod. 'Yeah ... I just don't know what to expect ... or how to behave.'

'You'll be fine ... don't overthink it.'

'Easy to say, but I can't help it ... I'm nervous as hell.'

His tone changes abruptly. 'Look ... they're moving up ahead.'

Sure enough, the impenetrable mass of cars and trucks is finally stirring; two minutes later we, too, are on the move. As is so often the case, there is no visible clue as to what caused the extended standstill, or what unclogged it, but our speed gradually picks up and, before long we're cruising at a reasonably acceptable fifty to sixty miles per hour.

My thoughts turn back to Liam, and we exchange few words for the rest of the journey.

***

I call Liam when we are almost there; when we arrive, he's already outside, waiting to greet us.

He's unrecognisable from the fragile wreck we had left just four weeks ago. His previously skeletal frame has filled out considerably, and he is standing tall and upright with no need to lean on anything or anyone for support. The straggly beard has gone, and his hair is neatly trimmed.

Mark stops the car to let me out, and he goes to park up.

'Hello Mum,' Liam says, as he steps forward to enfold me in a hug. 'It's been a while, hasn't it?'

The emotion is just too much; tears spring from my eyes. But they are tears of joy: joy at seeing the boy I once knew reincarnated before me.

'Hey, don't cry, Mum … I'm getting better … much better.'

'I know,' I sniff, holding him tightly. 'It's just … I wasn't sure how … or whether … oh, Liam, I'm so happy to see you like this.'

'Well, stop crying then. Now then, what about this picnic you mentioned?'

In the emotion of the moment, I've quite forgotten about our plans for today. There is a nice park just opposite the Helen Hope Unit, so I've prepared a picnic for us to take over there where we can have a good long chat and catch up on things.

Mark appears, carrying the cool box containing our lunch. He greets Liam with a handshake. 'Well, *you* certainly look a lot better than last time I saw you.'

Liam gives a small chuckle. 'Well, I could hardly look worse, could I?'

His words break the euphoric mood as the unbidden thought of what 'worse' would have actually meant enters my head. Neither of them seems to notice my involuntary shudder.

'Come on then,' I say, 'let's go and eat.'

***

We find a nice picnic area, furnished with those one-piece wooden table and bench affairs like you often find in pub gardens. Most of them are unoccupied, so there's no trouble finding a private spot to eat and chat. The food, to be honest, isn't great, the hours spent in traffic jams on a warm day having proved too much of a struggle for the coolbox.

It doesn't matter though, because the picnic is just a vehicle for spending some quality time with Liam. And it really works; he tells us all about the last four weeks, in much more detail than ever emerged during our phone calls.

Rehab life has been good for him. It has been structured, with reassuring routine. Every day he and the other patients have been encouraged to explore and validate why they are there. They have been shown that addiction has both mental and physical aspects and taught ways to divert themselves from the pervasive mental aspects.

He talks and talks; hours go by before he finally talks himself to a standstill.

He closes with a statement that I know will stick with me. 'I've learned more about myself in the last four weeks than in the previous four years. I'm determined to see it through this time.'

There have been so many critical moments in his relatively short life, so many times when hopes have been raised and hopes dashed, that I can barely allow myself to believe. And yet, hope and believe I do ... again. How can I not?

Chapter 78

'Resentment'

It's around two weeks since we went to meet Liam and scheduled to be another two before we see him again. I understand that he's still making good progress, but I'm beginning to sense that something is bothering him. It's nothing specific that he has said, but more a sense that there's something he *wants* to say but, for some reason, cannot. I decide to phone Jonathan to see if he can shed any light. As always, he is calming and reassuring, but what he has to say is deeply unsettling.

'As you know, we have regular therapy sessions with all our patients, to try to get them to look inside themselves and identify the root causes of their illness.'

I have no idea where this is going. 'So what is it that's bothering him? He seemed to be doing so well when I last saw him.'

'He is … physically … and he's faced down many of the demons in his mind, but there are some issues regarding his relationship with *you* which need to be exposed and … well, dealt with.'

My heart skips a beat. 'With *me*? What do you mean? We've been talking on the phone almost every day … he hasn't said anything.'

Jonathan's sigh is audible. 'That is, indeed, the issue. He *needs* to talk to you about it, but he seems unable to do so. I think he is afraid of hurting you.'

'Hurting me? What's this all about?' I demand.

'Please,' he says, 'try not to upset yourself. There is little value in me trying to express your son's feelings on his behalf; it needs to be a discussion between the two of you.'

Now I'm starting to get irritated. 'But what can I do if he won't talk about it?'

'I don't think it's a question of "won't", but of "can't". Look, here's a suggestion: why don't I try to act as a facilitator? We can set up an online meeting with the three of us. Maybe I can help Liam to push through his inhibitions and air his feelings.'

My simmering anger begins to subside; I remind myself that Jonathan is only trying to achieve the best for both Liam and me. And he's at least offering a positive suggestion.

'I ... well yes, if you think that might help.'

'I think it might.'

'OK ... when can we do it?'

'We have all the time in the world here ... you are the one with a busy schedule.'

Fuck the busy schedule ... nothing's more important than this.

'Tomorrow ... I'll take a day off work.' *They won't be happy about another short notice day off, but I don't care.*

'OK,' says Jonathan. 'Let me talk to Liam and we'll set it up. Do you use Zoom?'

'Yes, I have the app on my laptop.'

'Perfect ... I'll talk to Liam and make sure he's up for this. I'll confirm with a WhatsApp. 10.30a.m. good for you?'

The sooner the better ... I'm sick with worry now about what dark secrets my son may be harbouring.

'Yes, that's fine,' I say. I feel anything but fine, though.

***

I'm already sitting at my laptop fifteen minutes before the meeting is scheduled to start. My heart is hammering furiously as my brain embarks on an endless, circular trawl through the possible things which might emerge and how I might respond. It's pointless: I just don't know what this is all about.

Finally, the time comes, and the faces of Liam and Jonathan appear on the screen. Liam looks physically well, his cheeks fuller than last time I saw him and his skin tone healthier. The slight frown and visible beads of perspiration on his brow, though, betray the nervousness he is feeling. To be fair, my own image does little to hide my anxiety, either. Jonathan, by contrast looks, and sounds, calm and relaxed.

He kicks things off by explaining that some of the feelings Liam has revealed during the therapy sessions need to be aired between the two of us.

'Liam, you are doing incredibly well, and your physical condition has improved enormously, but as you know, it is important to explore and address some of the mental aspects which may have contributed to your previous addiction.'

Liam nods, though his eyes are downcast. 'I understand.'

'Now, you have shared with me some feelings which you have experienced during your illness which relate to your mum, but which you haven't shared with her.'

My heart's pounding even faster now.

'When you get out of this place, which I hope will be soon now, her continuing love and support will be key to helping you have the strength to stay dry and never again succumb to the lure of a drink.'

'I know,' mumbles Liam; he looks up, and I sense eye contact even through the screen.

'So,' continues Jonathan, 'I want you to tell her directly some of the things which emerged during our therapy sessions. Don't hold back … your mum's stronger than you think.'

He turns his attention to me. 'And Madeleine, try not to be defensive. Take what Liam tells you as what he has felt in the past, at a time when he may not have understood your situation or what you were having to cope with. You may feel much of it is unjustified, which is undoubtedly true, and you can feel free to say so, to explain what else was going on in your life. The point of all this is to get each of you to understand what the other has been experiencing and build a foundation for the future.'

God, now I'm really shitting myself. *What kind of monster does my son think I've been?*

'So, I'm going to stop talking now. Liam, it's over to you,' says Jonathan.

Liam is silent for several long seconds before he begins, falteringly, to speak. 'Look, Mum, I don't want to be hurtful, but there were things … things that made me feel … unwanted. In some way, I want to bury them, but Jonathan says it's important that we get them out in the open ... so you understand what I was feeling, and at the same time, I understand what *you* were going through.'

I'm still on high alert, but now I'm ready to face whatever he's about to say. 'It's OK ... let's get it all out.'

He doesn't reply, so Jonathan prompts him. 'Go on Liam ... she's ready.'

I can see Liam's Adam's apple bobbing up and down as he summons the resolve to spit it out. Finally, he does.

'Well, I always felt like I was second place to Amelia. You always put her needs first. You never seemed to even notice what was happening to me.'

I bristle at that but try not to show it. 'Liam, she was a *small child* ... what was I supposed to do?'

'I don't know ... just pay me a bit more attention, I guess. You didn't even notice my drinking until it was already too late.'

I bite my tongue and pause before responding. 'For heaven's sake, I was on my own ... your dad was not around, and I was left to provide for four children ... working all the hours God sent.'

'Well you still had time for boyfriends, didn't you?'

That stunned me. 'Was I not allowed to have *any* sort of life of my own then?'

'Well, I didn't see it like that,' said Liam '... you're my mum and I just felt your kids should have come first. It seems you had little time for any of us except Amelia ... and *I* was bottom of the pecking order.'

'Oh, Liam, do you realise just how hard it was for me, as a single mum, to provide for four kids? I had to pay the rent, put food on the table, and still try to find time to show you all the love I felt inside. I tried ... I really tried. I studied so I could get a decent career, none of you ever went hungry, you always had some gifts to open at Christmas and birthdays. I did my best for all of you.'

'I suppose ... but at the time, I didn't really appreciate that—'

I cut him off, my sense of righteous indignation coming to the fore now. 'Why am I blamed for everything that goes wrong, despite all the sacrifices I have made? What about your father? How much time or attention have you had from him over the years?'

'Well, I'm not saying it's all—' he begins, but I'm on a roll now, and I cut him off.

'Sweet F.A. – that's how much. He's moved on with his life and forgotten all about yours. His new partner and her two kids ...

they're the only ones he's interested in now. Do you know how much maintenance he's been paying over the years?'

'Well, no ... I didn't really think about that,' he replies, weakly.

'No, I'll bet you didn't. Absolutely nothing ... that's how much ... for all three of his kids. At the same time, he's been taking his new family on expensive holidays ... Dubai, New York, and God knows where else.'

Liam hangs his head, shaking it slowly from side to side. 'I didn't know ...' he mutters.

'Well there's a lot you didn't know ... like the expensive gifts he bought his stepdaughters while he never even sent a birthday or Christmas card to you.'

'Please don't be so angry, Mum.'

'Well, I *am* angry. *I'm* the one who has stuck by you through thick and thin, yet *I'm* the one who's the focus of all this resentment.'

'Sorry, Mum.'

At hearing those words, and the remorse in his tone, my anger subsides, as quickly as it had flared up. I pause and take a long, slow, deep breath.

'I'm sorry too, I didn't mean to rage at you like that. How is it that I never properly understood what you were feeling?'

'And I never properly understood what you were going through, either.'

We both fall silent, which provides Jonathan with his cue to get involved – he had been silent through all of the previous exchanges. 'The answer to that question is that you probably both bottled it all up instead of talking openly about it. And the truth is that when you were drunk most of the time, Liam, you probably wouldn't even have been capable of doing so.'

Liam nods, something resembling an ironic chuckle passing his lips. 'Hmm ... I guess you're right.'

'Look,' continues Jonathan, 'that was painful ... of course it was ... but you've made a huge step forward today. Now that's all out in the open and you are fully sober, Liam, you and your mum can continue to talk about it ... finally slay the dragons that have been eating away at you.' He pauses for a second or two. 'But that's for another day.'

Liam and I are both exhausted, and readily agree to call it a day, so we wind up the Zoom call.

But it's affected me deeply. I sit for a while, staring at the blank screen of my laptop, questioning everything I've ever done as a parent.

Had I really been blameless in Liam's descent into addiction?

Could I have done more to prevent it?

Should I have acted earlier or more decisively once his addiction was clear?

Maybe the answers to these questions are not what I would like to acknowledge, but the truth is that no-one prepares you or trains you to fulfil the role of being mother of an addict. You have to learn on the job.

The one thing that I *am* sure about was that his bloody father should have done more, and my resentment of his disinterest has now reached new heights.

This morning has been a gut-wrenching experience; I hope it's been worth it.

Chapter 79

'Coming home'

Two weeks have passed since that painful Zoom meeting, and it turns out that Jonathan was right: it has lanced the boil which was festering in Liam's mind and unlocked a much-needed openness in our relationship. Our daily phone calls have taken on a very different character; instead of just discussing mundane details of his daily routine, and mine, we are exploring what is good and bad in our relationship and building a foundation for the future, based on love and mutual respect.

And now, his rehabilitation is judged by Jonathan to be complete; he is sober, physically fit, and ready to come home.

The home he'll be coming back to, though, is looking very different from the one he left behind. Mark has completely renovated and redecorated his flat. Gone are the jagged holes punched in the plasterboard walls, which are now repainted in a pleasing pale grey shade. Gone is the dirty, bloodstained floor covering, now replaced by new carpet throughout. Gone, too, is the blood and urine-stained bed, replaced with a new one. Gone is the harsh overhead lighting, replaced by subtle, low-level lamps which lend a much more agreeable ambience. The transformation Mark has achieved is amazing, and I can't thank him enough. It's a comfortable and welcoming environment for my son to come home to, reflective of the hope that the future now holds.

*****

When we step through the door of the flat, Liam's reaction is heartwarming. He gasps as he takes in the scene, casting his gaze back and forth, apparently lost for words. He seems almost overwhelmed,

Finally, he turns and hugs me. 'Thanks, Mum … it's … fantastic!'

'Don't thank me,' I smile, 'Mark did it all.'

He seems a bit dazed and confused; perhaps it's all too much to take in.

He turns to Mark, 'I … don't know what to say … it's … thank you so much.'

'You're welcome,' says Mark. 'After all you've been through, and the tremendous effort you have made to get sober, you deserve a decent place to live.'

I notice a tear welling in the corner of Liam's eye as he does something quite unexpected: he steps forward and gives Mark a hug. Now *I'm* the one who feels the emotion burgeoning within me.

'Come on,' I say, anxious to move on before *everyone* starts crying, 'let's just leave the bags, and get over to the house for dinner.'

'I'm cooking dinner,' announces Amelia. 'we're having chili con carne.'

'Well, haven't *you* grown up while I've been away,' says Liam, managing a smile for his little sister.

'I was already grown up,' she asserts, which provokes a chuckle from Mark. 'I've been helping Mum with cooking for ages, and now I can do chilli con carne, spaghetti Bolognese, and macaroni cheese.'

'Well let's go then,' says Liam.

***

With a little help from me – I had to get her to exercise some restraint on how much chilli powder to add – Amelia does, indeed, produce a very good chilli con carne.

Liam is hungry, and more than does it justice. He's tired though, and this is a very big day for him, and for all of us, so conversation over dinner is limited.

Mark and I usually share a bottle of wine when we have dinner together, but this time, like Liam, we just have sparkling mineral water, unsure about how Liam would react to a bottle of wine on the table.

As I pour the water, he comments on it. 'I know why you're doing this, but you don't need to worry. One of the things that we concentrated on a lot in rehab was the need to get comfortable with others drinking alcohol around you while resisting any temptation to join in. You don't need to make allowances for me.'

It's music to my ears, but still, we stay with the water.

By the time we finish our meal, Liam is practically falling asleep at the table, so I take him straight back to his flat, leaving Mark and Amelia with the clearing up.

Having dropped him off, I hug him, kiss him, and tell him how proud of him I am, before leaving.

On the way home, it starts to sink in just what a pivotal moment this is. Now he is in control of his own future, he is free and untutored, he has access to shops, old friends, and – if he chooses – alcohol.

By the time I get back, Mark has gone home, and Amelia has gone to bed, so the house is eerily quiet. It's late and I have work tomorrow, so I go straight to bed myself, but I can't get to sleep; the thoughts which were troubling me on the way home linger and multiply.

I try to clear my mind, console myself with Liam's progress, his new skills, and his three months of sobriety, but my brain keeps flipping. The demons rise up and torment me throughout the night; they find problems to counter every solution and outwit any positivity I can muster.

Sleep continues to elude me, and the night seems to stretch ahead interminably. When the first slivers of morning light insinuate themselves around the edges of the curtains, I can stand it no longer. I get up and prepare to face the day ahead.

I have to go to work today but there is no way I can go until I've spoken to Liam. I'm dressed and ready to go at least forty minutes before I need to set off for work, so I call him.

No answer.

Come on Liam ... pick up. He doesn't. *Don't panic ... he could be in the bathroom, or still asleep.*

I decide to leave it for five minutes. Those five minutes feel more like fifty. I've already done my makeup but, for a few moments of distraction I decide to touch up my lipstick a little more.

I try Liam again.

No answer.

Now I find myself succumbing to the demons which tormented me through the night. I put the phone on speaker and lay it on the dressing table, letting it ring and ring while I get up and start pacing back and forth.

Still no answer.

Liam pleeease. Suddenly, my composure collapses; I hurl the lipstick, which was still in my hand, against the wall. It clatters to the floor, leaving a pink streak on the wall.

A familiar voice intervenes. 'Oh, hi Mum.' Hearing his voice, bright and clear, is like having a vice around my lungs suddenly released.

'Liam! Is everything OK? I thought you were never going to answer.'

'Oh, sorry … I was asleep. I was really tired last night.'

'But you're OK?'

'Yes … that new bed is super comfortable, and I can't believe how amazing my flat is. Say thanks again to Mark for me.'

I shake my head, stifling a small chuckle; here's me panicking about all sorts of terrible things that might have happened and he's just enthusing about the makeover of his flat.

'Glad you like it,' I say

'I love it. I'm thinking I might get a desk and chair to go against the back wall for my computer … I think there's enough space there. And one or two pictures on the side wall would be nice.'

'Fantastic!' I enthuse. 'Yes, make it your own. Oh, Liam, I'm so proud of you.'

'Couldn't have done it without you, Mum.'

My heart soars, and a tear escapes my eye. I take a second or two to compose myself. 'Well, let's call it a team effort, then. Look, I have to go to work now. Take care, and I'll call you this evening.'

'OK … bye.'

After I hang up, I reflect on the challenges which still lie ahead. There is the obvious temptation of alcohol at every turn, especially once he starts socialising again. But there are other, more mundane issues, such as sorting out his accumulated debts, dealing with daily bills, shopping, cleaning, washing, and more. It's so long since he has had to do these things for himself. Will it all be too much for him to cope with? It is, to quote an oft-used cliché, the first day of the rest of his life.

I know I cannot do everything for him. Now, he must learn to be an independent responsible adult – to reconnect with society. But I'm still his mum; I'll be there if he needs me

Chapter 80

'The first nine months'

At first, I call Liam every day, but I soon realise that he needs his space, and time to adjust to his new environment and new life, so the phone calls gradually become less frequent.

Before his discharge from the Helen Hope Unit, he had been given plenty of information about support groups and local meetings for recovering alcoholics. To my delight, and a little surprise, he appears to be making full use of these facilities.

He seems to be coping well with the daily chores of life which most of us take for granted but had been alien to Liam for years. And he is gradually getting on top of his finances – with a little help from me!

Jonathan, from the rehab centre, is keeping in touch with Liam from time to time. He seems to have a deep and genuine desire to make sure that the early recovery turns into something durable and lasting.

***

At the time of writing, Liam has been sober for almost nine months. He occasionally – maybe more than occasionally – feels the urge to drink, but with the help of the support network around him, he is able to say no.

And now, he has been offered a role with the very addiction service that supported him. It's unpaid work, but he wants to give back by helping other addicts. I'm so, so proud of him.

At the time when I started writing this book, helped by my good friend and author, Ray Green, I had no idea how it would end.

Actually, an alcoholic's journey never really ends; there is always the danger of relapse, if he or she falters in their resolve. For now, though, for Liam, for me, it's about the best possible outcome we could possibly have hoped for. Liam knows he could easily have died.

He supports the writing of this book.

__Epilogue__

'And what about me?'

As I said, an addict's journey never really ends. Liam is still recovering, but so am I. The Helen Hope Unit provided such a wonderful service for Liam, but those close to him, including me, have suffered greatly, and the scars do not heal easily or quickly.

Jonathan says I just have to 'let go', to move on, but that is far more easily said than done.

I have lost good friends, driven away by my chaotic situation. The job of 'mother of an addict' was thrust upon me, a job for which I was ill-equipped and untrained, so I made mistakes – of course I did. I faced judgements that I should never have had to face, yet I supported an addict through it all, with unstinting love. And now I'm supposed to 'let go'.

Well, I don't want to let go; I'm a different person now. I want to acknowledge this extraordinary journey, learn from it, help others who may be facing a similar situation. I want to fight back, challenge society on its laws, its easy accessibility to drugs and alcohol. 'Letting go' is not an option for me. And neither is presuming to offer Liam forgiveness. My son does not need forgiving for becoming addicted to a highly glorified drug which is there in every supermarket, every pub, and every social occasion.

My relationship with Liam has come through, against the odds, stronger than ever. It is underpinned by an unshakeable love and a strength which has seen us emerge from the darkness – and the very real risk of his dying – to an optimistic future.

Liam, you have taught me so much about love, pain, hope, and strength. Every step of our journey has been difficult, sometimes unbearable, but we are stronger for it.

If any of you reading this story are facing a similar situation, I hope you will take some solace in knowing that with solidarity, resolve, courage, and above all, *love*, you *can* overcome the most daunting of challenges and claw your way from the darkness to the light.

THE END

About the Authors

Madeine Fisher is a single mother of four: three girls and one boy. She lives in West Sussex, England, with her youngest daughter and her beloved labrador cross, Sky; the elder children have now flown the nest.

Before the kids arrived on the scene, she did a variety of casual jobs, including care worker and merchandiser for a Formula One team! But with a growing family to support she needed a stable career and studied to qualify as a nurse, a profession she has followed for many years. Most recently, she works as support lead at a centre which supports adults with learning disabilities. However, her most important job has been caring for her kids.

She had not written any books before 'Love versus Liquor' but when her son fell victim to alcohol addiction, it was the start of a heartbreaking battle to try to save him. The tussle between a mother's love for her son and the vicelike grip of addiction became the focus of her life for several years, and a story begging to be told. She has been helped by her good friend and author, Ray Green, to tell that story.

If any of her readers are going through the heartbreak of a loved one seized in the grip of addiction, she fervently hopes that this book may provide some support, solidarity, and hope.

About the Authors

Ray Green is married with two daughters and lives in West Sussex, England. He graduated from Southampton University with a BSc in Physics and then went on to a career spanning some 30 years in the electronics manufacturing industry. For much of that time he was operating at Director or Managing Director level in several different companies, so he is well qualified to give an insight into the world of business and corporate politics and intrigue.

His business career culminated in his participation in a management buyout of his last company. It was an incredibly tortuous process, and the experience that provided the inspiration for his first novel 'Buyout' in which the principal protagonist, Roy Groves, battles similar issues in a fictionalised management buyout. The sequel 'Payback' tells what happens when the human desire for revenge takes hold. Ray's third novel 'Chinese Whispers' explores the shocking consequences when legitimate business is infiltrated by organised crime. The fourth book, which completes the 'Roy Groves Thriller' series, is a comedy-thriller charting Roy's fortunes after he decides to quit the corporate rat race and retire to an upmarket expat community on Spain's Costa del Sol.

'Lost Identity', the first book in the 'Identity Thrillers' series, is a tense psychological thriller set in the criminal world of drug trafficking and murder. And the second, 'Identity Found' is the thrilling sequel. The third, 'New Identity' is the thrilling, shocking finale to the trilogy.

His seventh novel 'The Ultima Variant' is a gripping Coronavirus conspiracy thriller. It might not be as far from the truth as you'd think!

'Love versus Liquor' is, of course, very different indeed to his previous work, being based on the true story of a mother's battle to save her son from alcohol addiction. Learning of her story and helping her put it into words has been a rewarding and emotional experience.

www.ingramcontent.com/pod-product-compliance
Lightning Source LLC
LaVergne TN
LVHW040039090426
835510LV00037B/158